The Most Popular
Songwriter
of whom you never heard

*A*dvantage™
INSPIRATIONAL

Paul Serwinek, Ph.D.

First Printing: February 2009
09 10 11 12 13 14 15   10 9 8 7 6 5 4 3 2 1
Printed in the United States of America

FORWARD

I'd like to tell you how this book was conceived. I was in church one day, minding my own business. I t was a Sunday school class. The writer of the lesson mentioned in passing the issue of why a God of love and omnipotence allows evil. He then just happened to mention a scripture in Habakkuk. That thought really intrigued me. I hadn't read the Bible book of Habakkuk in years. I later looked up the scripture and thought, "Wow! I've never heard that before!" I kept reading. I then read God's reply to Habakkuk explaining how God often manages international/political events that pertain to his servants. Again, I exclaimed, "Wow! I've never heard THAT before!" In fact, I realize most Christians, unless they read it for themselves, would probably deny this insight was even in the Bible. I surmise not a few mature Christians, ever comprehend what God confided to Habakkuk. "This is unbelievable", I exclaimed in excitement. The further I read, Habakkuk also taught me nuances on how to pray. Some of these were major insights. How do you handle it when everything seems to go wrong for you? What do you do when you feel you're the only one going through a particular trial? The answers were all here.

I realized I had to do something. Being an in-depth student of the Scriptures for many decades and being a social psychologist by training, I realized there was practical information here that was must be disseminated now, right now. The very questions asked of me so often by new or seasoned Christians were answered here in new, clear ways.

I beg you to read with an open mind though . I've got to caution you, some of the things God says in this little book may be difficult for you to accept. Be patient. Some of the interpretations suggested in this little book may not be to your liking. Be magnanimous. After all, none of us has all the answers even though some of us think we do. Permit me a little leeway here as I write before you jump to conclusions.

One of the main reasons I had to write this book is because I see the need to put some Bible vernacular in the language of our day. Take a simple word like 'grace', what is grace, what does it mean? We use it all of the time but ask many Christians and some will give you an answer like, "Grace is well…just grace". But what does it really mean when God says to Paul who was asking for a miracle and the answer came back, "My grace is sufficient for you." God was saying he wouldn't grant the miracle but "my grace will be sufficient". In fact, our discussion will clarify other understandings of God's workings. I'll also be cognizant of the evolution of language in especially since the original King James version of the Bible was published 400 years ago. I'm excited to proceed. I hope you are, too.

Now a few thoughts on to whom this volume is directed. So many of us are suffering from discouragement – we've lost a job, our health is poor, maybe we've been dealt a great injustice. The Bible prophet's ideas are for you. He's suffered as intensely as any of us. Let him answer you. Sometimes it helps just knowing you're not alone. There is someone else who felt exactly like you. You say, "Why me?". I know someone who said it with as much exasperation as any of us could ever muster up. The exciting thing is what he concluded after venting to God. His words have been repeated by millions ever since but few have ever been introduced to the writers context and the insights that burgeon from the actual events. You can't help but read Habakkuk's story without feeling a surge of personal adequacy and the true significance of your life.

What I'm hoping you'll do is at least consider our Bible writer's unique and special spin on some of life's major issues. Don't automatically shut out his viewpoint or our interpretation as being too different from your previous training. As Christians, we want to expand our personal understanding on how our Lord might react under various circumstances. It's possible you may acquire a whole new set of possibilities as to how God controls without actually controlling. Keeping open to God's possible actions and reactions helps us to appreciate the wisdom and versatility of our God. We come to know him better. We become more of a friend as we learn to understand him. That's one of the benefits of this volume, I trust.

These are some of the other ways our writer, Habakkuk, will help you:

- He teaches possibilities on how to make our spiritual progress more fulfilling.
- He suggests a new outlook and answers to why God allows evil.
- He assures us God will never leave us abandoned.
- He demonstrates how separate Bible writers can apply God's words very differently but very harmoniously.
- He models what humility in practice really means.
- He has an amazing affect on our faith (Faith always trumps fate.)
- His experience observed helps raise our self-esteem & banish feelings of inadequacy.
- He explains in refreshing new ways how we might overcome the struggles most of us experience.
- His story suggests fantastic possibilities for what an average person, like you and I, can do with his/her life.

That last one is a paramount lesson I've learned from this 3-page Bible book. God invariably uses little people, insignificant people throughout history to accomplish great things, significant things. What an inspiration. I can't wait till you are inspired by Habakkuk to realize that God's still has something in mind for you to yet accomplish. You're significant after all. "I may not be famous but I always can be significant." The motivation to do something worthy of the Lord is the greatest legacy Habakkuk passes on.

So I dedicate this book to, first of all, those in my personal life that helped me to see how average individuals can live significant lives. I dedicate this book to my parents who, God bless them, never realized the legacy they left behind. My father never finished high school but was admired for his determination by all who crossed his path. I remember my mother, who though she had rather poor health throughout her life, and never learned to drive a car, nevertheless she gave me the drive to explore my place in the universe and in God's family. I dedicate this book to my wife who I know, due to unfortunate upbringing still doesn't what she's already accomplished in her life even though she's the perfect model of a Christian mother and the fulfillment of what I needed as a wife. I must also dedicate this book to my children, Matthew, Alissa and Kathryn. I know they will accomplish significant contributions to humanity just by being themselves, unique in their own way. Finally I dedicate this book to everyone seeking further meaning for their lives and who ,for various reasons, feel inadequately prepared in their present situations for the fulfillment of marvelous dreams hidden within them.

TABLE OF CONTENTS

Chapter One

THE MOST POPULAR SONGWRITER

We've all been there before. Things aren't going really well. You're trying, but things just keep getting worse. Doesn't it always seem that everything happens at once? You've been there, haven't you? You lose your job of eight years, but the guy who took more than his share of coffee breaks and was conveniently out of the office every time a major problem came up...there just seems to be no justice. You try but you're the one they let go when sales are down. Of course, as if that's not enough, within a week you could almost predict either the brakes on the car go or the hot water heater at home will start leaking. And if *that's* not enough, your fifth grade son is having problems. He's been getting into trouble and his teacher has been sending you notes, with the latest appearing yesterday. You've got problems. Nothing is going right. We've all had this happen at least once in the past. For some of us, it seems to be a regular occurrence.

Take heart, friends, you're not the only ones! This is a regular occurrence in our society. Millions go through something similar every single day. If it's not a job, it may be an illness, or it might be a pending divorce. We've all exclaimed, crying out in unison, "Why me?" In my family, this always happens. Just when we think we've made it through the worst, something else happens! But wait a minute! I've found something I think will really help you at times like this. Whether you're going through difficulties now, or for the next time you feel that way (for some of us it's a regular occurrence), this is written with you in mind.

What I found, and I'm using the term advisedly here, what I literally found while reading my Bible was a little tiny book written specifically for us when we're down. For some of you who haven't read the Bible through, you may have never heard of the book's name. It was written over 2600 years ago, which goes to show that life problems and emergencies happen in all societies, in all cultural settings and in all times.

This little Bible book was written by a rather obscure individual. He was just like you and me - nobody special. He wasn't famous in his day, and his name isn't famous today. He endured suffering probably as difficult as any of us have had or could imagine. Somehow he made it through and somehow, in spite of the suffering, he was able to be happy. It was as if he was able to conquer the suffering. I wish I could tell you his story had a short-term happy ending. I don't know if it did or not, but based on speculation it probably didn't. But he conquered the pain; he conquered the anguish. Consequently he's one of my heroes today. He wasn't a hero in his own time; he was probably herded with the masses. He was just a solitary man in a raging sea storm hanging on for dear life, just trying to make some sense of it all; one man in a crowd of suffering, angry people. He kept crying, "Why me, why now?"

Do you know why he deserves to be a hero? First, he endured suffering stoically - without continually whining and continually feeling sorry for himself. He was a hero because he put in writing what he felt, complaints and all. But most of all, he was a hero since he found the solution. He found a way to be happy, he found a way to be joyful in spite of it all. Can you believe it? He found the answer! He lived the experience to prove it worked. But best of all, he wrote it down. He gave us the recipe for happiness regardless of who we are, where we are or what we're going through, and it works every time! But you've probably never heard of him or, if you've heard his name, you've probably never realized how indebted you are to him, especially if you're a Christian.

And here's the astonishing thing: among the few lyrics he wrote was a short sentence, a brief phrase that has been at the forefront and featured prominently throughout history at the most cataclysmic turning points chronicled. This little phrase became a rallying cry that spawned revolutions and has changed the course of history many times over. But he was never given credit for what he was inspired to say. He was never quoted as an authority. Each time his phrase was rediscovered it inspired millions. It did its job. The phrase, when replanted in the hearts of a new generation, took root, changed lives, changed societies, even changed civilizations. That's powerful! So powerful that I know when you read and understand what he said, it will change <u>your</u> life beyond belief.

MAKING A DIFFERENCE

I can't wait to tell you the story. But first, I want you to understand the significance of this story, his story. Here we have a man that lived in obscurity. He wasn't wealthy, had no power to speak of, lived an ordinary life and probably wondered why he never had the chance to do something great. He probably doubted his usefulness, seemingly lost in a sea of "nobodies." However, don't forget, he was happy; he had meaning in his life. He did just fine. So in spite of his obscurity, in spite of his suffering and in spite of seemingly having nothing to show for his life, he emerged an unsung hero, albeit a hero. I have often mused, after I discovered his story for myself, "If he only knew what he would accomplish. If he only knew he wasn't ordinary, if he only knew he was passing on a legacy, if he only knew." But then it keeps coming to me; this is the beauty of his story. His story can be replicated in our lives, on a smaller scale, just the same.

I have a hunch that's one reason why his story is included in the Bible for our encouragement. There's a special incentive for us in this relatively obscure book of the Bible. The point I got when reading and understanding it has been here for each of us to discover for ourselves. For each of us to say, "I'm not so different from him. And maybe because I'm not so different, things can work out for me like they did for him. Maybe I can live the secret of happiness as he did, the secret he shares with me. Maybe I can live my life even if in relative obscurity, with little notoriety, but maybe, just maybe, I can pass on a legacy like he did." He never knew what a difference his life made, how many people were affected, in how many monumental ways.

I find myself musing, "Can *I* make a difference, can I pass on a legacy; will my life be lived with meaning?" I know many of you will say in unison with me, "I don't care if I'm obscure, I don't care if I'm not famous. I just care that my life has meaning. I just care that my life makes a difference to somebody, anybody." And our unsung hero just happened to stand up, through what he wrote, to say, "Take heart. I was just like you. I was just an ordinary guy. I never realized what I said would make such a difference. I didn't realize it at the time, I didn't even realize it before I died, but it happened. I don't care that I didn't get to be famous. I don't care that nobody gives me credit. I'm just so happy I made a difference."

I now appeal to you, my friend; it's all going to come true for you beyond your wildest expectations. You can make a difference; you *will* make a difference. Just follow the advice of Habakkuk. Yes, that's his name. He'll probably never have a movie made about his life but he was happy just the same. Hence the title of this volume, *The Most Popular Songwriter You Never Heard Of.* We'll be talking about the life of Habakkuk, how his life experiences had many similarities to those of most of us. We'll examine his life, his contributions to Christian thought, and his secrets for being joyful regardless of the circumstances. We'll spend a little time on his story and the history of his times but we'll spend most of the time on the few simple lyrics he wrote. Yes, he was an amateur songwriter among other things. I firmly believe the few simple phrases he has passed on to us will make a big difference in your life.

I'm going to say this often and I mean it, "Little people can make a big difference in the lives of others." This, to me, is a major message of the three-page long Bible book called Habakkuk. Habakkuk was a simple person. He didn't stand out prominently in his generation. But with the inspiration of God's Spirit, he was destined to accomplish great things. One little person, Habakkuk, influenced generations to come. Truly this little person made a big difference with God's help.

I really feel our Lord wants us to understand from reading this simple account that even you and I, who are simple people, can make big differences. I can just see some of you now shaking your head in amazement over that statement. "How could I ever make a big difference?" you retort. Nevertheless, you can. Habakkuk made a big difference in the lives of others with whom he lived. No doubt his family, friends and fellow workers in the temple where Habakkuk worked were positively affected by his example and his encouragement and his joy under duress. He went on to be used as an instrument of the Lord, helping generations to come. Millions of people are better off because he lived. Truly, one little person made a big difference with God's help and Spirit.

Now stop for a moment. What I'm saying is: any ordinary person can do what Habakkuk did on a smaller scale. The work, that difference you make, can be a big difference in the life of another. While Habakkuk made a difference in the lives of countless others, the most immediate difference was the positive results in the lives of his family, friends, fellow workers and fellow worshippers. What he proved is any person can make a big difference in the lives of others around him or her. Making a "big" difference to the Lord doesn't refer to quantity but to quality. Habakkuk did both, helping many and having a profound affect. What Habakkuk's Bible book is saying is that each of us, like him, can make a BIG difference in the lives of those with whom we come in contact. This is what I hope you will come away with here.

I guarantee if ever you sense that you have made a difference, it will affect you profoundly. In fact, you can prove it to yourself. Isn't it true that every time you make a difference, even a small difference, it just "makes your day"? Sure it does. What the Lord wants us to realize is these little differences we make a day at a time accumulate to a big difference in the lives of those close to us and even to those who just come into contact with us. Furthermore, those differences you make don't just make your day (you feel you have an effect) but they really make your life! And if you can look back and feel you made a difference in someone else's life, even just a few people's lives, you sense your life was not lived in vain.

I firmly believe what all my searching in scripture, research in psychology, interviews with others have demonstrated is that what every person really cherishes is a sense of significance. And most don't even know it. All anyone wants is to feel deep down that he or she has made a difference. It's that simple. Some people accumulate wealth, some people accumulate power, some people cherish influence, but all these are substitutes for a sense of value. What they really want is peace of mind, to know they made a difference, that their lives were not lived in vain, that they had an affect on the world around them, that their presence was felt. All these desires can be summed up by the word, "significance."

Stop and think about this for a moment. Isn't it true? Isn't that what you want? If you're a devoted Christian, isn't it the one thing you'd cherish more than anything else, to come to that point, when all is said and done, that you'll hear the words that Jesus predicted all would wish for? To have the book of your life opened and for the Master to say, *"Well done, good and faithful servant! Come and share your Master's happiness!"* (Matt. 25:21) That's it; it's that simple. If you can take just a moment to meditate on this, you'll see it's true. I know some will say, "I just want to praise God," or "My goal is to glorify God." That may be true, but isn't it also true your motive deep down is to have that feeling of satisfaction to know you've done and done well what you've been destined by God to do?

LEARNING FROM HABAKKUK

I have always found that I can learn something stimulating from any mature Christian I meet. Their experiences have been different from mine. Jesus has dealt with them somewhat differently than He has with me, based on their life experiences and where they are on their journey. That being true, just imagine how much we can glean from what Habakkuk tells us about his journey. He writes with the candor of every Bible scribe, admitting his doubts and questionings. You're going to find he asked the same age-old questions, but his answers may surprise you. Furthermore, the Lord's response to him is especially relevant to us.

For example, Habakkuk, you will find, was the first Bible writer to use the phrase, "live by faith." You've repeated it and you may be familiar with how other inspired Bible writers took up the banner and amplified the meaning. I'll go so far as to say, if you can comprehend what that phrase, "live by faith," meant to Habakkuk, you will experience immediate blessings. You'll also find how the phrase suggests a way of living. The practical benefits now, at this moment and every day, are profound. Habakkuk, by his life, demonstrated the practical application of faith. The Lord helped him to endure apprehension and uncertainty by employing the directive, "live by faith." I guarantee that examining Habakkuk's life experiences will give you new insights into the meaning of that divine directive and you personally will be able to use it more effectively in your own life. I'm excited to guide you into new applications of what faith implies for your journey.

However, as I mentioned, other Bible writers, the most prominent of whom was the apostle Paul, took up the directive, "live by faith," and updated it, based on their personal experiences with Christ. Remember, Habakkuk wrote some six hundred years before Jesus' coming. Habakkuk didn't have the benefit of Jesus' life and death to instruct him. Paul under inspiration actually modified the phrase and amplified it. He realized that what Habakkuk wrote as a practical directive for day-to-day living had more profound theological implications. Paul proved that "faith" had implications more encompassing than Habakkuk could ever imagine. By our contrasting what Paul meant by "live by faith," with what Habakkuk understood the term to mean, we receive a whole new appreciation for what the coming of the Christ, Jesus, truly meant for humankind. I expect your gratitude for the Lord will go up a full decibel! I can't wait to share that with you!

Here is another inspiration that came from Habakkuk. He dared to ask the age-old question, "Why, if there is a benevolent God, is there evil and wickedness in the world?" I say, "dared," because Habakkuk was bold enough to ask that question directly to God Himself. In his suffering and as he lived among the wickedness, he felt exasperated. Here were people purporting to be "God's people," yet they took advantage of the poor and marginal members of society. Why wasn't God acting when malevolent men, who claimed to be pious in the synagogues, stepped outside into the real world and be so hateful and hurtful? This is how Habakkuk put it, *Your eyes are too pure to look on evil; you cannot tolerate wrong. Why then do you tolerate the treacherous?...*(Ha. 1:13). Habakkuk agonized, why, if he, a human, could hardly tolerate the evil, could God seemingly tolerate it without acting? Habakkuk blurted out his question and then seemed to calm down by saying, in effect, "Now that I dared to scream this complaint to You, I'll wait for Your answer". His exact words, *I will stand at my watch and station myself on the ramparts; I will look to see what he will say to me...* (Ha. 2:1). And what an answer Habakkuk got back from the Lord! You've just got to listen to and comprehend this answer! Whenever you feel like blurting out a similar complaint to God, I hope you'll keep in mind God's answer. The answer made sense to Habakkuk; it calmed him. It will calm you, too.

THE MOST POPULAR SONGWRITER

At the end of Habakkuk's manuscript is a notation to the director of music indicating that this short writing (or at least parts of it) was put to music. Habakkuk evidently wrote the lyrics, though we can't say whether he wrote the actual music or whether his lyrics were just coupled with an existing Hebrew chant. Nonetheless, he is the songwriter (lyricist) you never hear of but whose words are among the most profound and popular in history to this day. He was indeed the most famous songwriter of whom you never hear.

This is the point I was alluding to when titling this volume, *The Most Popular Songwriter You Never Heard Of.* Habakkuk was that songwriter. The context of Habakkuk's writings gives us a good idea of when he lived, where he lived, and perhaps his occupation. First, we are quite certain Habakkuk wrote about 600 B.C. as a member of the nation of Judah, one of the two nations that claimed to be God's representatives on earth.

Also, from what we can ascertain from his Bible book context we conclude Habakkuk was of the tribe of Levi, given the divine assignment to work in conjunction with the temple in Jerusalem. One of the Levite assignments was to take charge of the music used in worship and celebrations. You'll notice that the notes at the end of Habakkuk Chapter 3 show parts of his writings were put to music and used in temple ceremonies. So among other things, Habakkuk was a liturgical songwriter among God's people, the tribes of Israel. What is interesting is that Habakkuk's songs no longer are popular, and in fact may never have been popular in his day. Probably in temple worship his songs didn't actually give credit to him as the writer, but at least one of his lyrics did become incredibly popular - so popular that millions of Christians throughout history have repeated his words themselves or at least have heard them spoken or sung. Habakkuk never in his imagination would have dreamed his writings would come to be so motivational. Again, God often uses the little people, humble folk, to do great deeds!

What I'm saying, though, is that Habakkuk was no superior man; his words of concern were voiced no differently than yours or mine might be. Still our Lord chose to use his words, collected, published and preserved, to encourage us. I say this to capture that recurring theme that reading Habakkuk calls to mind. God uses the little people to do great things. Habakkuk wasn't a celebrity in his day. He's never even mentioned by name by any other Bible writer. The Bible is filled with stories of men and women of faith, but nowhere do you read Habakkuk's biography; all we have is speculation. He is not even mentioned by name in the "great cloud of witnesses" held up in Hebrews as part of our heritage as people of faith. He was little in deed, but his influence had repercussions beyond what we might have imagined.

Turn with me now to the Bible verse at Galatians 3:11. This is one of many places in scripture where the apostle Paul argues for a foundational doctrine of the Christian faith. He supports his premise by quoting previous scripture as a precedent. Paul asserts, ***Clearly no one is justified before God by the law, because, "The righteous will live by faith."*** Guess whose song St. Paul was quoting here? That's right, Habakkuk's! One of our projects will be to compare and contrast Paul's and Habakkuk's understandings of the term "faith." You're guaranteed to glean some fascinating nuances on faith from this. Also, the conversations with God Habakkuk recorded under inspiration give us an unusual picture of the Lord. Employing the terminology of his day, he conveyed the power, the majesty and yet the patience and caring of our Father. That in itself will be a real inspiration to you. Let's examine together Habakkuk's story and his ideas from God. I've always found I benefit any time I listen to a mature spiritual person recount his story to me. Let's let Habakkuk tell his story.

MESSAGES I HOPE YOU NOTED:

- **Ordinary People Can Make Extraordinary Differences.**

- **One Meaning Of Meaning In Life Is Significance.**

Chapter Two

THE STORY BEHIND THE STORY

Let me tell you Habakkuk's story. I can assure you he's someone you can relate to. As will be true of most of us in our lifetimes, Habakkuk was never famous in his era. You'll not find a biography written about him or an autobiography written by him. All we have that survived is a short 3-page manuscript. And all I can tell you about him must be gleaned from circumstantial evidence. Like so many the Lord has used in the past and so many He continues to employ in His endeavors today, Habakkuk was just an ordinary man. He wasn't rich or famous, wasn't a king or a prince. He doesn't refer to himself as a sage or prophet, though, looking back, we'd readily call him both. Habakkuk was one of God's little people called to complete a giant task, though he didn't even know it at the time.

At the end of Habakkuk's manuscript is a notation to the director of music indicating that this short writing (or at least parts of it) was put to music. Habakkuk evidently wrote the lyrics though we can't say whether he wrote the actual music or whether his lyrics were just coupled with a Hebrew chant. Nonetheless, he is the songwriter (lyricist) you never hear of but whose words are among the most profound and popular in history to our day. He was indeed the most famous songwriter of whom you never hear.

Not much is known about the personal life or details of Habakkuk. Scholars debate many ideas, some of which seem highly probable, but the prophet himself offers his readers little clue about his origins. For instance, some scholars translate the name "Habakkuk" as a form of the Hebrew word for "embrace"; others take it to refer to a garden plant or flower. The name appears to be of foreign origin, leading some to speculate either an Assyrian or Babylonian influence on Judah, the mixed heritage of Habakkuk's parents, or even that the prophet himself was a foreigner. The consensus of Habakkuk's tribal affiliation is that of the tribe of Levi, based on mention in an apocryphal addition to the book of Daniel titled *Bel and the Dragon*.

THE STORY BEHIND THE STORY

The story of Habakkuk in the Old Testament stands as one of deep faith and honest pleading with the Living God. However, the story is even more meaningful when one looks "behind the scenes" and surveys the backdrop against which it was written. Political instability and societal corruption within the nation of Judah, combined with political threats from outside its borders, created a ticking time bomb that finally exploded in Habakkuk's time. Facing this tribulation, Habakkuk pours out his distress to God, trying to understand how the Almighty God in whom he and his countrymen have placed their faith could allow such a terrible reality to come to pass on His people. A primary factor driving Habakkuk's struggle of faith and subsequent conversation with God is the declining spiritual and moral state of the nation of Judah. He laments to God in Ha. 1:4: ***Therefore the law is paralyzed, and justice never prevails. The wicked hem in the righteous, so that justice is perverted.***

This statement reveals several aspects of Judah's societal corruption. The people were treating one another with disrespect, leading to all kinds of violence and destruction. The result of this behavior was severe injustice. This was bad enough, but compounding the problem is Habakkuk's observation that the righteous had shaky legal recourse from the wicked in Judah's courts. As he says in verse 4, ***Therefore the law is paralyzed, and justice never prevails***. What should have been a safe conduit for the innocent to seek aid had become incapable of serving its purpose.

Commentaries on Habakkuk note that the Hebrew words for strife and conflict (see Ha. 1:3) are legal terms. Habakkuk's use of these words, followed by his observation that strife and conflict *abounded* in Judah, indicates that litigiousness was rampant throughout society. Not only were the righteous being taken advantage of or altogether ignored in court when they had been legitimately wronged; they also suffered what one commentary calls "mock legal battles." Thus Habakkuk cries out to God for help and understanding. He is deeply distressed and confused by what is happening in the society around him and wants God to answer.

Political Trouble Inside Judah and a Threat from Outside

Internal societal corruption was not the only cause of Habakkuk's concern. To understand Habakkuk's distress over the state of his country it is helpful to also look at Judah's internal political woes. And when Habakkuk looked beyond his troubled country's borders he saw a looming threat on the horizon: Babylon.

In the seventh century B.C. Judah had seen its share of political turbulence. That century began at the end of King Hezekiah's reign. Under his rule, Judah resisted being subject to the power of the Assyrian Empire, which was the dominant political force in the region at that time. As a result, Judah had to pay a heavy tribute to Assyria. One positive of Hezekiah's rule was the religious reform that he brought to his country. Under his order, no foreign religious practices were allowed, a problem with which Israel and Judah both had struggled.

The two kings following Hezekiah – Manasseh and Amon – took the opposite route. Beginning with Manasseh, not only did Judah become subject to Assyria (a fate which Hezekiah desperately sought to avoid), its spiritual life also became corrupted. Foreign religious practices were reintroduced to Judah's culture.

After King Amon's rule ended, a man named Josiah took the throne. Josiah is one of the greatest kings in Judah's history. He reversed Judah's course, both in relation to its politics and its internal spiritual state. Politically, Josiah made "vigorous moves toward national independence" from Assyria, finally achieving it when Egypt rose to power and removed Assyria from the region's political landscape. Spiritually, Josiah brought restoration, justice, mercy and enlightenment back to Judah's national consciousness.

Unfortunately, Judah's fortunes took another turn for the worse when Jehoiakim succeeded Josiah to the throne. Jehoiakim reversed the reformed policies brought about by Josiah and replaced them with "injustice, covetousness, murder, oppression, and violence." This is the sad state of Judah as Habakkuk seeks the Lord's counsel for the problems he witnesses inside his nation.

From outside Judah, another threat appeared. Though Egypt had knocked Assyria from the international power scene, it was soon to be conquered by a more powerful nation: Babylon. Babylon moved into the region and conquered Egypt, and "by 597 B.C. [King Nebuchadnezzar] had added Judah to his empire." As Habakkuk saw this reality coming, he boldly questioned God's motivations for using such a country as Babylon to punish Judah for its corruption and sin. He was unable to reconcile how God could do so when Babylon was more culpable than Judah.

The context of Habakkuk's writings gives us a good idea of when he lived, where he lived and perhaps his occupation. First we are quite certain Habakkuk wrote about 600 B.C. as a member of the nation of Judah, one of the two nations that started out as the twelve tribes of Israel many years before. Though the nation had many glorious and prosperous years in the past, it was now living in the shadow of its past glory. Rather recently Judah had been ravaged by and considered a vassal state of the Assyrian Empire and was now living in an area dominated by the new world power, Babylon.

Judah yearned for the independence and prosperity it once had. Here was a country that traced its ancestry back to the patriarchs of old, beginning with Abraham, to whom God gave the promise, *"...I have made you a father of many nations,"* (Ge. 17:5). God even promised this ancestor of Judah the land in which he was now living, *"I will give as an everlasting possession to you and your descendants..."* (Ge.

17:8). What a tragedy, Habakkuk and his countrymen thought, from being a nation chosen by God and distinguished by past prosperity to have fallen to such a lowly state - a people not only having lost their freedom but in the midst of poverty partially due to the exorbitant tributes exacted by the conquering nations around them, each taking their turn pillaging and looting, and then requiring a yearly ransom from the nation.

Fortunately, most of us living in the Western world might find it difficult to relate to the plight of Judah. Economically only a small percentage of the population of the Western nations including countries like England, Canada, France and the U.S. live below the poverty level. We also have freedom that is envied by much of the world. Such was the heritage of the land of Judah in its finest hour. Now it had seemingly lost everything. Countries in the former communist bloc of nations can easily relate to Judah's situation. Take a country like Poland, which has for centuries been used as a pawn by neighboring countries. In modern times controlled by Germany before the Second World War and occupied by Russia and communist troops after the war, Poland's freedom has been at the whim of dictatorial regimes until its recent reprieve to relative freedom. Such was the lot of Judah. It could only mourn and wonder. How could one nation descend from prosperity, being the envy of the civilized world at one time, to excruciating poverty and depravity during a single lifetime?

DON'T MISS THE TWO SIMULTANEOUS STORIES

The Old Testament is on one level a history of good times and bad. The Bible chronicles on a national level what can happen to all on a personal level. When a nation or individuals forget their root values and no longer live by the proven principles of success, degradation, loss of happiness and fleeting fulfillment result. Elsewhere I have written about these basic principles of living first articulated in the Bible and then embellished by writers, historians, philosophers and social scientists in the ensuing two millennia.

We have Habakkuk's testimony from his perspective. Habakkuk lived in the good times and the bad. He tells us from his own experience how life had deteriorated in a few short years. Josiah was Judah's last king mindful of the Lord's way. He insisted that his subjects adhere to the principles of living spelled out in the Ten Commandments and the other Old Testament standards. Under Josiah, citizens of Judah felt satisfied with the political and social environment in their country because relative justice and fairness was the standard. However, once Josiah died, his two sons were successively installed as puppet kings acting under the behest of foreign empires. They had no zeal for God's morality and no longer continued publishing and modeling the principles of living meticulously recorded in scripture. Without reference to the laws of life, Judah soon deteriorated. Habakkuk's eyewitness account reports, *...Destruction and violence are before me; there is strife, and conflict abounds.* (Ha. 1:3).

Unfortunately, few recognized the contrast that Habakkuk insightfully heralded. This is just another example of one of the basic biblical themes repeated over and over, a history spanning thousands of years. Another Bible writer, David, gave his assessment based on his observations over a lifetime. Speaking from a positive rather than negative perspective, Psalm 37:25 testifies, *I was young and now I am old, yet I have never seen the righteous forsaken or their children begging bread.*

Only prophets and seers granted special wisdom seemed to discern the contrast. Time and time again, when the nation of Israel lived by the blueprint for living set out in scripture, their lives prospered. When the nation from the leaders on down accepted, valued and attempted to live by the standards and principles that appealed to the spiritually-minded among them, the Bible could report the inhabitants *...lived in safety, each man under his own vine and fig tree.* (1 Ki. 4:25). Every time the leaders scorned the living principles, the recommendations for living from a higher Source, the result was always disaster.

I want to emphasize a point here. From a macro national level to a micro individual level the results are similar. As a nation, when the Jews respected God's guidelines for living, they were rewarded and experienced prosperity and peace, and satisfaction prevailed. A disregard for the divine guidelines resulted in distress, destruction and disaster.

The principle, as stated repeatedly in scripture, is that an individual "reaps what he sows." So what seed we plant will result in a corresponding crop. There is no difference between planting corn seeds and reaping ears of corn as the crop and planting negative thoughts in our minds and reaping negative crops of economic and social hardship. That was the outcome of the Jews in Habakkuk's day. They never discerned the connection. When an individual emphasizes selfishness and material thinking in his life, the results will always be the same: a crop of distrust, disloyalty and a sense of distress. Habakkuk's writings highlight the fact that when his countrymen no longer followed the model of their God-fearing king, Josiah, who had died, their community suffered the consequences. Selfish thinking, material rather than spiritual thinking, and dishonest thinking brought ruin to a stable nation. The same results are even more certain and more direct when considering one's personal life. How one thinks, what one emphasizes, what is of most concern will predetermine one's life outcome.

I plead with you to learn the lesson that the entire Old Testament sets out as a rule of life. The history of the Israelites, generation after generation as their dealings were chronicled methodically, proved every time the nation turned from the guidance of God's higher principles of living, they suffered. No sooner did they repent and promise to observe these higher principles than they saw prosperity and wellbeing return. Any and every autobiography penned in scripture was a restatement of the law on a personal level. Each writer admitted when he observed God's higher standards he felt the serenity and peace of mind that comes from God. As soon as he felt cocky enough to go it alone, without God's guiding light principles, he faltered. Time and time again as a recurring motif, scripture warns us (and Habakkuk was one of those doing the warning), avail yourself of God's help and proceed with confidence and wellbeing or forget the higher standards, do it with your own wisdom and reap the return of distress and calamity.

I have to admit I've learned this lesson well. Fortunately I learned it at a relatively young age. But my years of experience dealing with people in business, professional and personal settings have cemented the principle of reaping what you sow. This simple notion asserts that whatever we put into our lives will affect our life outcomes. This works in so many ways. To the extent we treat others as friends, they will consider us their friends with all the attendant benefits. To the extent that we are honest and trustworthy, we enjoy loyalty and trust from others. To the extent we work to build a spiritual facet into our life values, we begin to gain wisdom not clouded by the clutter of the world around us. To the extent we strive for the higher, all-sustaining values in our lives, true feelings of wellbeing and genuine self-esteem will appear and will crowd out the demand for transitory needs such as never-satisfying material possessions. And to the extent we shun the tendency to feel we have all the answers to life's questions, we begin to see evidence of powerful help from higher powers and sources working in our lives.

These thoughts went beyond the thinking of those in Judah in Habakkuk's day. They were so busy sowing efforts to get ahead, planting treacherous plans to cheat their fellow men and women, that when they threw down seeds of hatred around them they got, not what they bargained for, but what they planted. They never really learned this immutable law of the spiritual world. I hope Habakkuk's eyewitness account is not wasted in our lives. I know the Lord purposed for Habakkuk to write his experience as a reminder to each generation that picks up and reads the account. Whenever a community of believers reads Chapter One, verses one through four, about the violence and lack of civility and says, "that sounds like our time," the words of Habakkuk are meant for them. What believer in our age doesn't have feelings that resonate with Habakkuk's when he said, ***"Destruction and violence are before me; there is strife, and conflict abounds."*** (Ha. 1:3).

In Habakkuk's despair, he hears the Lord's short-term solution to his plight. The retaliation by the Lord on Habakkuk's people would be accomplished by another marauding nation. He records The Almighty's words to Habakkuk clearly and decisively, *"I am raising up the Babylonians, that ruthless and impetuous people,"* (Ha. 1:6) and further, *"...Their hordes advance like a desert wind and gather prisoners like sand."* (Ha. 1:9). If it is true that Habakkuk wrote this prophecy about 605 to 600 B.C., he had to wait some fifteen years to see the prophesy fulfilled. The traditional date for Babylon's destruction of the temple in Jerusalem, the capital of Habakkuk's nation, was 586 B.C. At that time Babylon did as Habakkuk had prophesied; they "gathered prisoners like sand," devastating Judah and taking captives into exile in Babylon as slaves. This interim solution (the solution to the injustice in Judah by the Babylonians) was too bittersweet a solution for Habakkuk. "What about the Babylonians? Habakkuk asked. God made it clear these Babylonians would not be immune to the spiritual law of God themselves. God made it clear by addressing these words to the Babylonians, *"Now it is your turn! Drink and be exposed! The cup from the Lord's right hand is coming around to you, and disgrace will cover your glory."* (Ha. 2:16). The Lord here used words reminiscent of the phrase we often use in our age yet often forget, "What goes around, comes around." God taunted the Babylonians by saying, "the cup (of God's vengeance)...is coming around to you." History tells us, as foretold, Babylon was not allowed to bask in their glory for long; they were conquered by the Persians within the lifetime of some of their Jerusalem captives.

Habakkuk was not privileged to see the complete story - the episode of Judah's faithfulness to God and then unfaithfulness, followed by God's allowing the ruthless Babylonians to act as his henchmen to bring annihilation on Jerusalem and the surrounding countryside, to the eventual payback to Babylon for its wicked ways, which allowed the Jews to return to their homeland to start over again, this time to attempt to live by the Lord's righteous laws. We don't know if Habakkuk lived to see the first step to universal justice (when the Babylonians destroyed Habakkuk's capital city). In a way we hope not, since all participant observers in that event suffered excruciating pain from starvation and beatings. It's quite certain he did not live to see the second denouement (resolution) of God's plan. However,

Habakkuk saw the unraveling of history in his mind's eye years in advance. Habakkuk had to be a contented man for him to say, resolutely, *"I will stand at my watch,"* (Ha. 2:1). In other words, to say, "I'll be patiently waiting to see how it all works out." He would not be able to pen the words of encouragement to all generations, *"...the righteous will live by his faith,"* (Ha. 2:4) without heeding the directive himself.

ONE OF MANY SPIRITUAL PRINCIPLES TO LEARN

Through scripture one discovers little principles, little maxims, little suggestions that turn out to be milestones in life. Here's one of them. This spiritual principle that Habakkuk and all those in a close relationship with their God know, "You reap what you sow," works in many aspects of life. We've talked about how a whole society, the kingdom of Judah, suffered its backlash. But most important, understand that the principle is especially applicable to individuals. As I mentioned, I've had to personally learn the rule as it unfolded in my world. I've been forced to admit whenever I've acted without regard for others or for the Lord, the final outcome has always been disappointing at best. I remember the times I took the easy way out, doing the minimum and not considering the welfare of others. Invariably it always came back to bring regret. Whenever we forget the welfare of others, for example, we're forgetting the Lord's command to show love. Under those circumstances, how can we ever expect God's special assistance when we need it? Acting, or should I say reacting, as we think of our own welfare only, will always lead to a whole new set of problems once the "reaping rule" begins to work itself out.

A good example of that is the act of lying. I've analyzed the little white lies I've told in the past and in most cases I realize I've just reacted without thinking, feeling that a lie was the easy way out. Either I didn't want to put myself in a bad light or I was too lazy to provide all the details to a business associate or I was fearful of the other's reaction to the truth. In every case I've always suffered for not living by God's law. Fortunately, I normally don't knowingly transgress the laws of life

(I've found these laws to be set down clearly in scripture), but when I do, whether knowingly or unknowingly, the rule of reciprocation always exacts its due. As a result, over time I have not intentionally lost friends, nevertheless, I have in actuality lost business associates and possible friendships and associations that traced back directly to my actions.

As I've admitted, I realize now that the occasions where I, out of laziness, apprehension or oversight, have not disclosed full truth in dealing with others and they found that out sometime and somehow down the line, my reputation was reduced in the minds of these others. They may treat me with less respect; they may be more guarded and less spontaneous when dealing with me. The point is that a possible mutually successful relationship or friendship was curtailed due to my actions. As the Israelites and as Habakkuk observed on a national scale, the law of reciprocity worked without regard to the society or to the individual that attempted to dodge its certainty.

A perfect example of the results of breaking the standard of truth and its unfailing consequences is preserved for us in historical form in scripture. I'm thinking of the story of Jacob and Esau. The two brothers were sons of Isaac, the son of the patriarch, Abraham. Jacob always dreamed of having the most valuable gift his father could ever pass on to his children, the official family blessing and designation as heir and administrator of the family estate. Jacob reasoned that since he had been divinely promised this blessing, though his brother Esau was legally in line for the special privileges, it would be acceptable to do whatever was necessary to get what he thought was rightfully, though not legally, his. Jacob, with his mother's help, used a deception, a lie, to trick his father into officially giving him the family birthright.

He reasoned that to employ a lie to get whatever was rightfully his would really not be a major indiscretion. But how wrong he was. His deception set up a chain of events that forced him to flee for his life and go into exile in another country to escape the wrath of his brother. Jacob was forced to spend many years away from his family, living in fear of reprisals from his own brother. He, too, had to endure similar deception and unfair treatment while in exile. After many years of suffering, Jacob did get his coveted blessings, but he had to admit he would have been far better served by waiting on God to orchestrate events so that his promised blessings would be realized, rather than taking matters into his own hands by lying and deceiving. You can read the story for yourself starting at Genesis, Chapter 27. And remember when you read that no one is ever immune from the reciprocal treatment set in motion whenever an individual disregards a divine principle of living for self-aggrandizement.

I've mentioned but one of a number of what I consider universal laws of life and relationships: to uphold and share truth rather than deception. There are others found throughout scripture. As a starting point I'd direct you to Exodus, Chapter 20, where you find the list of the Ten Commandments. This is a good primer cautioning the reader that our relationship with our fellow humans and our communion with God is affected by our understanding and application of these principles. Whether you prefer to interpret these commandments literally or more generally, each states a principle of living that cannot be transgressed with impunity. So, for example, one of these "commands" is to keep the Sabbath, to rest from working one day out of seven. This can be observed literally by desisting from all physical labor one day per week. Many Christians would also suggest that the important principle here is the idea of recognizing we can't do it all ourselves; we must learn not to vest supreme confidence in ourselves. At times we must desist from our own efforts and acknowledge the need of the help of a higher power. That is an example of observing the Sabbath commandment in principle.

Psychologically we observe the Sabbath when we make room for recreation and relaxation in our schedule. Here we "rest" in deference to how we were designed by our Maker. These are examples of principles. Please don't use my rationale to say I'm not advocating a literal Sabbath observance or seventh day rest. That's the responsibility of each person to determine individually. What I am saying is that the principle cannot be ignored with impunity. Now it's your turn. Look up the Ten Commandments in Exodus, Chapter 20 and see if you can isolate the principle of life highlighted in each. Then acknowledge that if you knowingly or inadvertently sidestep any, there will be consequences to deal with in the future. Remember the Ten Commandments are just a sampling of the laws of living preserved in story and history for your personal benefit. I encourage you to be a life-long student of the idiosyncrasies of each.

THE LORD'S MESSAGE...BE PATIENT

The story of Jacob I previously mentioned was very familiar to Habakkuk when he complained that the Lord was taking too long to mete out justice. God actually reprimanded Habakkuk for a momentary wavering in faith when He admonished in Ha. 2:3, *"...Though it linger, wait for it; it will certainly come and will not delay."* What the Lord was saying is a message to each of us. Be patient, says our God. Don't be anxious. Remember I'm in control. I'll see that it happens at just the right time. Don't doubt the mission's success!

From a human standpoint of limited perspective things may appear to be postponed. It may appear the Lord is "lingering" as God says in Habakkuk. But that's only from the human vantage of finite time. From God's standpoint it "will not delay," it's on schedule, it's certain. You and I as human spectators need not doubt or complain. We need only do one thing as God says in Ha. 2:3, just "wait for it." We work on our patience and build our faith by waiting. According to God's schedule it will be right on time.

I know that's easier said than done. I've always found that I need only to get busy with a new project occupying my mind and the wait is much easier. Dwelling on the problem only makes matters worse. Praying for patience, praying for help to be settled about what you have no control over, will work. Remember the experiences of those imprisoned for the Christian stand they have taken. One such prisoner spent fifteen years incarcerated before justice was done and he was released. He said that fifteen-year period brought him closer to his God and taught him how to live with patience. His experience taught him how to be patient. During his ordeal he used the time to prepare for the work ahead.

There is always plenty for us to do while we wait. When we occupy our time helping others and fulfilling assignments set before us, time becomes immaterial. Keeping busy doesn't allow us to dwell on the injustice or the suffering. Anything we can do to keep our minds off ourselves and our inconvenience helps. A good friend told me he has learned to take one day at a time. "I can always be inconvenienced for one day. I can always suffer for one day, that's all I have to endure, one day. When I've successfully completed one day, I always find the next is easier, but I don't think about that. I just think about the one present day I'm living. I always find the Lord gives me the faith, the strength, the patience to deal with the one day. And if I must find the next day I'm still in the same predicament, I start the process over, but again, just for one day. I can say, 'Lord, it's a new day, but it's still here, just help me this one day. Help me find what to do this one day so I can be constructive and make a difference while I wait.'"

This is good advice for all of us and for all occasions. If circumstances dictate you must suffer with physical frailties, the Lord is telling you through Habakkuk, "wait for it;" wait for relief, it will come. If you suffer injustice, wait for it; the end of your injustice will come. When you see others suffer injustice, again, wait for it; the end of injustice will come on schedule, on God's timetable. He even promises that you'll never be required to endure beyond your capacity; He'll always give you the strength. *Cast your cares upon the Lord and he will sustain you; he will never let the righteous fall.* (Ps. 55:22).

BONDING WITH HABAKUKK

I personally can't help but be energized when I read Habakkuk's story. He admitted he complained, he admitted his patience was short, he admitted he was short with God, but once he spoke aloud and had time to think about it, he looked at things differently. In Chapter 3 of his book, after all was said and done, Habakkuk ends with a prayer to his Lord. He lets God know he hasn't forgotten what the Lord has done in the past for His people, the Israelites. One by one he recounts the many times God had come to the aid of His people as if to say, "If You did this in the past, how can I doubt that You will come to our aid now?" Habakkuk only has praises for God after he's had a chance to meditate on his predicament and after he's realized: Who is he to question the strategies of God?

I don't know about you, but I can really bond with Habakkuk since I've dealt with adversity in a similar way. I can admit it now after reading Habakkuk's confession. I don't feel like I'm the only one to be so shortsighted at times. Thank you, Habakkuk, for helping me see I'm not the only one to feel like complaining to God. And how many times have you felt the same way? You've been hurt; you don't deserve such treatment. Why does the Lord allow this injustice? After you complain and get it all out, you admit it's not the Lord's doing, He didn't perpetrate the malice; He just allows it. But you do realize, like Habakkuk, that your God will give you the strength and wisdom to deal with the adversity. You then have no problem saying like Habakkuk, "Sorry, God," and then, *...I stand in awe of your deeds, O Lord.* (Ha. 3:2). Habakkuk went on to recount one by one the miraculous interventions by the Lord in the history of the Israelites. How could Habakkuk even think that his Heavenly Father wouldn't do the same again?

Finally, listen in on this man of faith talking to God as he admits that even if he's left with nothing, no crops to eat, *no grapes on the vines, no sheep in the pen, and the fields produce no food* (Ha. 3:17), "I won't lose faith," Habakkuk says, *yet I will rejoice the in Lord, I will be joyful in God, my Savior.* (Ha. 3:18). After reading that, your first impression might be to say, "Isn't that a little arrogant on Habakkuk's part? Come on, now." I could say the same thing. After all, isn't he just feeling good about himself? At the moment he feels pretty confident but when he is confronted with a major test of his faith, a time without food or some physical abuse, will he be saying the same thing? First, remember that Habakkuk is praying to God directly here. He's not boasting to you or me; that would be quite different. And though he may be feeling confident at the time of this utterance, he's still talking to God in prayer. To make this promise to God (I will rejoice in You, no matter what) without believing it with every fiber of his self would be far more foolish than arrogant. It would be extreme blasphemy to God's face, tantamount to suicide. Besides, history would not have kept his precious place in Hebrew worship literature if he had reneged on his promise to God.

I'm inspired by Habakkuk's resolve. It provides all of us with a benchmark of what faith really is. I have often tested myself using Habakkuk's benchmark, his example. I ask myself, "Can I say like Habakkuk no matter what, no matter what suffering I go through, no matter what abuse I experience, no matter what injustice I'm confronted with, I will "be joyful in God my Savior"? That's the kind of faith I want, don't you? I want to have confidence that no matter what, my God will be my Savior. I pray if you don't have that yet, work toward that goal or benchmark. Pray for it daily. I can promise in time you'll be able to say those words just as readily and sincerely as Habakkuk did.

FEELING ON TOP OF THE WORLD

Habakkuk then leaves us with one last fantastic thought. He uses a metaphor, a practice I'm sure we've all seen. Remember the picture of a mountain goat or mountain deer on top of a mountain, surveying the landscape far beyond. From its vantage point you can see miles in each direction. What serenity, what strength, what power and what confidence are evoked by that picture! In the last verse of Habakkuk's writings is a phrase or mantra worth repeating often. *The Sovereign Lord is my strength; he makes my feet like the feet of a deer, he enables me to go on the heights.* (Ha. 3:19).

So how can you possibly feel on top of the world when all is glum? Habakkuk's faith transformed him. Habakkuk's faith made him feel "on top of the world." No one or no thing could shake his confidence since his confidence was in the Lord. He felt energized and able to take on anything with God's strength behind him. And that is what our Lord wants for each one of us. He wouldn't have inspired Habakkuk to proclaim this if it wasn't in reach of all of us. What a horrible trick to play as if to say, "Habakkuk was special but you'll not be able to attain to his level of faith." No, God wanted that for all of us. I promise you if you stick with this analysis of Habakkuk's inspired words and thoughts, you'll be able to experience the same confidence, strength and energy that Habakkuk displayed. By your reading, prayer and meditation to God in conjunction with Habakkuk's outline, I promise you'll have the strength and joy he experienced!

Habakkuk knew what God had done in the past (all of Habakkuk, Chapter 3 is a recounting of that). So he knew what he could expect from God in the future. You'll be able to say with Habakkuk, too, "I'm going to come out on top, if I just stick with my Father." I know I'll one day figuratively be standing on top of a mountain surveying the country with the sun of God's love shining down on me, with no one around, only me and God (with that bright sun reminding me that God is right there with me). Can't you just picture the light breeze and yourself there thanking God and feeling so grateful you were willing to follow the path set by each man and woman of faith, people of faith like Habakkuk. I can't think of a more motivating and exciting picture than that, promising you what is in store as you "live by faith" as Habakkuk beseeches you to do. However there's a story within a story that we don't want to miss-a national story and an individual one.

MESSAGES I HOPE YOU NOTED:

- **The Lord Uses An Average Man To Spread A Message That Spans The World**

- **If You Think Things Are Hard Today, Remember How Horrendous They Were In Habakkuk's Day**

- **Seemingly Little Bible Principles For Living Are Giant Steps For A Successful Life**

- **Though Living Over 2500 Years Ago, Habakkuk Is More Like You And Me Than We May Realize**

Paul Serwinek

Chapter Three

IS TALKING BACK TO GOD
AN UNFORGIVEABLE SIN?

When I read the writings of Habakkuk I'm reminded that the book is comprised of two prayers and two answers from God along with a final summary by Habakkuk. This Bible book was written, among other reasons, to teach us how to pray. What I take away most vividly from Habakkuk's writing is the kind of relationship he had with the Superior Being of the universe. To this day my upbringing doesn't make it easy for me to talk to God the way Habakkuk did. But it wasn't just Habakkuk, Gideon, David, Moses, other pinnacles of biblical heritage have portrayed to us that when it comes to prayer, no holds are barred; just about anything goes. I don't know about you, but I wasn't brought up that way. I was taught to approach Our Majesty in a polite, dignified manner with respect and decorum. But I don't see that with Habakkuk and the others I mentioned. They pray to God like they talk to a friend or spouse, thanking, praising but also venting and pleading at times.

For example, note Habakkuk's initial entreaty to the Lord in Ha. 1:2. Again, Habakkuk complains to the Father in Ha. 1:13. These prayers were anything but perfunctory prayers. We can all learn from Habakkuk here. He didn't just repeat the same words and phrases, but told God exactly how he felt. I've always found that putting into words our true feelings is the best first step to dealing with those feelings. Enunciation brings to consciousness what you are feeling. One of the major psychological problems of our times is the tendency to suppress what we feel. Sometimes it's done consciously as a ploy to avoid having to deal with problems. However, most often we subconsciously suppress our concerns not even recognizing we have issues to resolve.

I've often found that I can go for days not feeling my normal, optimistic, excited self only to realize at a particular moment, "Hey, I'm not happy!" I've forced myself to confront the emotion. I analyze, "Why is it I'm feeling 'down'? What has happened?" At times, I can trace it to a disappointment a few days before, or it might be something I'm worried about – for example, if my children are on a trip in another country or maybe I'm having an issue on the job. I have a tendency to collect these concerns; they build up, like a snowball rolling down the hill, gaining weight and momentum till the sheer force of them as one giant snowball starts to impair my performance in other areas. So when I finally awake to my predicament and my concerns, and finally realize consciously that I must confront them, my disposition has improved. It's amazing that just being able to put into words all those built-up concerns will immediately alleviate a good deal of the pressure. Habakkuk has taught us to take those concerns up with our Father. I'm finding I'm not as reluctant to talk to God, feeling like I'm bothering the Lord. I'm less likely to stoically insist to myself, "I'm a grown man, I should be able to deal with this myself." I know better, I know I can't, and so I'll now preface my entreaty to the Lord with the words, "I can't do it anymore on my own, that's why I'm coming to You. Lord, how should I look at this problem, what can I do, or is there anything I can do?"

WHAT'S THE PROBLEM?

This is what Habakkuk did. He was agitated to the point he could pour out his soul to the Lord. The first chapter of Habakkuk starts right out with Habakkuk complaining to his Lord and he pulled no punches in baring his soul. Ha. 1:2 starts out, *How long, O Lord, must I call for help, but you do not listen?* I think we've all felt the same way at one time or another. The difference is Habakkuk complained directly to God. He was so upset that his words of prayer came out quite bluntly. He intimated, "You're supposed to be my Lord, You're supposed to help me, at least You've promised me You would, but I keep calling on You and You're not answering." Haven't we all felt that way at times? Habakkuk demonstrates to us it's not unusual to feel that way and it's permissible to question the Lord that way. From Habakkuk's words we can assume he'd tried to be patient, waiting for an answer, but it just hadn't come. Haven't you said or wanted to say, "I can't take it any longer. I don't know what I'm going to do!" Well, Habakkuk is suggesting to us, it's okay to talk that way to God. God knows you're upset, God knows we're at our wit's end with nothing more we can do but importune Jesus passionately, skipping the formality, just saying what we feel.

In Habakkuk's instance, he was complaining about the violence and injustice in his society. In effect, he says, "I've pointed out the violence to You, and I've shown You the injustice, but You seem to do nothing and just tolerate it." Again, we've all felt that way, as if God doesn't care. What Habakkuk was saying was tantamount to accusing God of not caring. From the Lord's response, we're assured that that's the furthest thing from the truth. He told Habakkuk by inspiration exactly what He was going to do to resolve the injustice in Habakkuk's world. Happily, Habakkuk wrote to assure us that if we persevere in prayer, an answer will always come, though maybe belatedly in our estimation.

I can add my experience to Habakkuk's here. I remember praying literally for three or four years for help. I beseeched our Lord regularly, begging Him to open my eyes to the next project he wanted me to work toward for His glory. I felt at times that Jesus just didn't care. I kept this inside, feeling depressed and dejected for periods of time. I got to the point, I admit, of being exasperated like Habakkuk. Fortunately, I didn't give up, though I did lack my initial enthusiasm at times. But in time, an answer came.

I happened to be seated in a banquet hall (it wasn't even a Christian gathering), and across from me was seated an older gentleman and we began to talk. As it happened, he was a Christian and he began to tell me excitedly about the work he was doing with the Gideons (the Bible placement society). I was impressed with his work and with his enthusiasm. I then admitted my predicament: I'd been praying for an answer, I wanted my enthusiasm back, I wanted a work sanctioned by the Lord so that I'd feel like an instrument of the Lord again. The gentleman, Bill was his name, confessed it wasn't long before this that he was in a similar quandary. He advised that a book he had recently read had helped him clarify his thinking. In fact, he volunteered to send me a copy. Well, when I received the volume, *Half Time* by Bob Buford, I too, found it was just what I needed. The book helped me clarify my priorities and suggested several directions to pursue. I was again on my way.

I look back on what some would call serendipity (being seated with the right person at the right time), but I now know it was an answer to prayer. Though the answer appeared to be belated, I can say it came at the time I truly required it. I know of Habakkuk's frustration, waiting for longer than I thought was necessary, but now admitting the answer did come when I really needed it. I didn't have to change plans or regret any lost time while I waited. I've learned it's not a denial of faith to call out to the Lord in frustration and impatience as Habakkuk did. Our God, our Maker knows that this is a natural tendency of an individual uncertain and unclear of his/her path. I can only encourage you to follow Habakkuk's example of fervent importuning of our God. This is just another aspect of "living by faith," exactly what Habakkuk recommends in Ha. 2:4.

STILL COMPLAINING

What Habakkuk next tells us, at first reading, suggests Habakkuk is not following his own direction, to "live by faith." We've read where Habakkuk first complained to God and in time he got a clear answer. Remember Habakkuk asked pointedly why the Lord appeared to just tolerate injustice, and in another chapter we'll considered the Lord's answer given under inspiration. The Lord made it clear he would require recompense from the selfish, unreformed upper class. The bloodthirsty Babylonian armies would be allowed to completely desolate the evil social structure in Judah. At first, that seemed to satisfy Habakkuk, but in time Habakkuk continued to feel sorry for himself. He again complained to God, almost as if he never heard God the first time. He concluded that God's first answer didn't sit well. This time, though, Habakkuk prefaces his complaint with an acknowledgement of The Almighty's power. He lavishes praise on God in preparation for his questioning of God's rationale for action. I know exactly how he felt. He thought, "I've got a delicate question and objections to throw before the Almighty and I don't want to appear too objectionable." In sincere deference to God, Habakkuk acknowledges the matchless sovereignty all believers come to appreciate. Habakkuk confesses that God alone is everlasting, He alone is the "Holy One." He is too pure to associate with any evil (Ha. 1:12-13).

Now this sets the stage for Habakkuk's complaint. The crux of the matter is this, according to the prophet (I'm paraphrasing here). "If it's true that You are too pure to associate with evil and I know You are, then why do You let the Babylonians, the most wicked and oppressive of the nations, act as Your agent to bring renunciation on Judah. My nation, Judah, is wicked, but the Babylonians are far worse than we are. How could You possibly resolve one level of wickedness by tolerating a more serious level of wickedness?"

Habakkuk restates the age-old question Ha. 1:13, "...Why then do you tolerate the treacherous? Why are you silent while the wicked swallow up those more righteous than themselves? In other words, why, if there is a God, does He allow evil to continue?" Isn't that the age-old question? And the Lord is not hesitant to answer. His reply in Chapter 2 makes it clear that the more wicked Babylonians will in turn discover justice being visited upon them as well. Speaking to the Babylonians, The Almighty now says, "Because you have plundered many nations, the peoples who are left will plunder you..." (Ha. 2:8). God assures us that wickedness and evil are tolerated only for a time.

I won't go into a detailed treatise on the question of evil. I've stated my explanation elsewhere and many other authors have gone over the issue in great detail, but let me enumerate a few points. First, recognize there is only a problem reconciling evil in a world created by a benevolent God if we believe this world and this life is the only life there is. The shortsighted view is that if the malefactor is not brought to total justice and his evil halted in this lifetime, evil has proved triumphant. Similarly, if pain and suffering continue in an individual's life without letup, evil and suffering appear to be the master. But this is only if we take a short-term, shortsighted view.

TAKE A LONG-TERM VIEW TO RESOLVE ISSUES

This is exactly what Habakkuk's story indicates. Humans, in their impatience, often allow themselves only to see the short-term view. At first, in Chapter 1 of Habakkuk, our author could only see the short-term perspective. His homeland was infested with malevolent, greedy men. The suffering they were responsible for seemed unbearable. Habakkuk cried out in agony because he could only see the moment, not the denouement, the full working out of events. Now add in the Lord's first reply to Habakkuk in Chapter 1 and it becomes clear. Yes, evil can prosper short-term, but long-term it is extinguished. The Lord says in effect, "At this very moment I am allowing the Babylonians to make plans to decimate this land of Judah". The selfish, money-loving upper class that was oppressing the common man would be the main targets of the Babylonians. God said, ***"Look at the nations and watch—and be utterly amazed..."*** (Ha. 1:5). The Judeans will be utterly amazed that in one fell swoop the evil in Judah will be extinguished. It wouldn't take years but in a relatively short time the whole area would be desolated. No more evil, no more injustice because no more inhabitants. It's that simple for The Almighty, but in good time. He would allow the greed and depravity of one nation to terminate the evil of another. Therefore, in the long term, evil in Judah was not allowed to flourish.

Habakkuk didn't get the point the first time the Lord presented the concept to him. He got to thinking, "All right, maybe one source of evil might be eliminated but what about the depraved Babylonians?" Habakkuk considered them even worse than his selfish countrymen. Habakkuk complained, ***"...Why then do you tolerate the treacherous?"*** (Ha. 1:13). Habakkuk was thinking only short-term again. Yes, in the short run, Babylon, more wicked than Israel, would be in power, but only for a short time. The Lord of all nations had already determined that the Babylonians would only enjoy a fleeting moment of success. This is how Habakkuk interpreted God's inspiration to him: ***"Woe to him who builds a city with bloodshed and establishes a town by crime! Has not the Lord Almighty determined that the people's labor is only fuel for the fire, that the nations exhaust themselves for nothing?"*** (Ha.2:13). In other words, the Babylonians' bloodshed would be avenged. Their slave labor built mammoth cities, erected with criminal behavior, this would only turn out to be the fuel for a mammoth fire, reducing Babylon to rubble. Again, in the short term, evil might flourish but long-term evil will flop.

This is the lesson all Christians must learn. What is reality at the moment can very easily turn to be non-existent in a short time. The Lord tells us even in this world, right now, evil only has a tenuous hold. Evil always gives way to judgment and justice. There is a progression of evil as Habakkuk points out. In his world, first the Israelite upper class and then the Babylonian warlords appeared omnipotent, but neither had a firm hold in the long run. The history of humankind has shown this to be true. Among the most heinous deeds of the twentieth century were the intended ethnic genocide by Hitler and the extermination of peasants by Stalin. Each tyrant only enjoyed short-term success. Hitler's rise and fall could be told in a relatively short period of a few decades. Though it took Russian communism generations (some seventy years) to rise and fall, neither dictator's political philosophy has stood the long-run test of time.

For those of you that may feel that these endless historical proofs of rises and falls of evil in the short term are not sufficient justice, don't fret. While the history of all known civilizations has demonstrated an evil bent, no one brand of evil has ever endured. No one human dictator or suppressive society has lasted long-term.

What's more, consider the reasoning of arguably the greatest philosopher in secular academic studies ever to write. His name was Immanuel Kant. He proved to be one of those little people who made a bigger difference than he ever imagined he might. Throughout his life he never ventured more than a few miles from his childhood small hometown in Germany. Living in the nineteenth century, he never held political office and his logical, insightful reasoning may not be on the lips of many in future generations. But his vivid mind has helped put to rest the complaints of many secular philosophers concerning evil in the world. Though you don't hear much about him in the popular press, just as Habakkuk's accomplishments are not touted as significant, Kant helped many thousands of thinkers in the past two hundred years establish a faith built upon purely logical, reasonable arguments. Once a logical basis for faith was established, these logic-oriented seekers of truth were drawn to the Bible for further answers. Again, here's another instance of little people having big, far-reaching effects on society for good.

Kant reasoned this way: every society or group of people known to him had a concept of justice and fairness. Societal laws are in fact based on the endowed belief in all peoples that justice is a goal to be attained. Modern scientists use the term, "hot-wired." When an individual comes into this world, he or she is "hot-wired" with the concept of justice and a few other basic ethical building blocks in his or her genetic makeup. Only this explanation can account for the ubiquitous existence of justice concepts present in all peoples. Kant then reasoned, if justice is not ever fully attained in our individual lifetimes, that concept would have little value. Kant next reasoned that because all injustice and evil is never fully eradicated in the short run, it must be in the long run. The only way all people would see and cheer true justice and the elimination of evil is if life goes on beyond our merely 70-80 year temporal existence. To him, the existence of evil and injustice now was the best proof that there was a life beyond the present physical life.

Kant carried with him the hope, the faith in a long-run establishment of justice and repeal of the reign of evil. His faith was first energized by a series of logical step-by-step constructs, but augmented by the testimony of scripture. Kant did an invaluable service to many who would never consider examining the scriptures until they had a logical, clear, non-emotional basis for their search. Thank you, Immanuel Kant, one of the little people destined to help seekers of faith and truth in our modern world.

EVIL, BUT WHAT ABOUT FREE WILL?

Permit me to give you one more basis for accepting the presence of evil in a world controlled by an all-powerful, benevolent God. This is the idea of free will. Consider this: evil in a world of a benevolent God is only possible with free will. By free will, I mean choice, and choice usually demands accountability. So for God to expect accountability from His creation, all must be able to choose whether or not they wish to serve Him. You can imagine God, as we envision Him, also having a choice. He could have designed human beings so their actions could be limited by instincts such as found in other forms of life. Birds learn to fly and migrate and animals forage for food using instinctive behavior that's built into them. Our Creator could have also envisioned humankind as a race of robotic creatures. Within them would be programmed certain capabilities. Deviation from these activities could have been eliminated and therefore not possible. Robots, as they are employed now in manufacturing, for example, are capable of limited choices, if any, and perform a specific set of operations with no deviation. When there is a malfunction, the robot is simply repaired and never permitted to disrupt the assembly line.

Another possibility our Creator might have entertained was the concept of a creature having choice, not programmed with a limited number of mental decision capabilities but designed to identify possibilities and make decisions based on possible outcomes. Such a creature would be far more advanced than a robotic model and therefore more interesting to construct and observe. The downside, of course, is that with choices come fewer restrictions and the possibility of making wrong choices and a series of wrong choices might affect others in negative ways. These negative actions and outcomes that limit the actions of others and cause pain (whether physical, mental or emotional), are what we might say is a working definition of evil.

So here we have a seeming dilemma for God, though I'd stress the word "seeming" since with the higher power we've come to expect of our God, difficulties are easily rectified. Nevertheless, the Creator's choice was to settle, not for an inferior robot model, but to produce (create) the more advanced and delightful version.

With this version God would deign to relinquish some control and endow His creatures with capabilities heretofore reserved for a relatively select few beings, mainly the capability and intelligence to make choices. Given the possibilities, there really was no choice at all on God's part. Far superior intelligence and choice in the human race would introduce far more beauty and variety into the world, but also allow for evil and pain. For God, this enhanced the joy of having His creation willingly serve Him out of volitional choice, rather than by computer-like, predetermined programming. Free will allows for good choices with positive consequences or the absence of good choices leading to negative consequences.

As our friend, Habakkuk, found, though, the Lord in His love and mercy does not merely permit us only to experiment with choices, He provides communion and guidance for those that wish to avail themselves of them. Yes, there is evil and pain and suffering but there is also the promise from The Almighty that He will help us through any wrong choices and evil consequences we might encounter. In 1 Corinthians 10:13, He promises that He would not allow suffering beyond what one could endure. He would intervene where necessary so evil would not be perpetrated to the extent that it would eliminate humankind's gift of free will and choices. In fact, that's why those in a relationship with God never dwell on the evils in the world. They have the added assurance that their God is in control and allows evil, but limits its effects on those who seek His help.

With all Habakkuk's complaining and talking back to God, you still can feel the quiet reassurance in Habakkuk's entreaties to his God. He admitted, "You cannot tolerate wrong." He just had confidence within himself that God, the God he'd become familiar with, would not desert him. So while Habakkuk asked the rhetorical question, "Why then do you tolerate the treacherous?" (Ha. 1:13), he knew the answer.

He knew he didn't have to suffer evil on his own. He knew he could have God's guidance to make the right choices. He knew that God would not allow him to suffer beyond his endurance. He knew there would be an end to suffering. He knew his endurance of suffering would lead to a relief beyond his most optimistic expectations. He knew The Almighty would work along with him to insure that good would come to Habakkuk. ***...in all things God works for the good of those who love him.*** (Ro. 8:28). Finally, he knew he had a constant Companion with him every step into an unknown future.

He knew all these things. What I ask you, the reader, now is, "Do *you* know all that Habakkuk knew?" That knowing comes from a relationship with God. Just look back at your past experience walking with God, if you've had that privilege. Have you made it through serious difficulties? Has He helped you with choices? Has he seen to it that your situation is not hopeless? Those experiences build a relationship with God. A continuing relationship with God builds faith and provides the optimistic assurance that events in your future will be met with divine help and protection.

To those of you who have not had the privilege of a relationship with God yet, don't worry. You'll have that opportunity. You'll come to find as Habakkuk did, that "the righteous will live by his faith." We'll talk a lot more about that later. But God assures you that all you need to do is take the leap, though it might be a blind leap at first, and proclaim within yourself that you desire to explore a relationship with your Heavenly Father. Just ask as Jesus' disciples did, ***"Increase our faith!"*** (Lu. 17:5) They knew it wasn't always easy, but they knew enough about Jesus that He'd help them through any difficulty. Still they prayed beseechingly, "Increase our faith!" I can tell you from my experience that any request for more faith from God never goes unanswered. I've always found events and circumstances work out to assure me I'm not alone. Millions of other Christians worldwide assure you of the same. You will come to have the quiet assurance Habakkuk had.

I'LL WAIT AND WATCH

Let me now recount what faith did for Habakkuk. Remember now, in Habakkuk's story he tells us he complained bitterly to the Lord about the predicament Habakkuk's nation was in, suffering caused by injustice rampant in the land. God replied to him under inspiration to say the injustice would be rectified. But that didn't seem right to Habakkuk. He actually had the audacity to talk back to God, complaining that God's solution didn't appear fair, it just wasn't right. Now notice what Habakkuk says after he gets everything off his chest, so to speak.

This is what faith is really like. Habakkuk realized he probably wasn't going to see a resolution of the Israelites' situation in his lifetime. He realizes his own life would probably not play out the way he'd want. He wasn't going to see a happy ending anytime soon. On top of that, he thought God's solution wasn't a credible solution. What would you do under those circumstances? What if you were close to the end of your life due to sickness or an accident? Let's say you had a rift in your family. Your children wouldn't talk to you or maybe not to each other. You had tried to make amends but it just wasn't going to happen. You didn't see a happy ending for your earthly ending. Could you still continue to love the Lord? Could you still have faith that matters would be worked out after you were gone? Could you still leave this earth with peace of mind? Putting yourself in this position will allow you to feel how Habakkuk felt.

Habakkuk's response was, *I will stand at my watch and station myself on the ramparts; I will look to see what he will say to me, and what answer I am to give to this complaint.* (Ha. 2:1). That really is faith, isn't it? In effect, he was saying, "It doesn't seem right but I know You're always right. I expect it's not going to work out the way I'd like but I'm going to wait. I'm going to watch to see how You'll work it all out. I can't do anything else. I'll act like a sentinel stationed at a rampart of the city walls anxiously awaiting the resolution of the conflict. I know You'll give me a fair answer to my complaint. And since I'm not the only one complaining, I'll give Your answer to these others complaining with me." That's faith! Habakkuk could be calm even though he knew suffering was ahead. He just knew the Lord's answer and His final working out of the details would be fair and would be right. He said, "God, I can't do anything more but I know YOU can and will. I'm just going to wait for You to show me and I'm sure I'll be satisfied with the outcome."

So what about you? You may be going through major difficulties now. If not, you will be sooner or later. It's never fair if you or your friend contracts cancer, for example. How will you handle it? Habakkuk showed you how. He didn't just say, "I'll tell you what to do." No, he demonstrated by his own example. He lived his sermon, so to speak. That's faith, just knowing God can help. His way will work out best. Though you don't know at the moment what His way will be, you have that calm sense of assurance that it will all work out in the end. You can say, "There will be a happy ending to the story, my story, though I don't know it yet." If you don't yet have that assurance, trust me, trust Habakkuk, you <u>will</u> be able to trust the Lord. Keep praying, "Lord, give me more faith". Be resolved to work patiently building a relationship with your Father by starting to talk to Him in prayer often. Read His Word, the Bible, regularly and meet in association with others who are also trying to build their relationship with the Lord.

Every time you doubt, remind yourself Habakkuk doubted and every other Bible writer doubted. Habakkuk was no different from any of us, he didn't consider himself anyone of special virtue and confessed his doubt. That's one of the main messages of the whole Bible including Habakkuk's writings. With God's help, we can all overcome our doubt. We can be calm in spite of frequent doubt.

MESSAGES I HOPE YOU NOTED:

- **Talking Back To God Is Not A Sin**
- **The Lord Promises To Intervene In Evil**
- **Habakkuk Resolved To Watch And Wait, Can We?**
- **Would You Rather Be A Robot In Bliss Or Put Up With Evil To Have Free Willl?**

Paul Serwinek

Chapter Four

THE LORD ANSWERS PRAYERS IN THE MOST UNUSUAL WAYS

Permit me to preface this chapter on prayer as God's communication mechanism to us by saying that one of the major bases of your faith in God is or will be your personal relationship with your Creator. A time will come when your basis for faith will be questioned. Someone might question you on a seeming contradiction in the Bible. One verse appears to say "X" and another verse on the same topic may say "Y." Remember, your faith is not based on the fact that you are a Bible scholar with all the answers. Another time a friend might say he doesn't need to believe in a God because the theory of evolution makes belief in a God redundant. Again, your faith in a Creator is not based on your being a biological scientist with all the answers (the fact is, many scientists do have a strong faith in a Creator!).

Your faith is based on and is as strong as your personal relationship with the Lord. Of course, you're able ***...to give the reason for the hope that you have.*** (1 Pe. 3:15). Your beliefs have a solid foundation in fact and logic, but what anchors your faith is that personal relationship with our Lord. There will be times when a life experience, e.g. the death of a loved one, might momentarily shake your faith, but your personal relationship will bring you back. Or when you don't have a ready reply to a person demanding a logical, fact-based, scriptural answer on the spot, even this does not deter you. You know you can get that logical explanation if the questioner is sincere. But you also know that "knowing all the answers" has little to do with bolstering your faith.

RELATIONSHIP

It's all in the personal relationship. A relationship is built through time and experience and intimate contact. Your relationship with Jesus may have initially begun at a moment in life when you had nowhere else to turn and Jesus was there. You'll never forget that time, will you? Another possibility is that your friendship may have begun as a young child. The security of a father and/or mother guiding you, protecting you, and telling you about Jesus was your entry into God's world. You'll never forget the happiness, the carefree days of your youth when your every need was provided and you equate that with God since you had believing parents. Your experiences were different than mine but the feelings we experienced were very much the same. A feeling of security, trust, peace of mind, contentment - that's what we hold in common. Though that experience may have occurred in a moment in your case, or over a period of years as in my case, the experience is undeniable.

That's what we mean by relationship. No one can take that away from you. No one can taunt you, "That really didn't happen!" You and only you know, since you personally experienced it. For those of you who haven't yet experienced those moments of sublime peace and calm, I can only say you will. All you need to do is tentatively, hesitantly say in your mind, "God, I'm not sure about this but I'm telling You I can't do it on my own anymore, I need Your help. Through Jesus, please help me." If you say that sincerely, you know you can't fake it with God; He'll respond either in the moment or in the period of a few days. You'll know that God cares for you and no one will ever be able to take that away from you.

Once you start in your divine relationship you'll need to nurture the friendship. The more you learn of Him from friends, church or scripture, the more substance your relationship will have. And the more years you can look back on and say, "God helped me through this", or "Jesus protected me through that" or "I didn't know what to do so I prayed and it all seemed to work out for the best," - those are experiences no one can take away from you. You'd respond to any doubter, "Why would I ever give this up? Yes, I have had problems and setbacks and major trials, but I came through them, I've learned from them and I still feel the Lord is in control." That's a relationship. That's what all of us are striving for.

Habakkuk was such an example of godly relationship. He tells us something about his relationship with the same Lord with Whom you and I are building a relationship. His story is about to bolster our faith. He teaches the need to work regularly on that relationship. He teaches that friendships can have ups and downs and disappointments, and maybe a little bit of anger and bad feelings. But friendships grow through such experiences. Have you had the joy of an enduring friendship of twenty, thirty or forty years yet? If you have, you've invested a great deal of time and effort and you're not about to let that friendship unravel. That's what Habakkuk demonstrates to us. Watch and see, even when Habakkuk's best Friend, the Lord, seemingly disappoints him, Habakkuk gets upset, bursts out in anger but after a moment of contemplation, shrugs it off and apologizes. It's as if the blow-up never happened. Let me tell you the story. Listen carefully because I guarantee the exact same thing will happen to you sooner or later.

Have you ever had to pray in desperation as Habakkuk did?

First, let me say I'm glad Habakkuk had the courage and the humility to confess his foolishness. This way I don't have to give you an example of my own, since I might not have the courage to tell you the whole truth as Habakkuk did. In Habakkuk's own words, this is exactly what happened. You know the basic premise since you were introduced to Habakkuk back in Chapter 1. Remember, Habakkuk was indignant at the violence and injustice among his Jewish people. In particular, Habakkuk admitted the injustice at law was particularly difficult for him to stomach. Ha. 1:4 mentions his assessment of the courts: *...justice never prevails. The wicked hem in the righteous, so that justice is perverted.* I think we'd all feel as Habakkuk did then, if we were in his position.

There is something particularly intolerable when justice is perverted. Justice is a principal human value programmed into us by our Creator. Injustice just can't go on! Enduring injustice is tantamount to enduring physical pain. Some might even consider welcoming death rather than be forced to endure injustice over time.

We've all experienced injustice sometimes like Habakkuk, and under those situations a believer would naturally pray. Habakkuk did just that. He "cried out" (those are his words) to the Lord. In short order he received an inspired message from God. There will be an end to the injustice in Habakkuk's nation. The Lord added, "You'll be around to see it." In scriptural wording, God said, *"...I am going to do something in your days."* (Ha. 1:5). In other words, "Habakkuk, in your lifetime you will actually see the end of injustice. You won't die wondering when and if recompense will be meted out. You will see it, I promise." (Excuse my paraphrase). What a special concession to Habakkuk. His prayers will be answered in his lifetime. As you know, not every believer is allotted such a concession. Many Christian martyrs were tortured and died long before their peers saw the end of injustice, while the martyrs only saw the denouement through their eyes of faith.

Believers are assured their prayers are always acknowledged. I use that word, "acknowledged," advisedly. Our Lord will always let us know in one way or another that our petition was heard, whether by the working of events around us or by the words of a human messenger, perhaps a friend who is inspired to use the right words informing us of an answer. The answer may also come in a calm, settled feeling that envelopes our very person. Prayers of God's people are always answered but...the "but" is that the answer might be "No." Father knows best! Our Father might have a better, superior idea than we might. I needn't say more about that, for a "No" now will eventually lead to a different "Yes" in time. Do you understand what I'm saying? God may tell us "No" now, but keep praying, for a different, often better "Yes" will arrive from Him later. But there's a second "but" - but we might not appreciate the meaning of the answer at the moment.

Sometimes God's answer is "Yes, but..." And sometimes that answer is harder to accept than a "No." Have you ever got a "Yes," but the consequences of that "Yes" weren't what you bargained for? It's like the older gentleman, aged 72, with a wife of similar age. The way I heard the story, he found one of those magic lamps. He rubbed it and the resident genie appeared and granted him one wish. "What I'd really like," said our fortunate friend, "is a wife that's about 15 or 20 years younger than me." In an instant, after the poof of smoke dissipated, the gentleman looked at his hands and then at his face in a mirror to find that he now had the body of a 92-year-old man. Hence the saying, "Be careful what you wish for, you may just get it!" That goes for prayer too; be careful what you pray for since you may just get it!

Sometimes we don't anticipate our Lord answering that way ("yes, but"). However, it does happen and it did happen in Habakkuk's case. True stories, such as Habakkuk's, are set down in scripture to prepare us for all eventualities. We think we have it bad. Habakkuk suffered, was told he would suffer more and then he was told, "Your prayer is going to bring you more suffering than you bargained for but, yes, your prayer is to be answered." You have to feel sympathy for him but remember, as a reward he became "the most popular songwriter you never heard of." I know he'd consider that a wonderful outcome, as all outcomes end up being wonderful for those with a close relationship with our wondrous Creator.

In case you don't recall, this is what happened. The political networks in the judicial system in Judah were without a doubt corrupt. The Lord, Yahweh, whom the Israelites had originally proclaimed their counselor and protector, had every right to intervene. He had many options, but as those of you who have been blessed with a healthy relationship with our Father will concur, God often uses other humans as the instruments of His bidding. Rather than merely exposing the injustice and treachery in Habakkuk's nation, as Habakkuk would have had God do, God had a more far-reaching solution. In God's estimation the political and judicial systems in Judah were decayed beyond repair.

The only logical solution (and Habakkuk couldn't see this at the time) was to destroy and purge the system and start all over. Habakkuk was praying for a short-term solution while God settled on a long-term solution.

The Lord simply used the Babylonian Empire as His purging instrument. Here was a simple, logical resolution. Babylon was then the major world power centered in the Middle East. Relations between the Jews and Babylonians were strained at best. God simply withdrew His protection from around the Jews and allowed human nature to run its course. Since the Babylonians were fierce, ruthless warriors, it would take no prophetic ability to predict what would happen to the Jews. History tells us Babylon completely ransacked the cities and villages of Judah and the rallying point for all Jews, the magnificent temple in Jerusalem, was ravaged and decimated. When the temple, the pride of all Jews, was desolated, the conquerors met little resistance taking the best of the Jewish nation into captivity as slaves to Babylon. What a horrifying outcome for a once great nation! Jerusalem and Judah were no more. When they would be rebuilt years later, it would be with a fresh, pure approach to governance and legality free from injustice and favoritism. Habakkuk's prayers were answered, God's preference for justice was vindicated, and the natural end result of all human injustice could not be thwarted.

You could say the moral of the story is that phrase, "Be careful what you ask for, you may get it." But that could be a rather pessimistic view sometimes. A more appropriate way to style this true story is to say that prayers do come true and often in unexpected ways. Also, a history lesson is the perfect example of a maxim I firmly believe. Every human story has a happy ending or a sad ending; it just depends when you end the story. Here's what I mean. If we end Habakkuk's story with God's assurance to Habakkuk that a resolution to injustice would come, that's a happy ending. But if we end the story where Habakkuk first thought the story would end, it was a sad ending. See, Habakkuk knew when the Babylonians came to conquer it would be a sad day for the Jews, his people. Habakkuk complained a second time to God about the inherent injustice of allowing the Babylonians to pillage. Habakkuk couldn't see the next happy ending that would come when the Jews got another chance to start over and do it right this time. Throughout history there are always those cyclical spirals of alternate happy and sad endings. With God, though, there are only ultimate happy endings and because of God, humans have a choice to wish for their stay here on earth to have a happy ending. We'll have more on that later.

Let's get back to Habakkuk's story. We left him when he was incredulous hearing God's response to his first prayer. "Okay, Habakkuk, you're getting your wish soon, injustice will end in Judah." "But, God," Habakkuk objected, "That's not what I had in mind. The ultimate example of injustice is the Babylonians; they're far worse than my Jewish people." In Habakkuk's own words, *Is he* [the Babylonian] *to keep on emptying his net* [like a fisherman], *destroying nations without mercy?* (Ha. 1:17). If we end the story there, as Habakkuk was prone to do, that would be ultimate injustice. Habakkuk couldn't see the full picture. Habakkuk was tending to end the story too soon.

Isn't that human nature? The visionary prophet Habakkuk could only see so far in his vision. He saw over the first hill on the horizon but there is always another hill or obstruction on the horizon that man can't see over, a second hill. A prophet can only see as far as God's Spirit takes him on occasion. Maybe Habakkuk was impatient in not waiting for the end of the story before he complained. You can almost imagine God chuckling (I can indulge in such an anthropomorphic image since the Bible does) at Habakkuk's second complaint.

The Lord's second reply is sprinkled with a set of "Woe to's" addressed to the Babylonians. *"Woe to him who piles up stolen goods…"* (Ha. 2:6). *"Woe to him who builds his realm by unjust gain…"* (Ha. 2:9). *"Woe to him who builds a city with bloodshed…"* (Ha. 2:12). The beginning of the happy ending Habakkuk wanted is found in the Lord's proclamation to Babylon, *"Because you have plundered many nations, the peoples who are left will plunder you."* (Ha. 2:8). For Babylon, period, The End! But that's just the beginning of the end.

THE REST OF THE STORY

Other Bible writers fill us in on the real ending to this episode of encounter with The Almighty. The real ending was actually a new beginning. Yes, the Jews saw their lands desolated and were taken to Babylon as slaves. Yes, they lost everything including many lives, but while in captivity they were blessed, and as an ethnic group were able to keep their identity. Before seventy years had passed, history tells us, the second part of God's prophecy through Habakkuk came true. In one night the Babylonian Empire was no more. The new conquerors, the Persians, were somewhat more ethical and humane in their treatment of captives. And this is the unbelievable part (you just know the Lord exerted His influence here) - the Jews were set free. Imagine, when would a conquering people willingly give up their wealth in the form of human capital? In those days, having slaves gave you power, comfort and ease. Why give that up without a fight? The Persians did, but why? That was God's doing; that's how He often works. By receiving from Him what is least expected, in the most unlikely way and in the most unfavorable of circumstances, those in a relationship with the Lord come out on the winning end.

Unfortunately, Habakkuk didn't get an opportunity to experience the end of the story, but I know he'd tell you that didn't matter. What mattered to him was the knowledge that truth wins in the end, justice wins in the end, freedom wins in the end. That's the end of the story in every human episode. Somewhere, sometime, somehow truth, justice and freedom will always prevail. I know some of you might not be ready to accept that unqualified statement. This is where faith comes in. Those of you already in a relationship with God, from your years of effort trying to get closer to Him, know what I mean. When I make the wild claim that every story, given enough time to play itself out, will always have a happy ending, many of you will concur. You may say, "I haven't heard it put that way before, but of course it's true, I wouldn't expect God to orchestrate the world any differently." In time, I hope all of you can say the same.

Prayers do come true. Habakkuk's prayers of hope, though he didn't know how, when or where, did come true. What Habakkuk had is what you're promised when, over time, you grow closer to God. You have the unshakeable confidence that good will prevail. As Habakkuk would tell you if he were alive today, "It doesn't matter if I see it with my own eyes, it just matters that I know it's going to happen. I know who's in charge." This is exactly what happened in just one of Habakkuk's happy endings, one he didn't get a chance to see. It was no different than the happy ending to his song and writings. How proud and grateful he must be to recognize his song with the lyrics of, "The righteous will live by his faith," has been translated and sung in most every language on earth today.

So this is what transpired among Habakkuk's people. While in slavery, the Jews, including the haughtiest and the most arrogant, were taught humility. They learned firsthand from the most proud to the least, what injustice feels like. They repented of their twisted human logic and begged for mercy. They vowed if they'd ever get a chance again, they'd do it right the next time. This hope of starting over is one of the things that preserved the identity and ethnicity of the Jews throughout their slavery. "Just give us another chance to do it right," they prayed for some seventy years before that chance appeared. Unexpectedly, the Babylonian Empire fell without a fight. Overnight the Persians were heralded as the new conquerors. In short order, the Jews gained favor among their new captors and in time they were granted their wish to go back to rebuild their homeland and rebuild a nation founded on justice, truth and God's standards. Habakkuk couldn't have imagined a more perfect ending, even if he were writing a story of fiction. But this is fact. The Lord, the Great Storyteller, can see to it His stories and images actually materialize.

THE BEST OF YOUR STORY

Now don't go away just satisfied with hearing a good, true story with a compelling, happy ending. This story on a lesser scale is played out hundreds of times every day. What transpired for the Jews as a nation in Habakkuk's age is replayed in individual lives daily. This isn't lost history, it's current history and it's future history. The Jews as a people forgot God. They forgot how precious truth, justice, peace of mind and inner security really are. They lost any sense of true happiness and fulfillment. Things got so bad that they lost their connection with their spiritual selves and their connectedness with the Supreme Life-Giver. Without a hold to His lifeline, they faltered and suffered.

You know the story, perhaps because it's your story or a friend's story. The Jews fell so low they found themselves in slavery. I don't have to tell you how that feels; many of you already know. The Jews were literal slaves, while individuals without Jesus are slaves to money, to drugs, to what we worry others think of us, or as scripture says simply, "slaves to sin." The Jews only then realized in their predicament how bad off they really were and repented. That's what many of us have done and that's what many of us will yet do. You either woke up or will wake up one day to your predicament. You'll finally admit, "I'm not happy, nothing I do gives me exquisite satisfaction. I keep trying but it's an endless circle of frustration. There are things I've done I'm not proud of and I've got few prospects for winning the lottery of life. If I could just start over again - this next time with a nudge in the right direction, I'd be OK." That feeling of helplessness was the turning point for the Jews and the turning point for anyone willing to accept Jesus in his or her life.

With that realization, the fortunes of the Jews began to change. When enough of the nation repented and desired a better world and a better life, salvation for them as a nation was in the development stage. It works the same for any individual traversing the same path, only better! With Habakkuk's Jews, it took some seventy years before enough of the nation had had enough of slavery and wanted out before it came to pass.

With individuals the transformation can be literally overnight. Immediately upon admitting the truth to ourselves of our personal slavery to whatever and admitting we don't have real life satisfaction, we want something better, and acknowledging we're sorry to ourselves, but most of all to God, a transformation can take place. Ask anyone who's experienced it. Immediately the weight of past mistakes can be lifted, a newly found feeling of true freedom is experienced, and a sense of optimism comes as a refreshing breeze out of nowhere. Remember? Remember, it happened to you, didn't it? Yes, it can happen to any of you when you are ready; no one can force it on you. When you're ready, God's ready. Just don't let it take seventy years like it did with some erstwhile friends of God!

PRAYING ABOUT INJUSTICE

Habakkuk has shown us his feelings and his prayers to end injustice. This is probably one area of our deepest concerns. Habakkuk intimates the horrible financial injustice and physical mistreatment of his fellow townspeople at the hand of their own fellow citizens. In most cases, the injustice we perceive and pray so fervently concerning touches us personally. Habakkuk prayed for his nation. We pray about illness, over personal affront and injustice and mourn, "Why me, Lord? Why was I singled out for this disease?" We cry over the death of a loved one, again perceived injustice, "Why did it have to be my child, Lord?" And while disloyalty is perceived as mistreatment in a close personal relationship, these are all aspects of injustice similar to Habakkuk's worries. But Habakkuk's writings reassure us in at least two ways.

First, the Lord made it clear to Habakkuk that He feels injustice, all injustice, and He pledges to resolve all. We may have to suffer. Habakkuk had to suffer, his friends did, too, but God gives solemn promise to transform suffering to smiling. Note His words per Habakkuk.

The second salient reassurance is that even when bad happens, God never leaves us. Just note Habakkuk's story. He cried, he suffered, he prayed, "How long, oh, Lord?" In the very next breath he tells us of God's answer (Ha. 2:36). Again, Habakkuk complained. In the very next breath Habakkuk informs us of the Lord's response to him. He was never left without direction. Assurances will come to us from all directions. Just stop and heed as Habakkuk did. Just look for these assurances when you are hit with personal unfairness, whether that unfairness is sickness, suffering or mistreatment you don't feel you deserve. I guarantee the assurance will come. It may come in the form of a word of encouragement from a friend, a Bible verse you just happen to open your Bible to, a sermon that seems to be speaking to you in particular, or a seeming coincidence of a sort that communicates to you, "I'm here, I care."

Just look for it, wait for it. I'm sure God inspired our average Joe, whose name was Habakkuk, to write reassuringly these words of God that are for each of us. "The Sovereign Lord is my strength; he makes my feet like the feet of a deer, he enables me to go on the heights." When we pray as Habakkuk did, we sense that reassurance Habakkuk talks about, the confidence that the Lord is our strength. This will give us the confidence to do what humans normally can't do. Just as a sure-footed mountain deer can negotiate high and precarious mountain crags and cliffs, something no human can do effortlessly, God's power and Spirit imbue us with the confidence and ability to do more, endure more than what a human is normally capable of.

INJUSTICE BEGETS...

Those words apply also to personal suffering, the injustice caused by our fallen nature, sickness and death, along with injustice perpetrated by others, about which Habakkuk most took exception with God. Especially note how God makes an interesting observation for Habakkuk about injustice. This eternal truth is really exciting. Habakkuk never thought of it this way and I know most Christians have never thought of this without God's insight. I know when I state this truth, you're going to say, "That's so simple, I know that already," but follow the idea through with me before you pass judgment.

God's insight is this, "In the human realm, injustice always, always begets injustice." God gave a graphic example of that to Habakkuk. He allowed Habakkuk to live with the suffering to be sure his account graphically got the point across. Look at Habakkuk's leaders - many of them were violently unjust to their fellow man. God demonstrates violence (injustice) always begets violence (injustice). That would be true for Habakkuk's peers. They were violent so the Lord allows that violence to be repaid by further violence. The violence of the Babylonians was soon to act as a scourge against Habakkuk's people, violence against violence.

"Now what about the Babylonians?" Habakkuk complained. God's law in the human realm is the same for everyone: violence begets violence. The Babylonians would not dodge justice. As Habakkuk was inspired to write off the Babylonians, *"Woe to him who builds a city with bloodshed and establishes a town by crime! Has not the Lord Almighty determined that the people's labor is only fuel for the fire...?"* (Ha. 2:12-13). "Don't worry", God says to Habakkuk, "violence will beget violence. The Babylonians used injustice to gain power and wealth but they'll get theirs in the same way, by violence." As we recounted previously, that's exactly what history tells us happened. The Babylonian Empire was pillaged by the Persians in due course.

VIOLENCE BEGETS VIOLENCE

Before we move on, I want to stress the value of this simple revelation to Habakkuk. The lesson is restated in scripture in different words and different ways. Paul states, *...A man reaps what he sows.* (Ga. 6:7). It always comes back! Negatively and positively the rule holds for all. Paul further says, *Whoever sows sparingly will also reap sparingly...*(2 Co. 9:6). Now, did you get the point? Our Lord demonstrated to Habakkuk that Habakkuk didn't have to act to be sure God's law of recompense would work. In fact, God didn't even have to act! You see, God has decreed this law as a law of the universe. When He set the world in motion, including the laws of physics, such as the law that "with every action there is an equal and opposite reaction," and many of other laws, He also set in place "cause and effect" laws that apply to human action. Reaping what we sow and injustice begetting injustice are examples. These are laws of the universe. They always, unerringly come to pass. The universal order cannot be flouted.

When you realize this, as Habakkuk was forced to, our lives as Christians will not be the same. I hope I'm not making this too melodramatic for you, but I'm afraid it might go by without your truly grasping it. If God hadn't inspired Habakkuk to write, it might have passed him by without recognition. God was saying to Habakkuk, "Don't worry about injustice. You don't have to act, I don't even have to act, just let the law of the universe work, be patient. Let the human drama play itself out in the human arena." Yes, the injustice of Habakkuk's leaders amassed wealth, but don't you think someone else will be just as greedy and covet that? And when the successor commandeers that wealth by unjust ploy and violence, won't someone else want what he got? Of course, you can be assured God's laws will be applicable here, too.

Sometimes the drama may take a little longer to play out than we'd like. The recompense on Judah took time, but Habakkuk no doubt saw it with his own eyes. The second recompense, the one against the Babylonians, didn't come till after Habakkuk's death; unfortunately he didn't personally have the satisfaction to see like-for-like meted out. However, a personal inspiration and revelation from his God served as a good substitute. Injustice always begets injustice. Like Habakkuk, we just must learn patience. When the appointed time came, our God didn't even have to act to assure Habakkuk that the justice/injustice cycle would run its course. Another Bible prophet, Daniel, relates how God did tinker with events a little to insure that Babylon's fall would come more swiftly and with a minimum of life lost once the crumbling of the empire had already begun to take root.

How thankful I am that Habakkuk agreed to write out his concerns and very personal prayers. To have insight into how God works is invaluable! Justice always triumphs; our God programmed the universe that way. When you see injustice flourish, be patient and just know injustice begets injustice. The unjust with power will eventually lose their power and if there was not enough time in this lifetime for the downtrodden to experience recompense, then the injustice will be rectified in the world to come. In the meantime, the malefactor, the agent of injustice, has to live his life now perpetually looking over his shoulder, so to speak, wondering where and when violence will be meted out to him. The sagas of so many criminal mob bosses bear this out very graphically. In fact, as scripture says concerning universal laws, ***...God cannot be mocked. A man reaps what he sows.*** (Ga. 6:7).

Finally, let's focus on the personal level one more time to be sure we realize how the law works. For example, if one is slothful and spurns the directive to be diligent in fine works, rest assured that laziness, a form of injustice, will not lie undiscovered; it will come back to haunt. God won't personally come down to zap you for flouting the law against indolence; nature will take care of that for Him in short order. When a woman lives a lie, cheating on her husband, God need not bother Himself to see that justice is done. His universal laws take care of that with no effort on His part. First, she is "rewarded" with less-than perfect reciprocal love, and having to live without freedom and peace of mind is a negative "reward" in itself. Sooner or later she is humiliated when injustice comes to fruition and if that discovery does not occur due to an untimely death, injustice meets its reward in the life to come. Habakkuk's insights help us to avoid tempting fate, avoid tempting God's laws. No, he may not zap you, but you'll get plenty of circumstantial or collateral damage in this life as a forerunner of recompense, and be blocked from getting what everyone truly wants, peace of mind. To be sure, the scales of injustice will be satisfied. Don't ever attempt to circumvent God's natural universal laws. Thank you, Habakkuk, for making that so crystal clear to us.

MESSAGES I HOPE YOU NOTED:

- **The Law Of "Reaping What You Sow" Works Without God Having To Lift A Finger**

- **Know That Violence Begets Violence for Those Who Perpetrate It**

- **Habakkuk Seemed To Forget That There Is Always A "Rest Of The Story" When It Comes To Violence, Don't You Forget**

- **Be Careful What You Ask For, You May Get It**

Chapter Five

FAITH FROM
A DIFFERENT PERSPECTIVE

Now we come to the portion of the book of Habakkuk that should have made him famous but didn't. Remember he's one of those little people like you and me. He never knew what a difference his life would make. Under inspiration he was given the directive to "live by faith." As you recall, Habakkuk lived in dynamic, tumultuous times. The poor and the oppressed were suffering more than ever. An invasion of enemy forces was imminent. The brutal enemy intended to decimate the name of Israel, threatening to obliterate the nation of Israel's very existence. What could one man do? How could Habakkuk protect his family? The answers were "Nothing" and "He couldn't."

The Lord made it clear to him that worse suffering was soon to follow. He was helpless, or was he? There was, in fact, just one thing he could do. The Lord told him, "Live by faith." Habakkuk did just that. He wrote in prose and in song this simple phrase, "Live by faith." As we'll see, that simple lyric was picked up and extended by a later Bible writer and that phrase has become a major rallying call of Christians ever since. Those little words first spoken by a little person have changed the course of history many times over in the intervening 2600 years till our generation. We'll talk more about that very soon, but let's dwell on this practical advice, so sorely needed by every one of us today.

First of all, what does it mean to "live by faith"? I know I don't have to explain the mechanics of the phrase to a spiritual person. She or he has already come to almost intuitively understand the meaning and the method. I imagine though, for someone who has not attuned her mind and emotions to something greater than herself, it would be difficult to explain. So I'll first direct my remarks to such a non-spiritual person, and I use that term advisedly. Let's say it's a woman. When I say unspiritual I'm not talking necessarily about a non-religious person. There can be a major differentiation between a spiritual and a religious person. An individual can very easily be religious and yet not be spiritual. She can very easily go to a place of worship regularly and follow the tenets of a belief system for motives other than to be closer to a universal higher power.

So talking to this non-spiritual person, whether she be religious or agnostic, probably the closest thing to the concept of "faith" that she'd be familiar with is the term "optimism." A person who possesses faith or lives by faith is a person who is optimistic. She knows or feels certain that in the end things will always turn out well for her and her affairs. I hasten to add here that the qualifying term here is "in the end." A person of faith can easily be entrapped by negative circumstances - the loss of a job, a divorce, an illness, a death in the family or a financial reversal. But she always believes that "This, too, shall pass;" that in the long run she will always emerge victorious. Just over the hill, blessings are in store. She knows "you can't keep a good man (or woman) down". A person of faith and an optimist have this in common; they expect the best. She is not deterred when beset by bitterness or submerged in suffering.

THE ETERNAL OPTIMIST?

I pause for a moment here to ask you, friend, especially if you consider yourself a person of faith, to what extent do you really know within yourself that suffering doesn't last forever, that justice will always prevail, and that the unethical will be unmasked in the end? To what extent do you really expect the best for yourself? That's faith and that's optimism. So in this past paragraph I've been describing faith from a strictly secular view. I've interjected a couple of questions for those who are spiritual. No matter where you find yourself at the moment, believer or non-believer, I hope you see the value of optimism.

For example, scientific studies find invariably that optimistic people are healthier, happier: they live longer and tend to find they do experience the optimistic results they envision. That may be an explanation for why spiritual individuals living by faith are again invariably healthier, happier and more satisfied with their lives compared to the general population. But that's only part of the explanation. A multitude of scientific studies on intercessory faith-based prayers detect a statistically significant body of evidence showing prayer has positive, healthful results in medical patients the prayer teams don't even know personally, compared to similar groups of medical patients that had not been prayed for. Scientists admit there is no known explanation for their findings other than a spiritual, faith-based interpretation.

This finding leads us to investigate what it is that differentiates the purely secular optimist from the faith-based optimist. There is one major difference. The faith-based optimist can point to a reason for his optimism. He would say, "It's not just cock-eyed, wild or delusional. I'm not just hoping for the best. I staunchly believe that it's not all up to me. I have Someone more powerful than myself wanting the best for me. Under these circumstances I just can't fail!" So while the optimist can claim "the glass is half full rather than half empty, so I have at least a 50-50 chance things will work out for my benefit." The woman of faith feels it's not just 50-50. She can claim, "If it were just chance, maybe it would be 50-50, but with the extra help I expect from a Source of infinite power, the tables are turned in my favor!" *If God is for us, who can be against us?* (Ro. 8:31). That's a really powerful statement!

So to you, who profess to be a man or woman of faith, I specifically ask you, "Do you have an unabated optimism when it comes to the direction or the path you're taking?" You really should, you know. Scripture tells us that *...in all things God works for the good of those who love him.* (Ro. 8:28). I, for one, believe that when scripture says, "in all things", it means just what it says. I know that some Christians don't believe as I do. They argue, "Let's not be presumptuous. There are a lot of qualifications needed to claim God really means He'll help "in all things." But I think that's equating our Lord with the television advertisers who say, "This is free." You know they aren't reading you the fine print. You say, "Sounds good but there must be a catch; it's too good to be true." I'm certain my Father is not like that. He doesn't tease with grandiose claims like, "I'll help you in all things," only to say, "Well, actually there's a catch attached to this promise… It does not apply to everyone who follows My tenets, it only applies under certain circumstances, at certain times and only with certain people." Not at all! Any person who's been in a close relationship with the Lord for any length of time will tell you God's not like that. He means what He says. You can count on it! Please believe that.

WHAT CAN YOU BELIEVE OF WHAT YOU READ?

I know some scholars have only the best of motives when they claim you can't take these scriptures literally. Some interpreters claim that when Jesus said, "Ask in my name and I'll do it," He really didn't mean that applies to all areas of life; that only applies to areas of life where worship is involved. They don't want you to be disappointed when it doesn't happen, they say. That appears to be a kind sentiment on their part. However, I'd say real kindness is shown to a fellow Christian by saying, "Let's face it, we're all sinners, but we're no worse than David who murdered an innocent man and used his position of power to commit adultery. Yet he was seemingly presumptuous to say in Psalm 119:132, *Turn to me, and have mercy on me, as you always do to those who love your name.* He wrote this when he was well along in years and even after surveying his life he still could say the Lord was with him constantly." I plead with you, man of faith, woman of faith, don't let anyone derail your optimism. Every servant of the Lord, EVERY servant of the Lord, when life is coming to a close, invariably says, "The Lord has dealt with me kindly. I've received far more from

Him than I ever dreamed possible!" I can only assure you this will be true of you also.

I once thought I had a real problem. I was brought up on reading the Bible. Since I didn't know any better, I believed what it said. When Jesus said in John 14:13, *"And I will do whatever you ask in my name..."* I was gullible enough to believe this. I didn't think God was teasing me or that those words were written for a select few, I believed them. When I got older, I started reading various Bible commentaries and some made me stop dead in my tracks. Some seemed to say I really WAS gullible! "You can't take that literally," one would say. Another would say, "What Jesus really meant when He said this was anything you asked about spiritual matters He'd assist, but certainly not day-to-day affairs." I had a problem. Had I been misinterpreting scripture all along? "This is serious," I thought. "I don't want to ask for things I'm not entitled to." I even began to think, "I'm really glad I hadn't read these ideas before, because I've gotten all that I've ever asked for from God and, in fact, an awful lot more! Had I been too presumptuous in asking?"

I began to think, "All I asked for was a marriage that was blessed by God and it happened. I just prayed that the Lord would help me start a business to provide for a family and it came true. I also asked that He help me so I was never beset by money problems. Every time I felt I was getting close to being out of debt something happened – the car needed a new transmission, the house needed a new hot water heater. I couldn't get ahead. I just prayed for some kind of help so I could escape the financial rat race. And my business just happened to become more successful. When I prayed for help to get a college education (because I felt something was missing from my life) while raising three children and running a business, it just worked out." I could go on and on. I believed the scriptures of promise without reservation, but did all these things happen by chance? I reasoned maybe one or two dreams coming true might just be chance, but when all these seeming miracles, every one, one by one invariably came to pass, that's more than just a coincidence. I realized I hadn't made any mistakes in my belief in scripture.

Given the interpretation of some learned scholars, compared to the childlike interpretation by someone seeking a little guidance, I affirmed I had stumbled upon the proper reading of scripture. I called to mind what Jesus said about *"Let the little children come to me, and do not hinder them, for the kingdom of heaven belongs to such as these."* (Matt. 19:14). Yes, I was just a little kid who didn't have any difficulty having faith, believing in miracles, believing that my Heavenly Father wanted the best for me. I looked back at myself at 21 when I prayed about my life's direction - yes, I was just a little kid. When I prayed for a career at age 30, I was still just a little kid. All along I'd have to admit I had the faith of a little kid; I didn't know any better. There was no question the best just had to happen and it did. I confess, I'm a whole lot older, but I still want to be that little kid at heart!

FAITH CHECK

I hasten to say, though, that faith is a lot more than just optimism. The Bible definition of faith, the faith Habakkuk was talking about 2600 years ago, is found in Hebrews 11:1: *Now faith is being sure of what we hope for and certain of what we do not see.* Notice that the Bible definition makes prominent the element of optimism in faith, by saying that faith is being sure of things "hoped for." The things "hoped for" are always optimistic or at least there is the element of the positive. Whether you are hoping for an event or insights, what is hoped for is always a positive consequence, whether for yourself or someone else. Being "sure" is an even more optimistic aspect. With faith, you are confident the positive outcome will transpire. For extra emphasis, the Bible writer avers that faith is "certain." The big difference with a man or woman of faith is that it's not enough to feel, "I really hope things will change; I hope my life will improve." Such a statement is not necessarily optimism; pessimists hope also. But faith is positive - "I am SURE, I am CERTAIN."

Pause for a moment and ask yourself, do you have "faith" or is it just "hope"? I know a lot of Christians who, if you use the definition provided in the Bible, are not yet to the level of faith. They are still at the hope level. You don't need to be a spiritual person to have "hope." I know because a number of my agnostic or atheistic associates will use the term "hope" often. They hope for better times or hope for an improvement in their situations, but they don't have faith, at least not the dynamic faith of the Bible. So, how about you? Do you have faith? By that, as the definition says explicitly, are you certain, are you sure? I implore you to work on that dimension.

How do you get to that point of certainty? It may take time, but it's by no means extremely difficult. The longer one associates with positive influences in life, strong faith is acquired with little difficulty. There are positive examples in the Bible. In Hebrews, Chapter 11, a number of sterling examples of faith are mentioned, not just the pillars of faith like Abraham, Jacob, and Moses, but also lesser known "little people" like Rahab and others. Hebrews 11:32 says, ***I do not have time to tell about Gideon, Barak, Samson, Jephthah, David, Samuel and the prophets.*** All you need to do is look up their stories in any Bible. Go to the index at the back of most Bibles or a Bible concordance and look up Rahab, Jephthah and others. Read their stories. Gideon, for example, at first wasn't sure or certain, but then it tells how his Father and Lord helped him to gain faith.

Spending time with positive influences by reading the positive examples in the Bible will help immensely. We are further drawn to faith by listening to others and their personal stories. The other week at church the pastor asked how many of us had felt the Lord work in our lives. Pretty much every hand went up. Hundreds of people could testify to how they were assisted when in need. At that moment, I commented to myself, "I wish I could hear each of their stories firsthand." Everyone, through their experiences acquired "faith;" became "certain," "sure," because of their personal experiences. Many will tell you they didn't have faith when they first asked for help. When they saw positive results in their lives over time, they acquired faith.

Just ask anyone who has a relationship with Jesus; she'll tell you with excitement what happened in her life, why she is sure and certain now. If you don't at the moment have such confidence, I know it will come in time. All you have to do to begin to experience that confidence and do as Jesus' disciples did. They simply asked Jesus to "Increase our faith." It's that simple - right now, don't wait! Just close your eyes and say that phrase, "Lord, give me more faith." Then when you think about it over the next few weeks, say the same thing either to yourself or aloud, "Lord, give me more faith." When you're in a predicament, remember to just say it. "Jesus, give me more faith." It's that easy.

Your Father will never let a request like that go unanswered. Within two or three weeks, if not before, you'll begin to feel the assurance that things are starting to work to your benefit. That gives you reason, then, to be certain. You have personal experience and that makes it easier to embark with confidence and expectation the next time. I implore you, realize that it's not enough to "hope." You have to have faith and be "certain" when you ask for help. Don't just hope; be confident. Promise yourself now you will work to get dynamic confidence, certainty, "faith." What a difference that will make!

A CLEARER PICTURE OF FAITH

I want to call your attention to one more distinction with the Biblical definition of faith. The Bible makes it clear faith is required in two distinct types of situations. A person of faith is certain about what is "hoped for" in the future, number one, and what "we do not see," number two. This is a major distinction between the faith believer and the secular "hoper." One difference we've already highlighted is that the believer is certain while the "hoper" is not. But Hebrews 11:1 shows the other clear distinction. The person of faith is also concerned about "what we do not see." In other words, a faith believer realizes there are events and activities going on that cannot be detected by normal observation - "what we do not see." She recognizes there are events happening behind the scenes, so to speak. There is more to universal life than just the physical. We may be able to observe the physical, the mental and the emotional aspects of human activity but we may not be able to observe or verify, with normal physical scientific methods, the spiritual aspects of life.

The spiritual is the "what we do not see." We can't see what happens when a person dies, the possibility that life can go on in another realm. We can't see the possibility of another realm, a spiritual realm that can affect or influence the physical. Again, the spiritual person has an advantage here. She is, first, at least open to the possibility of such a realm and secondly, as she ventures out to explore that dimension, her faith becomes firmly grounded. She begins to see "what he (the physical person) does not see". She begins to see (comprehend) that frequent apparent coincidences are more than just coincidences. When "coincidence" continues to happen on a regular basis, the observant person can conclude that there are other forces beyond the physical at work.

I remember the time my wife and I were in a quandary over where to move. We realized that the decision we were about to make would have a major affect on our life course. We had put out overtures in several directions. We felt like the traveler in Robert Frost's poem, "Two roads diverged in a yellow wood, And sorry I could not travel both..." When we realized a decision had to be made imminently, we prayed for divine guidance. The very moment we finished our prayer request, the phone rang. On the line was a landlord offering to rent a house we'd seen for a price below what he'd earlier quoted us (and that we couldn't afford). He also commented that he just felt moved to give a young couple a break and to rent to us. That was one of the first of many such "coincidences" that helped us to "see" (perceive) what we "do not see." I urge you, my friend, to go out on a limb and open yourself up to the influences of a Higher Power that cannot be seen. Your willingness to venture in that direction is an indication of a measure of faith.

I remember speaking to a group of men who had recently joined a faith-based initiative program, seeking help to clean up their addictions and aimlessness. For some, they felt as though the program was a last resort. They had tried for a solution in many other ways but with no resolution. Some admitted they had reluctantly agreed to enroll in this program. When I asked them, "How many of you have seen positive results so far?" every hand went up! When I asked, "How many of you have begun to feel a strength beyond yourself?" again, every hand went up. These men were building faith, a step at a time. Everyone had begun to "see what we do not see."

I have no reservations in predicting similar results for you if you are willing to just take that simple step to admit, "I don't know everything; for all I know, there may very well be a spiritual realm. I won't be so doubtful as to deny categorically or completely that there could ever be such a realm. Therefore, I'm willing to venture out in that direction. I'm willing to pray to God, if there is such a God, to show me, doubter that I am, that He is there. Show me in some way, I beg of You!" If you are truly open to the possibility, I know He'll reveal Himself in some way as He revealed Himself to the former self-described cellar-dwellers of society I spoke to. There was no longer a doubt that they had connected to a higher, beyond physical, Power. They **were** men looking for those subtle influences in their lives. Seeing what **most** would discern as a spiritual transformation also assured them **of the** certainty of the first part of faith referred to in Hebrews 11:1, "**being** sure of what is hoped for." And what they hope for, as do most all of us, is a meaningful, confident life unfolding with guidance and direction leading to the future.

So how do I describe the sense of connection that one feels when he starts to live by faith? Or what the dynasty of men and women of faith in Hebrews felt? We can't point to a definite proof of faith for, by definition, faith deals with the unseen. Very often, though, I have believers tell me when they pray in faith they are immediately enveloped in a feeling of calm, a sense of tranquility. Others have said they have the feeling that someone is near, someone who cares for them. There is a sense of benevolence, an assurance that events will turn out in the believer's favor. Still others say that they just know they'll make it through their adversity. "I just experienced an assurance that all would go well for me," exclaimed another. For those who experience it, there is nothing quite like the sense of wellbeing and the assurance of being surrounded by goodwill. Paul described it as, *"the peace of God which transcends all understanding."* (Ph. 4:7). Isn't that fantastic, wouldn't you like that sensation? You can. It's provided to all who are willing to start out on the journey of faith.

GETTING STARTED

Some say, "I'd be willing to try, if only I knew for sure." Unfortunately, there is no absolute proof to give you. Encompassed in faith, the great philosopher Soren Kierkegaard asserted, is the necessity of a "leap of faith." Take a chance! However, the closest thing to proof there is, is the experience of millions of people through hundreds of generations and thousands of years who have testified of the exact same experiences. Every one of them at one point or another in life had to take the "leap of faith." Even those raised as Christians, at one time or another had to put their beliefs on the line by enduring *the testing of* [their] *faith...* (Ja. 1:3). No one is granted the experience of faith automatically. That's why at times it's more difficult for people raised as Christians to have a strong faith. Not until they are old enough and on their own, or going through an experience where no one can help them make it through, are they forced to take the "leap of faith." That initial experience, that rite of passage, is a cherished memory to all who experience it.

I sense from my interviews with others who are not yet faith believers that there is almost a feeling of jealousy. They envy the sense of benevolence a believer has, and that sense of calmness and tranquility that is so inviting. They don't have it, and if they are honest with themselves they'll admit, "I'd like that, too!" But they can't bring themselves to take the leap, either because they feel it's a childish experiment or because they have never been able to trust anything but pure logic or mental exercise. Just ask anyone who is an agnostic or atheist, "Wouldn't you like to have the sense that things will go well for you, that someone is watching over you, that you're experiencing a sense of serenity and blissfulness?" Sure they would! I've had just a few claim they wouldn't, but I sensed they were afraid to admit that I had something they really wanted. So I say with no equivocation, a faith believer is the envy of all who don't yet have the assurance we do.

It is a sensation of inestimable value. I can only extend the invitation to you. It's a simple process. Pray out loud or to yourself asking the higher power, or God, to show you the way. Tell Him you realize you can't do it alone. Then find a Christian group that is Bible-based where there are believers who can testify to experiences of faith. They'll describe the process and the conviction in Christ Jesus that led them to the faith you want.

Our hero, Habakkuk, didn't have it quite as easy as we have it. This is his experience. As we've already recounted, Habakkuk lived about 600 years before Christ. Habakkuk writes, no doubt, after Judah's last righteous king, Josiah, had died. How extremely disappointing it must have been to witness a period of revival to the worship of the Lord, only to live through a return to the injustice and tyranny in the nation of Judah. The first five verses of the book of Habakkuk set the stage. Habakkuk speaks of violence, then injustice, followed by strife. Even the legal system appears to be paralyzed, due to the wicked and wealthy upper class of Judeans using their influence to pervert justice in the courts. The nation had been so close to returning to the tenets of God's laws, only to crumble and decay when Josiah's sons began to rule. Judah had been living as a vassal state under the oppression of the Egyptians, but that oppression was also becoming more demanding.

What extraordinary faith was required of Habakkuk to dare to believe justice would one day return to the Jewish nation. And even greater faith was required to believe that the outside vicious national oppression by first the Egyptians and then the Babylonians could come to an end. To hold the optimistic picture of a national restoration of self-governance when the nation did not have, nor could it have, an army to rival the opposing force, took extreme faith. To further believe that the nation could then rid itself of injustice was beyond the most benevolent of visions, but that's what Habakkuk saw. Somehow, some way, Habakkuk could have the calm assurance that though he saw desperation all around him, he could also see what could not be seen: a new generation of Jews, having no army, still able to rid themselves of oppressive foreign captivity. Habakkuk couldn't imagine how this could possibly happen, but he still could be certain it would.

That's the wonderful thing about faith; a believer needn't bother himself with the "how," but only the "what" and the "why." Habakkuk was certain the God of heaven could make it happen. And it *did* happen. Though Habakkuk personally didn't live to see the return, some of the next generation did see the rise of a new super power, the Persian Empire, who after defeating the powerful Babylonians, for some "unlikely" reason deigned to allow the captive Jews to return to their homeland. That's an exciting story on its own, recorded in the Bible books of Daniel, Haggai and Ezra.

SOME OF MY FRIENDS OF FAITH

Though Habakkuk was not able to rejoice in person or attend the inauguration of the new restored nation, he saw what could not be seen and rejoiced nonetheless. His story would be something like the story of a single woman, whose husband or boyfriend had left years ago, leaving her with small children in the midst of poverty in any one of the cities of the industrial East or Midwest of the Unites States. The woman had grown up in poverty, that's all she knew and yet faith in the God of miracles allowed her to see what could not be seen, a vision of her children going to college and rising out of poverty and starting new lives for themselves, free from the oppression of crime and poverty.

This story has come true thousands and thousands of times in America. Almost invariably the unlikely matron of the family, working perhaps two jobs but planting the vision in her children, will give credit to her Lord, Jesus Christ, for giving her the wisdom, courage and strength to salvage something better for her offspring. She had no idea how it could happen, but she knew "what" would happen, prosperity was promised to people of faith, and "why" it would happen. The Lord would not allow injustice to reign indefinitely. I lifted up her daughters, Dolores, May and Elizabeth, as just three examples of women I can recommend as having the faith of Habakkuk.

Let me tell you another true story. This one is about my friend, Ray. Ray has had serious health problems for a number of years. He's been in and out of the hospital numerous times battling heart disease and diabetes. In talking with Ray, you'd never guess he's ravaged by these ailments. He's enthusiastic about life and considers his ministry, visiting others who are hospitalized and providing encouragement to those despondent, to be an opportunity to show his appreciation for one more day of life. As tentative as his health is, Ray keeps on giving. He picks himself up from each setback and continues with his service. He's grateful that doctors are amazed at his ability to recover so quickly after each setback, never presuming on his amazing recoveries but only gives glory to the Lord that he personally has been so blessed. His comment is to the effect that, as long as he is kept alive with a power beyond his own ability, he knows that Jesus has further work for him to do. His positive and calm countenance is an encouragement to all he contacts. That's an example of a living faith, similar to Habakkuk's. Ray is the first to disavow any special personal ability other than his strong faith, which has been strengthened through years of building a relationship with his heavenly Father.

Here's another of my personal examples. To my wife and me, the raising of our children to be Christians and to make a difference in the lives of still others is the legacy we hope to pass on beyond any others. I remember, though, with great anguish when one of our daughters was finishing high school. She had gotten in with a dubious crowd who we learned later were involved in the drug culture. We confronted her but she insisted she was not an abuser. Trusting her disavowal, since we had no previous experience to doubt her word, we took action as best we could, even to the point of transferring her to a different high school for her senior year. Upon finishing high school, she informed us she was going to forego college for a time and travel with her "friends." No matter how hard we pleaded, begged and tried to bribe her from following her plans, she was firm. What do you do when a precious life you've nurtured, and dreamed would have a fantastic physical and spiritual life, walks out? What do you do but pray and ask for wisdom?

I remember I kept being reminded of King David's words of reflection after a long life with the thousands of acquaintances. He observed, *I was young and now I am old, yet I have never seen the righteous forsaken or their children begging bread.* (Ps. 37:25).

Scripture also says, ***Train a child in the way he should go, and when he is old he will not turn from it.*** (Pr. 22:6) I could confess to God that my wife and I had honestly tried to do that. We continued praying, not dwelling on the negative prospects. Through the ordeal, I was calmed by the faith I had built after years of experience with my Father. I kept repeating the words of scripture and just "knew" within myself that the Lord would protect her and bring her back to her senses in due time. My faith helped me to wait in patience; after all, there was nothing else I could do, I couldn't even call or talk to her without a phone number. Again, there was nothing I did (other than pray), but in time, we got a call from her saying she was ready to come home. Of course she couldn't admit she had made a mistake at the time, but that was the least of our concerns. We had her back and we kept on hoping, still ever sure that what we hoped for would come to pass. Shortly after returning home she started college and was instrumental in helping her boyfriend consolidate his own faith, graduated and became instrumental in helping several churches grow. She continues to make a difference in the lives of others.

Take this away with you – LIVE BY FAITH. When confronted with suffering, live by faith the way Habakkuk did. When confronted with discouragement, even as you see your peers appear to prosper by cheating, live by faith as Habakkuk did. When contemplating your family's future and your personal future, live by faith as Habakkuk gave us the example to do. When you are confronted with health issues or when unsure where your life is leading, live by faith. The Lord gave Habakkuk the recipe for strength and security when meeting adversity. This is His practical advice. "Living by faith' means recognizing that there is Someone more powerful than you in control. ***"He will not let you be tempted beyond what you can bear,"*** (1 Co. 10:13). Living by faith means really believing in the optimistic, positive and absolute best for you. Our God promises us that in any situation the end result, the long-run expectation, is that your portion will be the best conceivable. So the next time you're confronted with a seeming emergency, just repeat the words of Habakkuk, "live by faith". Keep repeating over and over, "I'm determined to live by faith, I'm determined to live by faith. Good must come if I just live by faith!"

MESSAGES I HOPE YOU NOTED:

- **A Spiritual Person And A Religious Person Are Not Necessarily The Same**

- **Christians Are Not Just Optimistic, They Have A Basis For Their Optimism**

- **There Are Major Differences Between The Faith Christians Have And The Hopes Non-Christians Have**

- **To Feel Real Happiness Is To Feel God's Spirit**

Chapter Six

ST PAUL TAKES UP HABAKKUK'S CALL

Here is where it gets really exciting. Habakkuk's life and his insights have already proved to be incredible, so practical and relevant. We have seen he was a man like you and I, with the same fears, the same concerns, the same insecurities. But this is what's especially powerful. God used this ordinary man. Habakkuk expressed his concerns no differently than you and I might. Yes, Habakkuk had an abundance of faith but as we detected in his writings, that faith almost seemed to waiver for a moment, didn't it? But he held firmly to his faith; he didn't let it slip away. What I'm saying, though, is that Habakkuk was no superior man, his words of concern were voiced no differently than yours or mine might be. But our Lord chose to use his words, collected, published and preserved for us, to encourage us. I say this to capture that recurring theme that reading Habakkuk calls to mind. God uses the little people to do great things. Habakkuk wasn't a celebrity in his day. He's never even mentioned by name by any other Bible writer. The Bible is filled with stories of men and women of faith but nowhere do you read Habakkuk's biography; all we have is speculation. He is not even mentioned by name in the "great cloud of witnesses" held up in Hebrews as part of our heritage as people of faith. He may have had little in the way of spectacular deeds to report, but his influence had repercussions beyond what we might have imagined.

This is the point I was alluding to when titling this volume, *The Most Popular Song Writer You Never Heard Of.* Habakkuk was that songwriter. From what we can ascertain from the Bible book context we conclude Habakkuk was of the tribe of Levi, given the divine assignment to work in conjunction with the temple in Jerusalem. One of the Levite assignments was to take charge of the music used in worship and celebrations. You'll notice that the notes at the end of Habakkuk, Chapter 3 show parts of his writings were put to music and used in temple ceremonies. So among other things, Habakkuk was a liturgical songwriter among God's people, the tribes of Israel. What is interesting is that though Habakkuk's songs no longer are popular and in fact may never have been popular, and probably in temple worship his songs didn't actually give credit to him as the writer, at least one of his lyrics did become incredibly popular - so popular that millions of Christians throughout history have repeated his words themselves or at least have heard them spoken or sung. Habakkuk never in his imagination would have dreamed his writings would come to be so motivational. Again, God often uses humble folk to do great deeds!

Look with me now at Galatians 3:11. This is one of many places in scripture where the apostle Paul argues for a foundational doctrine of the Christian faith. He supports his premise by quoting previous scripture as a precedent. This is what he said: ***Clearly no one is justified before God by the law, because "The righteous will live by faith."*** Now what do you think Paul was quoting to support his conclusion? When he stated what previous scripture had proclaimed, "The righteous will live by faith", guess whom he quotes? That's right, Habakkuk. Stop for a moment to ponder the implications of this act before we ponder the meaning. You no doubt have heard of the apostle Paul (or St. Paul). He, after Christ, was the greatest orator, salesman and publisher of Christianity to the known world in his time. Christianity spread like wildfire throughout the Roman Empire, due in large part to his indefatigable passion and activism. The apostle Paul (or St. Paul) was the man chosen by God to perform great deeds. He's a larger-than-life historical figure establishing and clarifying the fundamentals of Christianity, as he understood them from Jesus Himself.

What is so amazing to me is that God inspired him to quote the words of an obscure unknown to establish our understanding of Christian doctrine. The Lord had inspired this little guy, Habakkuk, to plant the seed that later enveloped the known world. Three times in scripture (also Romans 1:17 and Hebrews 10: 38-39) Paul quotes Habakkuk to make sure those simple words were heard, understood by and motivational to Christians then and throughout history. Millions throughout history have memorized those exact words written by Habakkuk and inspired by the Lord. "The righteous will live by faith." Thank you, Lord, thank you, Paul, and thank you, Habakkuk, for that simple phrase. It really means so much as we'll see.

PAUL'S SPIN

What's really fascinating is to note that Paul subtly extends the meaning of Habakkuk's words, "The righteous will live by his faith". (Paul omits the word, "his.") Paul lived after the coming of the Lord on earth and had the benefit of Jesus Himself clarifying and extending the understanding of Judeo-Christian doctrine. Habakkuk's words were something Habakkuk didn't fully comprehend when he was inspired to speak and pen them. Only Jesus' coming could embellish its meaning in all its fullness. Nevertheless, the Lord in His magnanimity used Habakkuk to articulate the idea first.

So here was Paul the apostle, attempting to introduce a revolutionary idea, first to the Jews and then to the rest of the world. Since it was new and different, some might be skeptical, but Paul knew it was critical that they understand the concept. The basis of all Christian theology was to be built on several major ideas. One of these Paul introduced by showing that it wasn't such an esoteric, unusual idea after all. It had a precedent in Jewish literature and scripture. The idea was Habakkuk's famous phrase, "The righteous will live by faith." This is how Paul responded in Galatians 3:11, the verse we just quoted. Writing to all ethnics, but starting with the phrase many Jews were familiar with, Paul reasoned like this: The wonderful blessings of Jesus extend further than what you, as a Jew, have already come to know and believe. Faith is the vehicle that will give you the strength and ability to get through anything.

You know that. But did you know this? Jesus, the Son of God, verified it, and our Lord promises to help us build this faith. Faith is really a free gift from God. Our Lord will graciously give it to you, if you will only ask. Maybe you never thought of it that way. You don't have to do it all on your own, and in fact, it's impossible to do it all on your own. Think about this: Paul intimated that the very phrase, "The righteous will live by faith", has within it the kernel of truth that to be considered righteous, no amount of works or deeds will suffice to elevate you to that level of righteousness. You may have repeated this phrase in the past and never realized you were admitting only faith and that no amount of deeds, no matter how stupendous, could earn you life. So your present life, your future life, as well as your faith, are free gifts from God.

This is the message Paul desired so passionately to declare. All we are and all we will be are due to the mercy of God. As hard as we try, as meticulously as we follow the religious laws, we can never be righteous enough to earn the right to life. Though you can't earn it, God proposed to give it to you freely. When you were born, your life was given to you without charge; it was free, and your future life, your deliverance and salvation from death and suffering is also a free gift. This is all possible now that Jesus has come. We can now call Jesus our Savior. He has saved us from death and suffering, not because we deserve it or earned it, but because He loves each one of us.

At first it may appear that Paul is taking creative license with what Habakkuk proclaimed, but that's really not the case when you examine both proclamations (Paul's and Habakkuk's) together. When Habakkuk said, "The righteous will live by his faith," he was intimating that righteous persons (persons who love the Lord and are close to Him) live day by day having faith or belief that the Lord will help them through all circumstances, sufferings and setbacks in this life. They have confidence that God will be with them and not abandon them. These righteous ones admit they can never do it on their own; what they have, their abilities, their wherewithal is due to their faith in the

Creator. They can't be righteous enough to deserve it; only their continued faith, belief and confidence in the Lord's magnanimity help them to get through each day of this life.

Paul now extends the meaning of, "The righteous will live by faith" to include a future life. He was saying that the righteous is given life only because life is granted by God. What's more, the righteous ones are granted future life, eternal life, not based on anything they can do. Again, it is given freely. So the righteous live now and right on into a future based on faith, not by what they can do. They have faith and expectation that when the Lord decrees eternal life in numerous Bible verses like John 6:47, ***"I tell you the truth, he who believes has everlasting life,"*** that promise applies to them. Are you, the reader, at that point yet? Do you see that God is speaking to you when He says, "Everyone who believes in him may have eternal life." If so, isn't that the most comforting promise you could ever have? And if you are one who is not yet at the point of assurance, trust me, you will be if you study the logic and reasoning behind the promise.

Note what the Message Bible says, quoting the words of Habakkuk by name, only translating them slightly differently. The person who lives in right relationship with God does it by embracing what God arranges for him. Doing things for God is the opposite of entering into what God does for you. Habakkuk had it right: ***The person who believes God, is set right by God—and that's the real life.*** (Ga. 3:11). So Paul emphasizes the "God factor" in human faith. God is the one who first "arranges for" the promise. Then faith comes. So first the promise of life and endless life, then faith comes to the righteous person. Lest we misunderstand Habakkuk, Paul argues that there isn't anything we can do to attain the promise. We just have to have faith.

SET RIGHT BY GOD

Several things I want you to ponder here. Another way to speak of the righteous person is, "The person who believes God is set right by God." A person is considered righteous not by his own deeds, but is "set right by God." God initiates the process; He doesn't wait for us. He devised the promise and all we need to do to get on the path to the "real" life is believe in God's promise. I know it sounds too good to be true. And if you are not yet at that point of believing, I know it's because it seems so simple and so easy. In our society we are forced to react cautiously when someone says something is free. Usually flashing lights go off! "It can't be free, what's the catch?" we say to ourselves. I've personally learned in a business I manage, I can't give anything away free anymore because people expect that either there's a catch to my offer or it's worthless and of little value. So I've stopped offering anything free of charge. That's what happens with many who first ponder and later accept the promise of "real life" from God. Because it's free, they drift in and out of a righteous relationship with God. They really didn't have to do much to initially accept the promise, so its worth (to them) may diminish over time. What a shame.

If it makes it any easier for you, my faith seeker friend, to accept the promise, let me tell you it's not that easy after all. As Habakkuk volunteered and Paul seconded, it takes faith; "The righteous will live by faith". That's not at all really easy. To keep believing when you're down, maybe depressed, to keep believing when your friends mock you, to keep believing when you're tempted to abandon your right standing with God or to keep believing when you are persecuted for your belief - that's not so easy, but it's worth it. The Bible speaks of the "real life." That's what I'd like you to highlight in your mind, "the real life." Believe me, it's worth anything to have "real life." Take it from someone who has lived both, I like to call it the "mundane life," as contrasted with the "real life."

The mundane life is the one where a person just goes through the motions of living. He or she eats, goes to work, sleeps and does things by rote. You know what I'm talking about. Why can't it be as if you're falling in love all over again with your partner every day, continuously? That's the way it is when you have the real life. The real life has a purpose to it; it has meaning. With the real life it's like you're starting a new job every Monday morning. You're excited and yet a little nervous because you don't know what to expect. The real life is like waking up and remembering there's a new baby in the house and he or she is counting on you to care for him or her. That's purpose and meaning. As a fellow worker with Christ you can have that purpose even after your kids are grown or before you even choose to bring a child into the world. The real life means you know you're going somewhere and it's an adventure. What serendipitous events or unexpected surprises, what new friends will happen on your path? What is the next project that God wants you to work on with Him? That's real life. It's exciting, meaningful, full, and God promises you that! All you have to do is adjust your attitude to prepare for it. You just have to believe!

So before moving on to Paul's legal argument on faith and salvation that was bolstered by Habakkuk's initial song, let me summarize what we have found so far. By claiming the righteous shall live by faith, Habakkuk was suggesting how a person in a right relationship with God would live in the present: he would live by faith and through faith. Paul then, by repeating the exact same words, was emphasizing how God lives, not just how His servants live. The righteous person will live because God chooses to live His example of love; He chooses to give life to the righteous. The righteous one lives today and into eternity because of God and through the faith they show in return. Habakkuk centers on living now, one day at a time. Living by faith that whatever the future will bring, he'll be able to confront it with God's help. His faith keeps him going, day by day. In contrast, Paul chose to center on our future life. The righteous person has hope for a future life because of God's free gift. The righteous person is not only granted life now but into a new world, a new life, eventually able to meet his or her Creator God and Christ.

IT'S THE LAW

Let's look at another passage of Paul's writing that uses the similar words, being saved "through faith," but here adds another word, "grace." Read Ephesians 2:4-5, 8-10 with us from the NIV. *But because of his great love for us, God, who is rich in mercy, made us alive with Christ even when we were dead in transgressions—it is by grace you have been saved...For it is by grace you have been saved,*

***through faith—and this is not from yourselves, it is the gift of God—
not by works, so that no one can boast. For we are God's
workmanship, created in Christ Jesus to do good works, which God
prepared in advance for us to do.*** Paul sets it out so clearly, doesn't
he? And to make sure we get the point about faith and works, he
stresses the word, "grace." Paul's reasoning is like this: He starts with
the predicament we're all in. In verse 3 he claims "all of us" are guilty
of indulging ourselves without thinking of anyone else but ourselves,
neither of God nor of our fellow sojourners on earth. We all have a
"sinful nature," Paul explains. I know sin is not a popular theme these
days. Most of us claim to have enough of a problem with our self-
esteem as it is, without exaggerating our depravity by throwing around
words like "sin" and "sinner." We might say, "I don't need to be
reminded of that!" But lest we forget the starting point and predicament
we're all in, the Bible frequently uses the word "sin." Its meaning,
according to scripture, is very simple: "missing the mark of perfection."

You don't need to dwell on it, you just have to admit it, per Paul.
Who is there that hasn't spent a good portion of his life satisfying his
own interests to the exclusion of others? Paul admits that we've all
been gratifying ourselves and that we sin when we "think only of
ourselves." So don't fight it, don't deny it, just admit it, says God. If we
can admit that to one part of our nature, we don't have to dwell on it.
God's plan is to save us from ourselves and from any repercussions of
our past. All of us, says Paul, have done things we're not proud of,
some of us perhaps worse deeds than others, but we all can admit
we've been petty, vain, conniving and calculating. We've hurt others
and we've been self-centered, as if no one else mattered but ourselves.
Logic even tells us a society can exist only as long as its citizens are
thinking of the welfare of others and not just themselves. You must
admit you've done things that if all persisted in doing, our civilization
would unravel. So Paul says that God says, "Just admit it." Whether
you insisted on a divorce because you thought more of yourself than
your children, or lied to conceal your culpability in a business deal, or
were so self-centered that you didn't do your part to be a productive

member of society, God says just admit and accept His plan of rehabilitation and move on.

It shouldn't be so hard to admit, "I'm not perfect. There are things I've done, things I'm ashamed of. There, I've admitted it." Can you then go further to admit, "I'm sorry - sorry for the problems I've caused for others, sorry for their suffering. I also admit there are consequences of my sin and self-centeredness." Whether you don't have a satisfying family life since you didn't treat your siblings, parents or children with the care and concern expected, or you've quit relationships and financial agreements unilaterally, you may be dealing with those consequences for years. What God says is, "Yes, you may have to deal with the consequences, it's not fair that I just 'Poof!' take them all away, but at least you don't have to deal with the debilitating depression and worthlessness you normally would if you chose to dwell on any breach you at least partly were the cause of." Christ said, "I'll take on that load for you. I'll also help you to rebuild."

I'm not just telling you this, God is. ***But because of his great love for us, God, who is rich in mercy made us alive with Christ even when we were dead in transgression—it is by grace you have been saved.*** (Ep. 2:4-5) As we were just commenting, many of us at one time felt lost, even dead. We didn't know how to get out of our depression, or at least we weren't excited about life, just thinking of the mess we had made of things. Or we were so self-centered that we were in effect living as if we individually were the only ones that mattered. You probably wouldn't be reading this unless you have admitted either consciously or subconsciously that you weren't truly happy at this time.

What's more, God says He can make you alive again, "alive with Christ," as He puts it here. Christ promises to help you start over, to be alive, excited again, enthusiastic again. Can you imagine - you didn't ask for it, and you didn't even know what the problem was. You probably didn't realize your malaise, your "funk," your daze or "same old, same old" was due to that subconscious desire to "gratify our sinful nature." That's okay, God's love and mercy is dynamic and is active; we need only be reactive. Yes, God is always active when it comes to our true needs. We need only be reactive, and follow His suggestions.

THAT WORD "GRACE"

Next Paul introduces terms that may be new to you, though most of us have heard them many times before. "It is by grace you have been saved." First, "saved." You can be "saved" from your condition of being a "nowhere man", a "nobody", a person with a past, a person with no particular place to go, especially "saved" from feeling depressed and dejected. Finally you can be saved from feeling you'll just wither away in death over time or what's worse, feel you have to be punished after death for an unsavory past. Saved, past, present and future, God declares. Saved from the guilt of past selfish actions, saved from future apprehension. What a wonderful proposition! It is too good to be true, if it weren't for the other word that Paul introduced - "it is by grace you have been saved". "Grace", you've heard it, haven't you? It would be too good to be true, if it weren't for "grace."

That term is so important that I prefer not to use it without a qualifying adjective. I'm telling you, don't ever use this term unless you know what you're speaking of. I'm saying Christianity has become so commonplace when it should be extraordinary because we throw around terms like "grace" without stopping to think what we're saying. Remember "grace" means God's extraordinary love, with "love" meaning an almost passionate desire on God's part to see things work out well for each of us. He's rooting for us, wants the best for us, hoping that we will let Him help us. That's true love! "Grace" also gives the connotation of unrequited kindness and concern. The grace of God means He wants to help, He's concerned for us but He'll never impose Himself on us. Christ is always there waiting and hoping we'll let Him in. As scripture says of Christ, ***"I stand at the door and knock..."*** (Re. 3:20). So, when you hear the phrase, "the grace of God," be reminded of God's unselfish, extraordinary kindness and the passionate love He feels for us. He so wants us to succeed, to make it.

That's not all. More is in store for us due to grace, Gods grace. What God's love (His grace) moves Him to do is share the best with us. As Ephesians 2:6 says, ***And God raised us up with Christ and seated us with him in the heavenly realms in Christ Jesus.*** Anyone that has started to build a relationship with God knows what this verse means. You've already felt it. When you come to know God you feel so very special, maybe for the first time in your life. You know how people like to say some experience was so wonderful that it was "like I died and went to heaven"? That's what scripture is alluding to here. When we really accept God's love and Christ's mercy to come and show us the way, giving us the guidance we so desperately need, how can we help but feel special? It really is just like God having "raised us up with Christ and seated us with him in the heavenly realms." I hope you can say one day, if not already. "You know, I really do feel like a king or queen or prince or princess because I know God and He really is on my side. He wants great things for me!" Heaven now and heaven to come, but that's an added blessing we'll talk more about later.

One other thing before we move on. Notice how Paul, who had this close relationship with God and Christ already, could speak of what's yet in store for us. Ephesians 2:7 says, ***...in the coming ages he might show the incomparable riches of his grace, expressed in his kindness to us in Christ Jesus.*** In the coming ages, He'll show us incomparable riches, beauty and true satisfaction. I have to admit, I personally can say I've gotten so much more than I ever bargained for already. I could never dream of what this happiness and satisfaction was like, before I came into a close relationship with Christ. I was never able to put into words what I was looking for, but God knew all along. I have to say if I've gotten incomparable riches already from Christ, riches that no amount of money can ever buy for anyone, what must these "incomparable riches" in store for the future mean? I'd get too excited to speculate about it.

Again, I shake my head in amazement to think that a little person like me, born in a humble family with a father lacking a high school education, with my own share of hard times, should wake up to the blessings and privileges I now have, all because I found out about Christ! I can't help but think that what God has in store for us is a fitting end of any story for anyone who's had a life of tragedy and suffering. How ecstatic they'll be to see what's encompassed in that phrase "incomparable riches" that God can't wait to give out. I can expect that even those who lived in sickness, suffering and squalor for all their short existence here will acknowledge that the "incomparable riches" make their suffering appear as a brief episode on a journey to a better place.

Yes, it really seems too good to be true, but it IS true! But how do we put ourselves in line for these unexpected lavish gifts? Scripture doesn't let us forget – grace. Ephesians 2:8 stresses the salient truth of Christianity, *"For it is by grace you have been saved, through faith – and this not from yourselves, it is the gift of God."* Here Paul comes back into harmony with our friend Habakkuk, since faith is mentioned again. Paul and Habakkuk are reading from the same page. Both are testifying it is by grace; it is the gift of God. All the good things of the future, per Paul, and the wherewithal to make it through the present, per Habakkuk, come down to faith. Salvation comes with faith. Salvation through personal suffering when all is crumbling around you, (Habakkuk's experience), and salvation through this world into the future, is not in our power to manufacture. There's nothing we can do. Paul emphasizes, "and this not from yourselves, it is the gift of God," God's present to us. We couldn't engineer it if we tried.

Habakkuk looked at his world and realized salvation from what his world was going to experience was not in his power to create. He could only live, live through the calamity, with faith in God or through the strength faith could give him. Paul assessed his degenerate, dying world and he also concluded salvation could only come from God. There was nothing he could do to change or forestall it. Salvation is God's gift to each of us wherever we are and whatever we're going through. But to actually get this free gift, you have to reach out for it. That's where faith comes in. Remember how Paul put it, "it is by grace you have been saved through faith". May we never forget those last two words "through faith." That's what Habakkuk was hoping to tell us and that's what Paul seconded. All we can do is have faith.

So that we get the point, Paul goes on to explain that salvation is *"not by works so that no one can boast. For we are God's workmanship..."* (Ep. 2:9-10). Paul makes it quite clear, doesn't he, that it's not by human works we gain protection and salvation from

God? There is absolutely nothing anyone can do to amass enough credit with God to earn God's free gift. First, it wouldn't be free if someone could possibly earn the distinction. Second, Paul is making it clear no one can amass enough good works or acts to counteract the negative actions he's done, either consciously, unconsciously as an oversight, or just not knowing any better. You just can't do it; no matter how hard you try. What's more, God doesn't want any person to boast, "I did it on my own". That would be tragic if it could happen, for one person to boast of being just a little better than others. God has thought of everything. Never will anyone be able to lord it over others due to his/her benevolent circumstances or even extraordinary effort. Also no one will ever be allowed in God's realm to feel inferior to others. Due to Christ's efforts, we all deserve full self-esteem. Each of us is as good as or as great as anyone else in God's estimation. He's treated you special and will continue to treat you special because you truly ARE. He loves you. What could make you feel more special than that?

TRULY SPECIAL

Think of this: if you're reading this book now, you are truly special. How many people in the world have the ability to read and think freely? You are one truly blessed. If you even know a modicum (a tiny bit) about God's love, whether told to you when you were young or whether you were found when you were older, you have much to be thankful for. I remember the day I happened to be in a room when I heard someone praying aloud in a group. At that moment, I felt a twitch in my stomach and the feeling came over me that I didn't understand what God's love truly was. I had known something about God, but at that moment I realized I didn't know enough. I felt I didn't fully know what I really should know. I then and there resolved to explore further my understanding of the true God of the Bible and His Christ.

To this day I often reflect on that day years ago. I feel really special every time I do, because I think, "What did I do to deserve being singled out, communicated with, and having my attention commanded to want to learn more?" It's the same with you. How did it happen you were born who you were, where you were, when you were, so that at some point you came in earshot of the message that could potentially save your life? You didn't deserve it any more than anyone else, any more than I deserved it. And the message Habakkuk learned, "The righteous will live by faith" and expanded by Paul, "it is a free gift of God," is a special message and you can't help but feel special if you understand what these words mean!

MESSAGES I HOPE YOU NOTED:

- **Heaven Now And Heaven To Come**

- **How Special To Feel God's "Specialness"**

- **To Habakkuk "The Righteous Will Live By Faith" Meant The Righteous Person In This Present Life Would Live By Faith And Through Faith**

- **The Apostle Paul Argued That This Phrase Could Be Extended To Promise Eternal Life**

- **Bask In The Grace Of The Lord**

Chapter Seven

ALWAYS JUSTICE IN THE END

There is still another place in scripture where the Habakkuk motif, "the righteous will live by faith" is found. It's in Romans. There is a very special story of how the upheaval of all human society came about as a result of this one verse and one idea, first stated so succinctly by Habakkuk. Before we begin that discussion I want to dwell for a moment on how the very nature of Habakkuk's phrase exudes power. Being clear and to the point is one of the main rules of communication and Habakkuk's faith phrase is an example of that. Habakkuk was not the first or the last to extol the virtues of faith. Long before Habakkuk, another was called the "Father of all who have faith." That, of course, was Abraham. Faith is mentioned a number of times in Genesis, the first book of the Bible, written long before Habakkuk's time, as well as in other books spanning a period of thousands of years before Habakkuk.

HABAKKUK'S HARMONY

However, when Paul produced an argument to demonstrate his notion of faith having saving power, he didn't quote one of those other men of faith, he quoted Habakkuk. Why? The main reason was that the way Habakkuk states the proposition was both clear and succinct. He put it clearly, crisply and practically. A simple clear phrase that carries an enormous thought in a small package is unusually potent. Habakkuk's "The righteous will live by faith" is focused, to the point, clear and practical all in one. That's real power. This reminds me of the personal computer. The PC didn't become the ubiquitous commodity of every home and office until the microchip was invented and perfected. Being able to pack an enormous amount of information into a tiny chip allowed computers to become more powerful and more practical. Habakkuk's phrase is no different. The phrase packs an astonishingly powerful message in a clear practical directive that leaves little doubt as to its utility.

Every time you quote the phrase, consciously with feeling, it unleashes an incomparable power. I have found when I'm worried, when I'm anxious, when I'm apprehensive or downright scared, I have repeated those words and immediately I felt I had summoned the power of God's Spirit to my aid. When I'm worried about how a negotiation might go, when I'm worried about the wellbeing, either physical or spiritual, of a friend or family member, I can chant aloud or in silence, "The righteous will live by faith!" Immediately I feel calmer, clearer. It's all so clear again. I can't do it! I don't have all the power and all the wisdom. This phrase reminds me Who does!

At one time and in one moment I can resolve not to be anxious, knowing our Lord is in control. I'm reminded to be courageous since my faith is coupled with the strongest Force in the universe. At the same split second it reminds me what I need to do this very moment – have faith! That phrase has the effort of a sunbeam splitting the gloom of a dark cloudy day. You've experienced that, haven't you? It's also like a fresh breeze coming out of nowhere on a hot, humid enervating summer afternoon. You've had that experience too, I'm sure. Well that's what "Habakkuk's harmony" does for me! And it will for you, too.

I implore you to identify this phrase as one of those little breath prayers similar to the ones made popular in the 1600's by Brother Lawrence, the Catholic monk. When you think of it or need it, give this one line back to God. When you need strength, just say it, "The righteous will live by faith." When you're disappointed by friends or enemies, just say it, "The righteous will live by faith." When you need inspiration to meet a challenge, just say it, "The righteous will live by faith." That one line whether offered as an affirmation aloud or in silence serves as a reminder of how you resolve to live that day. That one line can also serve as a one-line breath prayer to the Lord saying, "I want to be one of the righteous who will live by faith, help me!"

So as a prayer or as an affirmation Habakkuk's one line can remind you of what's most important and of the manner of living you envision for yourself – faithful living. And faithful living according to Habakkuk and ratified by Paul means leaving the day and the future in the Lord's hands, trusting Him to orchestrate an outcome for your best and for the best of those you love. And faithful living means to be optimistic, knowing that good will always spring from the bad – a good outcome is always possible from the bad. We need only be patient and wait for the unfolding outcome. Faithful living also means acting with an attitude of gratitude, knowing your future, your salvation, has already been arranged, through no toil by you, as long as you live with faith.

ANOTHER REMINDER TO THE ROMANS

As I mentioned at the outset of this chapter, there is another place where Paul quotes and takes up the call heralded by Habakkuk. This message is found in Romans, Chapter 1, and there is a special story that goes along with it. Paul equates the faith message as an integral part of the Gospel message. "Gospel" is another word meaning Good News. Paul avers that God's plan is Good News, It's Great News; it's the Best News any human could hear. Roman 1:17 says, *For in the gospel* [the good news] *a righteousness from God is revealed, a righteousness that is by faith from first to last just as it is written: "The righteous will live by faith."* There's Habakkuk again at the heart of Paul's argument and as a justification for his agreement. Paul, the apostle and pillar of Christianity, stands on the shoulders of our relatively unknown "little guy" we've come to see as a friend, Habakkuk. And this verse with the quote from Habakkuk serves as the theme of the whole book of Romans.

Paul says this is the "Good News," the good news we've all been waiting to hear. I'll call it the "Best News" because all other news, all other kindness from God rests on this news. This news helps to eliminate all the bad news that has happened to each of us and obliterate all the negative news we've ever been forced to pass on. This is the Best News, since this news reversed all the bad that has ever happened in the world. All the bad things that have ever happened to you, my friend, are erased and negated in the utterance of this one Good News!

Part of this Good News (Gospel) as Paul puts it is that "a righteousness of God is revealed." God is righteous; He always does what's right. And He, in His magnanimous kindness and mercy, declared the right thing to do was to grant forgiveness, a fresh new start and salvation to everyone who really wants it. God doesn't have to do that; He's not bound by any legal or logical doctrine to do this. In fact, what God offers defies all legality and it does not follow from logical argument. Paul then calls it the "rightness" of God. From God's vantage point, it's the only right thing to do.

If you're a parent you know exactly how God felt. Whenever you feel like it, you shower your children with gifts. You don't take count of the good things they did compared to the bad. In fact, when your children were babies they never actually did anything worthy of a blessing from you other than just being there. Here they are keeping you up at night, needing to be waited on day and night, costing you time and money and yet you want to give them more! That's a reflection of God's love to us. We may not be as "cute" as a baby is, but He thinks we're pretty special. And just as there is no logical reason for you to be "head over heels" in love with your newborn baby, God feels that way about us. What we do is a reflection of God in us. After all, He conceived us; we come from Him. We have His DNA - He gave it to us directly!

All this is encompassed in the words of Paul. "In the gospel (or as part of the good news or God's good news) a righteousness of God is revealed." A right act of God is revealed. More than just right, it's loving, kind and benevolent. It's just the kind of thing you'd expect from God, once you get to know Him. And that's part of it, this righteousness from God was "revealed," scripture says. He didn't wait for us to wonder about our future or what's to become of us. He revealed it first. It's revealed, it's proclaimed and even though most people aren't ready for it, it's there when they are ready for it.

The Good News revealed (as Romans 1:17 says) is "a righteousness that is by faith first to last" or a righteousness that involves "faith to faith," as some translate the verse. Faith permeates the good news. How? First, realize the way our Lord has set up salvation now and into the future. There is a transaction between you and the Lord (Christ); there is no middleman. Salvation is not dependent upon anyone else. You needn't count on anyone else. Just the two of you, you and the Lord, are part of this contract. Scripture speaks of God as being faithful (1 Corinthians 1:9). In other words, He inspires faith; He is constant. You can always count on Him. Once you have been in a relationship with Him for any length of time, you know that's true by your own personal experience with Him. In the meantime this assertion of God's faithfulness only requires faith on your part.

As discussed in the last chapter, that faith means a certainty on your part that what might appear to be "too good to be true" is too good, but it is also true. That will require an instant "leap of faith." But that's not too much to ask. Once a person gets herded into a corner by circumstances (or maybe you "paint yourself into a corner") and you realize you have no other choice, you'll muster the strength to take the "leap of faith." When there is no other option, you've tried it all yourself and it hasn't worked yet, when you've got nowhere else to go, yes, then you're willing to try this godly promise as a last resort. Fortunately the Lord accepts you that way. He's willing to start out as your second choice or last choice because He knows once you get to know Him, He'll be your first choice from then on!

As Paul observes, the good news is possible only by "faith to faith" or alternately "first to last." Our God is faithful and you are required to demonstrate faith, too. The good news is permeated with the idea of faith, very simply. The Lord in His faithfulness offers you the option of trying things His way for a change and you are required to accept that option in faith. As scripture says, salvation is a free gift. You only have to reach out and accept the present and say, "Thank you, Father."

HOW COULD YOU EVER BE ASHAMED?

I was especially taken by the verse just before Romans 1:17 where Paul quotes Habakkuk. He prefaces his quotation with this idea in Romans 1:16: ***I am not ashamed of the gospel because it is the power of God for the salvation of everyone who believes…*** It's very clear isn't it? The good news (Gospel) has to do with salvation for everyone. There are no limitations; everyone who believes is eligible. Nowhere do you find in scripture any "fine print" making it overly difficult to qualify. It's not like any of the advertisements on the radio that shout out a ridiculous low price with the announcer, then in a soft voice speaking 100 miles an hour blurting out all the qualifications, such as some ads for life insurance. A ridiculously low price is quoted, but they don't tell you only 5 to 10% of respondents will qualify since the rates are predicated on perfect blood pressure, perfect cholesterol level, perfect weight for one's body build. God isn't that way. His life insurance doesn't require perfection - actually it's just the opposite. God's insurance policy is designed for the person who is imperfect, and that includes all of us. God desires to include everyone. And all you need to get the free million-dollar life insurance policy (actually much more than a million dollars since your life is worth more than that) is to be alive. As they say, if you can "fog a glass " you'll qualify.

Note though, God does put one provision on the offer. "You must "believe." Paul proclaims it's for "the salvation of everyone who believes." There you have it, the one requirement. And this requirement will unfortunately disqualify many from acquiring the free gift. They must believe. That's another way of saying what Habakkuk attested to you before. You need to "live by faith." Faith is believing what may be hard to believe. However, what God has you believe is not difficult to believe because it's illogical or beyond reality. It's difficult to believe because it's just too good to be true. For some who have been hurt too many times or been taken advantage of once too often, this might be difficult. I think this is one reason Jesus remarked that a true believer must become almost like a young child, (Matthew 18:3-4) a child who is trusting and hasn't yet been hardened by the "school of hard knocks," so to speak.

And that's where we come in, you and I, we who are already believers. First we can assure those muttering under their breaths when they hear the "good news" for the first time, "Sure you want me to believe that, I wasn't born yesterday!" We can reassure by telling our story. Friend, we say, I know it seems too good to be true but once I was so low and so hurt and had no way to go. I was so desolate or depressed there was nowhere else to turn. When I was that low, I'll admit I had no other choice but to latch on to the "life raft idea" a believing Christian threw out to me. I was drowning and I knew it and I didn't have time to ask if this was too good to be true. And you know what, friend, this life raft idea of God's saying He forgave me, wanted me to start over with a fresh start and offered me His guidance from that point on, really helped me. I can attest it's true. It worked for me. I was saved and saved again. I was saved from my life of endless wondering with little hope and that proves to me I'll be saved from any future endless suffering or even death. "Trust me," you and I implore, "God's gift will do for you what it did for me!

That's our assignment, as it was Paul's, to proclaim to others the good news of salvation, God's plan for everyone to be saved, everyone who truly wants God's gift. But I can't go on without calling your attention to the curious word Paul used, and I feel he used it advisedly. "I'm not ashamed of the gospel," Paul remarked. I feel when he said that, he was talking to me very clearly. "I'm not ashamed, though I could be," as if to say "don't you be ashamed of what you have." Paul took his message to the thinkers, philosophers and sages of his day. I know when I've been demanded to do the same I've felt a twinge of waning self-confidence when I thought about what I expected to be a daunting task. To some thinkers in Paul's time and, surprise, surprise - it's no different today, this Gospel of salvation is too simplistic, it's too easily understood. "You expect me to believe that what philosophers have been struggling to comprehend for eons is so simple. It just can't be," some say.

Whether that word "ashamed" came into Paul's mind when he penned Romans 1:16 due to his experience with philosophers in his day or not I don't know, but that's immediately what was called to my mind. I've had people ask, after saying, "It's too good to be true," or "It's too simple," - "Why haven't all the thinkers of the past come to the same conclusions?" I've never had anyone retort that the gospel message of salvation I've brought to them was illogical. They admit it's clear, concise but just too simple, too simple and maybe they're also saying, but under their breaths, too good to be true.

I'm convinced, personally, that Paul had such experiences, and that explains why he used the term "not ashamed." Just as I've used the term myself to say I'm not ashamed, though if I dwelled on it I could be. I've needed to remind myself often, especially when others marvel that I could be so gullible as to believe something so simplistic. I need only remind myself it works, it's true in my life, I have verified it. I have been saved from the sense of emptiness, isolation and depression so many others complain of. I remind myself that studies have revealed that, especially among intellectuals, the feeling of emptiness and hopelessness is prevalent. No, I'm not ashamed of this simple, too easily understood message my Lord wants me to convey. I'm actually proud.

As an interesting aside, I can't help but draw your attention to the paraphrase rendition of Romans 1:16 found in the Message translation of the New Testament. The writer has Paul saying ***"It's news I'm most proud to proclaim, this extraordinary Message of God's powerful plan to rescue everyone who trusts him..."*** Though in the literal Greek manuscripts Paul uses the Greek word for ashamed and says I'm "not ashamed" of the Gospel, the paraphrase rendition of this verse is "I'm most proud of the message." I'm sure Paul was proud to advance the message of salvation, but "not ashamed," though it could imply being most proud isn't necessarily the same as being proud. They could be the same, but not necessarily. Similarly, when someone says I'm "really not unhappy" that's not the same as saying "I'm very excited" or "happy." I'm not in any way attempting to cast aspersions on a paraphrase rendition of scripture in the Message version (you'll see I refer to it often in this work), because another way of phrasing a term that has become trite can be presented in a refreshing manner when rendered just a little differently. I especially applaud the Message for speaking of the "Good News" and not the ubiquitous term "Gospel" that has very little meaning to the un-churched, especially young people.

Again, I go into this sidetrack to explain what I think God, through Paul, is communicating to us. Don't be ashamed of the message I want you to share. God knows some of us feel inferior, that we may not estimate we have the intellect of a self-described philosopher or the cold concise logic of a mathematician or what's worse, an attorney (Sorry I didn't mean to say that, it just slipped). But we have what those who don't know the Lord don't have: happiness, peace of mind, excitement about the future, confidence we can confront any adversity. We have what everyone wants and we have it now. When someone says to me, "What you have is an illusion," I say, "How can you possibly tell me what I'm now experiencing within myself? Since when have you begun to read another person's mind or psyche?

"It appears to me that, as someone who admits he doesn't have what I claim to experience now with God's guidance, you're not only acting arrogantly, but actually your comments belie a sense of jealousy on your part! What you're really confessing when you use the camouflage of arrogance and barrage of belittlement is that you're just plain jealous that I could claim I have something so valuable that you'd want too, but at the moment you're just too proud to admit your predicament." I always tell sincere scoffers, "You may not be ready yet, you may not have come to a defining moment yet in your life where you have to admit you don't have all the answers, you may not have hit a proverbial low point yet, but when you do, remember you once talked to someone who claimed to have stumbled on the answer. Either he was an idiot claiming to have found something so profound and valuable or he just may have found what he claims. It will be worth a try."

So don't be ashamed. Remember all us little guys, little guys, yet entrusted with wealth beyond compare. Remember our unknown hero, Habakkuk. He never attained the top of his profession. As a Jewish

Levite, which we're quite certain he was, in the scheme of things, he worked in and around the temple but he wasn't the High Priest, the top man, or we would have had some evidence of that in his writing. He was content to live as any other true believer of the word. But remember he was entrusted with a profound oracle. His vision and his godly direction could have come from the High Priest of the religious system of his day, but it didn't. God saw fit to entrust it to him to proclaim, "The righteous will live by faith."

Though he was privileged to be the first to discover those words, we are entrusted with the same message of faith. The Lord is employing an army of untrained, and in many cases undistinguished, scholars to proclaim a message so valuable and so profound as to claim it is the panacea for all problems. Yes, it sounds too good to be true – a panacea for all problems. How absurd to say such a thing! How simplistic! But don't be ashamed. I know and you know, at least if you've been on the journey of salvation for any length of time, that what we have may appear from the vantage point of the doubter to be a message to be ashamed of, it really is a message of which to be most proud.

THE POWER OF GOD

In the same breath that Paul averred he was not ashamed, he said, "because it is the power of God." I think God through Paul was saying to many of us what I confessed before: though you could be ashamed, don't forget what you have to offer – it's the power of God. As Paul said in 2 Corinthians 12:10 *...when I am weak then I am strong.* When we feel inferior or less or even ashamed for some silly reason, we are reminded of the power of God. Paul was exclaiming the message is the power of God, inspired by God and energized by God. If only a person is willing to listen to and accept the message of salvation, the power of God will work in him to eliminate any inadequacies. That power will hone his God-given abilities and potential to be adequate to the task of representing the message of Good News. We need not do it alone, we cannot do it alone. The power of God first initiated the plan of salvation, the power of God saw to it that the message of salvation would be spread against all odds, the power of God gives us the impetus and strength and ability to put our lives in harmony with the plan of salvation; and finally it is the power of God that gives us the courage and ability to share the message of salvation with others.

The apostle's insights here in Romans, Chapter 1 resonate well with the life story of Habakkuk. One of the insights Habakkuk grasped from his experience was the necessity to rely on the power of God. Can't you just feel the despair in Habakkuk's quivering voice when he cried out, ***How long, O Lord, must I call for help...?*** (Ha. 1:2) Like so many of God's servants on earth, he felt alone at the time, so alone that all he could do was cry out to God. There was no crowd to comfort him. He learned first hand the power of God, and was forced to confess that only the power of God could end the misuse of power in his time. You remember his acknowledgment that the power of the influential and affluent power brokers in his country along with the power of the world-renowned Babylonian Empire were no match for the power of God. He also acknowledged it was the power of God that sustained him. He poetically testified in Chapter 3, ***I will be joyful in God my Savior. The Sovereign Lord is my strength***. I hope you're getting the point. It's no surprise that persons of God by their experiences and through their experiences come to realize and appreciate the power of God.

MESSAGES I HOPE YOU NOTED:

- **You'll Never Know If It's True Till You Try It**

- **Is It Hard To Believe Because It Seems Too Good To Be True?**

- **A True Christian Has What Everyone Else Wants**

Paul Serwinek

Chapter Eight

ARE YOU REALLY LUCKY?

Hopefully you have begun to see how the apostle Paul employs Habakkuk's original comments on faith as a basis for his arguments on the power of faith. We've seen how Paul directly quotes Habakkuk in Romans, Chapter 1. However, reading further in Romans, the apostle paraphrases the refrain "the righteous will live by faith" and says in Romans 3:28, ***For we maintain that a man is justified by faith...*** So Paul goes from "live by faith," to "justified by faith," and thereby shows the two ideas are related. Let's take a moment to explore how these ideas can help us now.

TAKING RESPONSIBILITY

To some of you, Paul will be introducing you to a little different way of looking at yourself and looking at life. Our society has taken great pains to make us feel good about ourselves. When we make mistakes we're assured not to worry, it's not our fault. We're taught to accept that there is always a reason for our actions outside of ourselves. There are no misogynists any more. When I act to hurt others in my world I can always invent an excuse. It's not my fault; it's either my environment or my upbringing or some maladaptive behavior that can be attenuated with an assortment of drugs and chemical treatment. That's the real problem; it's not me. I'm taught to sidestep responsibility. I can always blame someone or something else. I will not accept the stigma of any hurtful act. I'm taught to take the credit when something good happens, but never ever the blame when bad results.

But isn't that a double standard? Logic tells me I can't have it both ways. If it's not my fault when I perpetuate an act that hurts those around me (I can blame my upbringing or the social network I was thrown into), then it's also not "my fault" when I do good. To follow this logic of no responsibility applied to the good act, a kindness I display, the care I take to help another in need is just a product of my genes and a product of the circumstance I find myself in. Do you see the problem, though? Such logic leads me to believe I am merely an automaton. I am not a volitional being. I am no different than a one-cell amoeba or even a speck of dust, both buffeted about by the winds or the current of the water around the organism. Now do you see why we live in a hedonistic society? Deep down, all of us are getting vibes from the philosophy of the age that we are really expendable, or of no consequence, so why shouldn't we just continue in a state of "feel good" for as long as it can be maintained?

Do you see what I'm arguing here? If I start with the premise that there is no need to take responsibility, the logical outcome is that we have little worth, for good or for bad. If our faults can be explained away completely by defects and environment through no fault of our own, and then if any cause for self-worth must also be attributed to biological and social causes we have no control over, what a quandary we find ourselves in! Do you see that's exactly the predicament the prevailing philosophers in our universities have placed us in through the one premise that no one is ever responsible? Of course, the end result of their logic is never emphasized. If it were, the world would be in anarchy and all social fabric would be torn to shreds.

For the last 200 years our greatest thinkers have been grappling with the results of their logical progression of thought, but to no avail. The next great thinker will come up with a fad to inure the pain of our existence, but it's always a variation of the same theme. We may not matter; inherently we are nothing, trying to extricate ourselves, to fight our way out of our meaningless existence, anything to help us feel better about ourselves along the way. They'll admit, though, abdication of responsibility leads to a meaningless existence. All you can do is invent for yourself some arbitrary meaning for your life and live by that. Perhaps it may make you feel better in the meantime. It doesn't matter what meaningful system you choose to live by, since they are all meaningless when you get down to it, but pick something, anything to help you get by, to pass the time till your personal end comes. What a way to live!

HUMAN REASONING

My assertion is that subconsciously most people in our world pick up the undercurrents of this worldview, though it's never explained to them what they are buying into. I see it in colleges today - professors with tenure who can never lose their jobs feel secure enough to denigrate any belief. It makes them feel superior to debunk beliefs; it gives them a level of power they could attain no other way. They have the power to tear down, yes, but they have no power to build up! Yes, they can tear apart any beliefs by starting from a premise they hold to be true, and using logic, any and every belief system can be decimated. But with what do they replace it? They have nothing they can substantiate as a replacement premise in its place. So by default the graduate has only one choice: take a materialist mindset, and try to make the most of it. Collect and accumulate the most you can of material accoutrements and hope that you'll be happy. Unfortunately, time and time again studies show material collecting is no different than garbage collecting; inherently it doesn't satisfy. But they reason, "What else is there? "

Let me just say one more thing before we leave the depressing consequences of innate human reasoning. Most of these scholars are not trying to tear down society. Many really want to help. They'll tell you, "We advocate the excuse of no responsibility because we want people to have self-esteem." They reason that the best way to build self-esteem is to negate responsibility. That helps to pacify inadequacy. They contend "people shouldn't walk around with negative feelings about themselves like weights on their backs. People who feel good about themselves are capable of accomplishing more for society. We must build up self-esteem at any cost!!" But the premise they build on, that there is no need to take responsibility, is a shaky and unrealistic foundation upon which to build a life. Unfortunately, when high self-esteem first was heralded as a goal by psychologists, they didn't realize self-esteem is not the real need of humans. Studies have shown time after time that the sector in our society with the highest self-esteem and self-confidence is the young male ghetto-dwelling gang members in our inner cities, who live a life of crime, think only of themselves, and live only in the moment, with no care for the consequences of their actions. You probably never heard that, but believe me, just a little research in psychology will verify what I say is true.

Again, what I'm saying is not that self-esteem or self-confidence is not desirable; what I am saying is that self-esteem is not the elixir of society. Self-confidence is not the desire or result of therapy. Self-esteem for self-esteem's sake is a double-edged sword as the self-confident inner city terrorists in our midst demonstrate. And certainly you must admit that eliminating blame and responsibility in order to produce self-esteem and self-confidence in our children is an idea that has been put forth without doing the necessary research and without considering the consequences.

A BETTER WAY

Christian thought built upon the foundation of the Judeo-Christian prophets and sages, like Habakkuk, had a better system. As a Christian, I believe God, knowing better than anyone else, since He was our inventor, has a better idea. This system is one that provides for an immeasurable increase in self-esteem and self-confidence without having to base it on meaninglessness. His system asserts that humans have value, have worth. There is an explicit meaning for life and a true inner satisfaction is the desired consequence. This system is built on two premises. The first is there is a Creator and Director of the universe, which assumes meaning, and the second is there is such a thing as responsibility along with consequences.

What I'm asking you to consider, if you haven't already, is that if a premise that asserts life has no purpose and there is no such thing as responsibility leads logically to a meaningless existence and meaningless human experience, you should consider the alternative, especially if our present existence has consequences that are not desirable. Please posit for a moment that there is such a thing as responsibility; that's what the Judeo-Christian worldview starts with. This isn't difficult, since we've seen that modern western philosophy is built on the arbitrary premise that there is no responsibility, with no proof whatsoever of this claim.

Modern philosophers merely say since we can't prove beyond any doubt there is such a thing as responsibility, we'll just assume there is none. If they could only bring themselves to reason, just as logically and perhaps more so, that we can't prove there is such a thing as responsibility beyond any doubt, but since their premise of no responsibility leads to a dead end and a meaningless existence, there is only one possible way to go. When you have two choices and one leads to no solution, you have no choice but to choose the other. We've proved by logic there is only one possible way to proceed. Unfortunately Western philosophy from the 1900s didn't stop to think it through. We've inherited their legacy of a dead-end existence.

But God says that doesn't have to be. He says, "Just try to start with a premise that may be difficult to accept (live by faith, ala Habakkuk) but trust Me, when you accept My reasoning it makes more sense and the pain evaporates." This takes us to the writing of St. Paul in Romans and the theme verse he chose for the book of Romans, Habakkuk's phrase, "The righteous will live by faith." Follow with me Paul's reasoning. The logic is clear and the only premise he begs you to consider is that there is such a thing as responsibility and that any person should be willing to accept some blame for the turmoil they have created in their own little world.

JUSTICE REQUIRES JUSTIFICATION

Further, in the book of Romans, Paul introduces a variation on the theme and melody that he inherited from Habakkuk. Whereas he said in Galatians that a righteous man lives by faith (using the exact words of

Habakkuk), he now introduces the variation. An example is Romans 3:28 where Paul proclaims, "For we maintain that a man is justified by faith." This newly introduced word, the term "justified," is rather unusual. It doesn't come up in normal conversation often, though it's easily understood. The root of justify is "justice." A man being justified indicates he comes to justification in the sense of being considered just or blameless. You've also probably heard of the term in connection with a crooked picture on a wall. You justify the picture by straightening or adjusting it. And similar to a crooked picture on a wall that looks out of place, a natural man in the context of God's universe is out of place. That's what Paul contends.

This goes back to the one idea with which we started this chapter; that we must take some responsibility for our own actions. We can't say, "It's not my fault!" The point is, hello…we're not perfect. In God's world we are similarly out of place and just as conspicuous as a crooked picture on the wall. But God wants you in His world; He wants to associate with you. He wants to come into your house and He wants to invite you to His. For that to happen you must conform to His perfect standard. For one thing, without perfection you'd feel out place in your own estimation. God knows that, so He invented a plan to justify you, straighten out your crookedness, so to speak, sand off your rough edges. But let the apostle explain it to you. In only a few Bible verses he makes it so clear and logical.

Starting with Romans 3:10 the apostle contends *…There is no one righteous, not even one.* Do you agree with that? In other words, can you think of anyone who has performed perfectly in all his actions? Of course not, you know from personal experience that the harder you try to conform to perfection, the more apparent it is you are not perfect. For example, God's perfect standard is love, yet how often have we acted contrary to that standard? Even toward the persons we care about the most, our spouse or children, we irrationally may loose our temper in a momentary act, without considering our loved ones' welfare. Every one of us has had the same experience. We admit with Paul, "There's no one righteous, not even one." If you've ever resolved to start out just one day trying to eliminate unjustified negative thoughts toward others, as I have, sooner or later you catch yourself failing, especially in your thoughts, though you may not act on those thoughts.

That's what Paul was showing when he says in Romans 3:20, ***Therefore no one will be declared righteous in his sight by observing the law...*** When he talks of the law, the Jewish set of laws is being referenced. The Jewish law delved into every aspect of human life – dietary restrictions, social behavior and criminal infractions - all were stipulated. However, this law, incumbent on a nation that considered themselves God's chosen people, went much farther. Attitude and emotions were also regulated. For example, jealousy and envy were strictly forbidden. Under these circumstances no one Jewish citizen could claim to have followed the law perfectly. They all had to admit to errant negative thinking and feelings at times. This in no way contradicts my previous suggestion. Try to go even one day without thinking (not just speaking aloud) any negative thoughts toward your fellow man. I dare you to try. You'll find that a thought of bigotry, arrogance, fault-finding or self-interest that could undermine the social structure will reveal itself at some point during the day. I'm talking about one day, let alone a lifetime.

Will you now repent and concur with Paul's assessment that "no one will be declared righteous in his sight by observing (or trying to observe) the law"? Paul says here that even in your own "sight," your own estimation, you could never claim to be righteous. All of us have more blame. For example, seldom is a disagreement between individuals totally the fault of only one of the partners. I've talked to friends who are marriage counselors and they will testify that they have never been involved in a divorce where only one spouse is wholly to blame. Their assessment is that both sides always contribute to a marriage's decay. One side may be more culpable, but both sides contribute in some way to the break-up. Given the fact that children invariably bear the emotional scars from a divorce, for at least a time, each spouse, whether the one most at fault or least at fault, has some culpability for the hurt brought on innocent children. I stress this, not to encourage you to carry around the baggage of blame, but only to encourage you to acknowledge to yourself the uncomplimentary side of your personality. It doesn't even have to be a divorce; even break-ups of a friendship involving no innocent children still hurt. Blame and negative feelings directed toward others always result. Again, no one side is ever 100% to blame. The other party at least must bear some of the blame for having allowed the relationship to decline in the first place!

Even with this guilt, we must move on. God does. All God cares about is that you admit, mainly to yourself, that you are not righteous, you are not perfect. That being the case, who will dare claim they are in a position to demand justice for themselves in all circumstances? If I now have admitted I have not always dealt with others completely justly and without malice or uncomplimentary thought, who am I to dare to assume that every other individual in society needs to treat me justly and fairly, when I can't demonstrate that I have always returned the favor. Do we get the point? If my own conduct isn't always beyond reproach, how can I insist on justice for me from others? Even worse, if I have acted unjustly and with hurt in the past, am I not admitting that justice demands that I be treated in like manner by others? That would be fair, wouldn't it? Fortunately our God, the source of all perfection, doesn't dwell on this negative predicament all are in.

As Romans 3:23 says, *for all have sinned and fall short of the glory* [perfection] *of God.* Leave it to God to provide a solution, a way for you to feel good about yourself in spite of your imperfections. And this novel idea of imperfections has taken on a whole life of its own in our modern, enlightened society. Adolescent self-esteem is dashed to pieces when they compare their appearance to that of movie star heroes. Every blemish, every imperfection is proof a boy or girl does not rank in the category of "special." TV commercials coax me to disparage my appearance since I don't have "six pack abs"; in fact, I don't even have all my hair! Don't get me started, let's stop right here. God doesn't compare us that way. We all are something special in His eyes. He claims we are all exactly the same when comparing our righteousness - not one has attained to perfection. But in God's eyes we are all incomparable when it comes to our abilities, strengths and experiences.

This then is exactly idea the apostle next suggests to us in Romans 3:21. ***But now*** [that is in spite of our degraded state] ***a righteousness from God, apart from law, has been made known...*** We can't extricate ourselves from the curse of comparing ourselves to others in appearance or ability. We can't even forget that we don't deserve special treatment by justice since we even inadvertently treat others unkindly by volition or neglect. "Leave it to God." A righteousness from God has been made known. We can't do it. We can't make ourselves feel special or worthy at a snap of a finger, but God can! He alone can offer us the righteous start we all lack. He alone can settle in our favor the issues we have with ourselves or the issues others may have with us.

This was God's plan from ages past, for the apostle, after heralding the good news of this great righteousness of God in Romans 3:21, adds the parenthetical thought, ***a righteousness from God to which the Law and the Prophets testify.*** So this wasn't something new that Paul conceived, but long before his time, the prophets foretold this. And who was one of the prophets, one of those chosen from the distant past that Paul could hear echoing? That's right, Habakkuk. Any reference Bible you pick up will point you back to this verse immortalized in Ha. 2:4: "The righteous will live by his faith." See, before Jesus' time no one knew for sure how God would do it, but any person of faith knew that He would somehow provide every person ever born with a fresh start, absolved of any baggage he had collected along the way. Just to give you another example of still another prophet seeing the future, we have David. He could feel that peace of mind that comes from a fresh start. Psalm 32:1-2 proclaims, ***Blessed is he whose transgressions are forgiven, whose sins are covered. Blessed is the man whose sin the Lord does not count against him, and in whose spirit is no deceit.***

ARE WE REALLY LUCKY?

To give you a real feel for what God is doing here, let me quote again this scripture, this time a paraphrase - the Message translation of David's hopes and joys put in the vernacular of our day. Listen to this.

Count yourself lucky, how happy you must be – you get a fresh start, your slate's wiped clean. Count yourself lucky – God holds nothing against you and you're holding nothing back from him. That's exactly how I feel as a Christian, and that's exactly how countless millions throughout history have felt – liberated. Free at last! Pulled out from the hole they dug for themselves or the hole someone else dug to put them in. When Paul was explaining this good news, he didn't say Christians are better; instead, what he was intimating was – "We're lucky." We're lucky (or more properly, blessed) because we didn't have to work it out by ourselves. None of us can claim righteousness on our own. God invented the phrase. We're just lucky that He thought so much of us humans that He made the plan a reality. If you accept the Christian perspective, you'll get up each day, as I do, feeling oh, so fortunate to be alive, with a fresh start and yesterday's errors forgiven.

Before we go on to how Paul explains how this became a reality, let's get one other thing straight. I want to be sure when Paul makes his point to you that you have no reservations that this promise <u>includes</u> you. I wonder how many of you who are already Christians and know what Paul is about to say, still find it difficult to imagine this wonderful prospect applies <u>to you</u>. This includes many of you who are thinking, "This sounds good, but is it just appealing to me selfishly? I see I'm being offered something from God and yet I don't even know Him, maybe never gave Him a single thought all these years, and now I say, 'This sounds good.' I can say selfishly I'd like it to be true. But doesn't God see through my motive – that I'm finally interested in Him for what I can get out of it?" Others of you may admit, "Yes, I accepted Christianity because I was told I'd go to hell if I didn't. That's pretty selfish isn't it?" To you I say you may not be getting the point of the apostle's phrase, "a righteousness from God."

I remember when I was a newer, younger Christian second-guessing myself. I mused, "What God is promising is too fantastic. How could anyone not want God's helping hand? But I still did begin to feel that peace of mind and excitement, just as scripture promised I would. But before long I started second- guessing myself with thoughts like, "I'm really no different than I was before, just as selfish, just as conniving," beginning to creep in. "How do I really know if I love God because I really feel that way, or just because of what He's given me?"

Have you ever thought that? I think many of us go through that period of questioning. Fortunately I realized that second-guessing, that excessive self-interrogation, was not going to be productive. I simply resolved this: what I'd been led to thus far all was true. I did receive what God promised me. Sometimes He's overlooking my current seemingly selfish motive for coming to Him because I'm getting the blessings described in ages past. It wasn't until years later in reading Paul's words anew that I got the point: it's "a righteousness of God." Nothing I did deserved the present blessings I was experiencing. I realized that even the initial selfishness that brought me to God in the first place (being no different than the selfish acts I perpetrated on others) was wrapped up with them in one package and taken by the Lord, never to be counted against me.

Guess what has also occurred in the intervening years of my walk with the Lord? Another day I awoke to realize my time with the Lord had molded me into a different person. I realized I no longer served God so much for what I was getting out of it as I had in my initial experiences with God. My motive is less selfish and more altruistic now. I can truthfully say the blessings serve less and less as a motivation. I'm acting more now simply because I want to. I just want to see the Lord's plan of salvation come to completion for His sake. He deserves the fulfillment of the plan He's been revealing in increments over the ages. I've given myself as a fellow worker of His, not so much for what I can have in store as a reward, (what He's already given me is more of a reward than I could have ever asked). I'm working now more because of gratitude and because I want to. It's the only right thing to do! I tell you this story so you have no reservation in accepting this "Righteousness of God." Don't second-guess it; just accept it. What I'm suggesting with my personal example is not to waste time second-guessing your initial motive or current motive in serving God; it's not productive. Just remember what happens to most all Christians: over time your walk with God will develop into such a love for God as you have for any close friend. Motive is never an issue again.

JESUS' SACRIFICE REASONING

I'd like to switch gears for a moment here. I've been talking to most of you readers with the assumption that you are believers, but for the rest of this chapter I'm going to speak to some of you that aren't quite convinced about the importance of Jesus' sacrifice. The major assertion that separates Christians from other religious or spiritual seekers is the belief that Jesus gave up His life as a sacrifice for the benefit of all who believe in Him. My purpose here is not to discuss the issue from a theological standpoint, but merely from a logical view. This is a rather esoteric concept and may, for some, require further biblical references. My goal here is to pass on the excitement I feel when I find that modern scientific research is proving the value of this Christian doctrine. This section will also be helpful for you believers, since the information here can be employed to discuss that topic with any non-believing friends from a strictly non-biblical and non-threatening position.

The issue here is the issue of forgiveness. In my studies and work in the field of social psychology, I frequently encounter the necessity for personal forgiveness. Fortunately, modern psychology has produced an avalanche of data demonstrating that individuals have a difficult time coping with relationships and attaining personal self-esteem without being able to forgive others or themselves for past transgressions. We now understand that an individual may not be able to grow emotionally and in self-concept if he is stifled by an inability to forgive others or self. Countless studies show that an individual may have every right to disparage and castigate another for a heinous offense against himself, but if he is not able to go beyond that hatred of the other and move on, he inadvertently hurts himself. Personal growth, emotional growth, is affected adversely.

This is especially true if an individual is not able to forgive herself for past actions. What she may have done may appear so horrible to her that no amount of therapy will convince her to forgive herself. Remember, I'm talking strictly from a social scientific standpoint here. These data are verified by rigorous research. Unless a person is able to reach the point of forgiveness, she cannot forget. If she cannot forget, that equates to carrying around harmful baggage that prevents nimble self-maneuvering in daily life. I've tried to convince others, when I've engaged in counseling, to simply "let it go," but they can't.

Imagine struggling with a person who has for years never let himself forget that due to his past inability as a parent, his son committed suicide. Or what do you say to someone who, in a fit of anger, murdered his best friend? Psychologists can work for years with such a patient convinced that they have all but coaxed the patient to move on, only to find that he relapses into total disintegration. What can you say? Have you ever had some part of your past life come back to haunt you, something you aren't proud of and something others won't let you forget? Psychologists will tell you such a situation can be very difficult to resolve. And yet, resolve it the patient must, if he is to grow. I'm not going to belabor the point of the importance of self-concept and self-esteem here. I trust most all will concede the critical need of a positive self-concept to be fully functioning.

Happily the one concept that works, and works consistently I have found, is an appeal to the Christian concept of Jesus' sacrifice. I find I can appeal to this, regardless of a person's own personal religious persuasion. Again, my goal here is to explain the concept without evoking a debate over whether Jesus is the Son of God or even what it means to claim Jesus is the Son of God. That comes with further meditation and soul searching. This is what Christianity can offer that no other religions can offer. Jesus, the Christ, in effect proclaimed, "I am willing to go through unspeakable suffering, martyrdom, death, to be punished for something I didn't do. And I'm willing to do this for you. I'm going to be subjected to inhuman torture and death because I'm not willing to deny truth. That's My only crime, not being willing to renounce truth, to keep quiet, nothing more."

How many other martyrs have experienced a similar fate, from biblical prophets to political martyrs even in our time? What happened to Jesus has been repeated countless times. We are all familiar with that. So it's not difficult to accept that such a fate occurred to Jesus. In fact, His followers after Jesus' death were willing to undergo the same fate rather than deny what they had personally witnessed. No more convincing proof need be offered of any event occurring than that the witnesses to the event are willing to die themselves rather than deny the facts of the event.

But here's the point of this sacrifice. Jesus said, "I am willing to suffer for you, be punished for you, tortured for you, die for you. I am willing to do this of My own volition, so you can have this priceless feeling of forgiveness for yourself and as an inducement for you to forgive others." When you feel, for example, that you committed an unspeakable crime, caused another person to suffer, did something you are extremely ashamed of, follow Jesus' advice. Jesus, in effect, said, "Ask yourself, what is the worst punishment you could imagine for your crime or culpable action? Do you feel you deserve to be tortured, to undergo a slow methodical torture of unspeakable pain and torment that eventually leads to death?" Most of us would be willing to concede that such a personal ordeal might be enough to expiate one's past transgressions. However, most of us lack the courage and conviction to undergo such a punishment.

Jesus said, "No matter. You don't have to subject yourself to such agony. I did it for you! So whenever you feel down and beyond consolation and dejected, just consciously apply My agony for your agony. Don't waste what I did. Please apply it to yourself, for yourself! I've undergone the most ignominious suffering for you freely and without coercion. So when you feel you should be punished or need to atone for your errors, apply my personal suffering for yourself. I only ask that you ask forgiveness, apply My punishment for what you deserve, and resolve to try to do better the next time. Finally, be willing to forgive still others. Remember, I am willing to apply My punishment for what you feel you deserve."

This concept really works! I've had real success using this concept in my personal counseling. Furthermore, countless millions throughout history have been able to start new lives without years of therapy by first understanding the concept and being willing to impute this act of Jesus for themselves. No other religion has such a powerful concept that can be used practically, efficiently and successfully. Other religions or non-theological therapies attempt to say, "You should forgive yourself". Or "God loves you." Or "It wasn't so bad what you did, and I think you should forgive yourself." But only one worldview offers such a reasonable, easily understood concept to promote self-forgiveness. This is the beauty of Christianity. It's practical; it works. Note that I did not appeal to the claim that Jesus is the Son of God and what that adds to the equation. There is no need to argue that issue here. It's a matter each can individually deal with once he understands the believable, reasonable basis for being able to start a new life. I'm proud to be a Christian due to the simplicity and beauty of this solely Christian doctrine of sacrifice!

MESSAGES I HOPE YOU NOTED:

- **You Don't Have To Be A Believer To Believe In The Power Of Forgiveness; Science Is Proving It All The Time**

- **God's Forgiveness, Self-Forgiveness And Inter-Personal Forgiveness - - Christ's Sacrifice Insures All Three**

Paul Serwinek

Chapter Nine

JUSTICE IN THE END

I'm going to make an astounding statement. This is what I believe, based on my reading of scripture. You may not agree with me fully or at all. I don't claim to have all the answers. I believe our Lord will restore in time all that has been lost to those who "live by faith." I believe He will recompense every person who ever "lived by faith" for all their suffering they have ever, ever endured. I'll show you how this is so, but now let's first get back to Paul's argument concerning God's free gift to each of us.

Paul has established for us that we are all sinners - we all miss the mark, we're all imperfect. As hard as we try, we fall short and sometimes that falling short hurts others around us. Out of deference for the others that are hurt, justice cries out for some recompense. And when I say we have all hurt other people, I mean hurt in a multitude of ways. I admit I have hurt others physically, mentally, emotionally and financially to a greater or lesser degree, many times not even realizing it at the moment. True justice insists that all these hurts be mended. And since our conception of God is as the protector and champion of justice, we would expect our God to insist on the same. He would insist that all hurts be atoned for or mended in one way or another, and He does. Fortunately as the source of all that is just and the guardian of what is right, He has the ability to right all wrongs. In fact, He promises us just that. Throughout scripture our Lord promises the restoration of all that is lost.

FOR HOW LONG WILL YOU TOLERATE WRONG?

Remember when we read Habakkuk's bewilderment earlier? Several times in the first chapter of Habakkuk our prophet and songwriter called attention to injustice. He asked that same question pondered by believers and nonbelievers alike. Both groups ask what Habakkuk did, "(God), why do you tolerate wrong?" (Ha. 1:3). Put another way, Habakkuk complained again questioning his Lord, "Your eyes are too pure to look on evil"… and … "Why do you tolerate the treacherous? (Ha. 1:13). Aren't those the same questions you've asked? Why if there is an all powerful, just God does He allow evil and suffering in the world? As I said, both believers and nonbelievers ask the exact same question but with different motives.

The nonbelievers ask the question of why with the motive of attempting to discredit the very existence of God. The nonbeliever has a vested interest in there not being a God. He or she does not wish to be accountable to any higher power. "How wonderful to think I can do anything I want and not be required to answer to anyone," they dream. They then use the existence of evil to justify their positions. Evil is employed as a basis for furthering their cause of complete individual liberty with no need to feel accountable to anyone, whether small or great. "I have all power within myself," they claim, either in word or deed or silently within themselves. They figure the more they can discredit the existence of a caring all-powerful God, the more justified they feel in maintaining their selfish course. To many then, the question of evil is not a question they want answered. It's used as a smoke screen, very often to hide a selfish and self-gratifying motive. I've often found when I open my mouth to respond in answer to their question, some are not patient enough to wait for an answer, further revealing their motive in raising the question in the first place.

Besides, raising a question one personally does not have an answer for is really no proof of the non-existence of any entity including the existence of the One we call God. I've learned when another raises the issue of "Why evil?" I first try to ascertain if they really want an answer or if they are using the issue as their personal smoke screen to justify their own actions. There are, of course, still others who ask the question of "Why evil?" with sincerity. What a joy it is to provide a plausible answer.

For many, the question of "Why evil?" is linked with an emotion of bewilderment. The query is not raised to question the existence of a God, but more to elicit a satisfying answer. Habakkuk was one of them. No doubt most of you readers are in the same emotional frame of mind as Habakkuk when you see injustice going unpunished. You can just feel the incredulity of Habakkuk when he says, "(I know) You cannot tolerate wrong (then) why do You tolerate the treacherous?" In effect he exclaims with us, "I know, Lord, You have a reason, please let me know it and please give me the patience to put up with it like You do. Please give me something to hang onto, to assuage my personal suffering and the pain of seeing others hurt." This emotion of disgust toward the treacherous puts us in the proper frame of mind to follow Paul's argument for the triumph of God's righteousness as predicted by the prophet Habakkuk among others.

Remember we used one argument to counter the question of evil earlier. That was the necessity of free will. Free will and choice always open the door to wrong choices and wrong choices lead to evil and unintended consequences. We won't repeat our reasoning here. We ask that you be open to still a different line of reasoning for suffering. Paul asserts that evil is tolerated due to "a righteousness from God" (Ro. 3:21). In other words, a righteous act of God, not by man, will rectify all injustices. God has the power to right all wrongs. Due to a yearning for justice and desire to make things right, a righteousness of God was made known.

The Lord's plan is to right all wrongs. Throughout scripture God promises just that. The last book of the Bible, Revelation, ends with God's promise and plan restated. Revelation 21:3-4 says, ***"Now the dwelling of God is with men, and he will live with them. They will be his people, and God himself will be with them and be their God. He will wipe every tear from their eyes. There will be no more death or mourning or crying or pain, for the old order of things has passed away."*** Then in Revelation 21:5 the Lord adds, ***"...I am making*** *everything new!"* Our God clearly states He intends to wipe away any and all evidence of injustice and suffering. That's why God can tolerate evil, because He can wipe away all memories of its rule. So radical is the renovation that God titles the event *"a new heaven and a new earth…"* (Re. 21:1). In this New Era, all those who have suffered in the past, all those victims of injustice and all those forced to endure treachery will be recompensed. All that they lost, all that was stolen, all the pain and deformity, all that was evident of injustice will be rectified. God's existence and His righteousness will once and for all be exonerated. The history of humankind on earth will record proof that justice, while requiring free will, must have limits. Right-ness or righteousness will be preeminent over free choice. Having allowed evil to run its course and having proven for all time that God's course is the best course, God can rectify each injustice one at a time.

This is the overwhelming promise of our Lord. It's so radical and so unfathomable that for some it's unbelievable. But it isn't unbelievable to all. Our friend Habakkuk reminds us, "The righteous will live by faith." I believe he was also consoling us by those words so all those yearning for righteousness need only have faith strong enough to conquer disbelief. Christ's promise may be unbelievable to some but it is believable to those with faith. Faith allows you to dare to believe what is unfathomable. While it's hard to believe without faith, the believer recognizes God's promise certainly answers any lingering question of "Why evil?"

Imagine what God is saying. Those who have suffered in the past will be brought to life again to see justice prevail. All who have died due to injustice or evil will have the opportunity to behold, in their own presence in the world to come, the unraveling of all injustice. All those who lost their material inheritance will personally experience it being restored in some way. All those who experienced the emotional and mental trauma of injustice will experience the unraveling of all the ill effects of that injustice. Christ promises that all who have ever in the past yearned for justice and righteousness will finally experience such a world. Revelation 21:4 makes it clear and all-encompassing when it says "pain" will be no more. The pain of losing a child, the pain of losing all you worked for due to injustice, the pain of suffering inhuman treatment, the pain of enduring being banished from your home or loved ones, the pain of being forced to watch as your friends and family suffer while you stand by helpless, the pain of torture and even death, always and inevitably the result of injustice, will be assuaged.

Can you now see why God can tolerate evil for a time? As any great craftsman or artist must exercise patience while he or she fashions the work of art, our Lord does the same. He patiently endures evil by dwelling on the good that will result. If any of you have ever seen the works of art of Michelangelo, e.g. his Sistine Chapel or his great statue of David, in person you cannot help but be amazed not only for the beauty but the patience and long-suffering endured to spend years before seeing the clear conception in the artist's mind come to fruition. Michelangelo was using the God-given quality of patience endorsed and evinced by His and our Creator.

Our Lord is indeed passionate about justice and that is why the apostle Paul in Romans lays out so painstakingly the argument for justice. And this is where what some might call a "catch 22" situation was confronted by God. We know our Creator despises injustice. The problem is, justice means not overlooking an injustice. Here we are back to the starting point of Paul's treatise on God's justice. Yes, with our hearts still tingling with the prospect of relief from injustice, Paul has the unenviable task of reminding us all, "There is no difference."

When it comes to sin and injustice, ***...There is no difference, for all have sinned and fall short of the glory of God.*** (Ro. 3:22-23). This truth is a rather rude awakening. For now God's attitude toward injustice touches us all. There are numerous times we have not gotten it right. There were times too numerous to count where we treated others unjustly. How many times have you or I slighted another? How many times have we lied to another? How many times have we played with the emotions of another, or let others down when they were counting on us? You get the picture.

COMPARING LIES

See, Christ demonstrated when He came that there is "no difference" between the gravity of lies – they all are unjust. A lie blurted out on the spur of the moment versus a premeditated lie can still hurt another just as severely. For example, screaming at a child in the midst of a heated argument, "You're worthless, you won't amount to anything," just one time, is all it takes. One time and the child could believe it for life.

Similarly what's the difference between deception and stealing? The continuous mega trials in the business world prove the point over and over. A corporate officer deceptively leads stockholders to believe a company is solvent, when in fact there are far more expenses than income. Not warning stockholders (omitting the truth) or deceptively covering up the profit shortfall bankrupts companies either way. Billions of dollars of employee pension reserves have been lost forever. Money that employees had counted on for their retirements is no longer there. Is the employee covering up business errors and failing to divulge corporate losses any different than the officers who have actually stolen millions of dollars from the corporation? The end result is exactly the same. As the Lord says, "There is no difference." The corporate employees ready to retire, either way don't have the funds promised them. What do they do now for retirement income when the pensions they counted on are lost forever?

Or how do you put a money value on a broken promise? I know of someone, you probably do, too, who put her spouse through college. She worked full-time paying academic expenses for her spouse and putting food on the table. No sooner did he graduate from college than he broke it to his spouse that he was also graduating to a new life style with a new companion. You can maybe put a dollar value on her lost time and the four to six years that she acted as the personal valet and servant for the unfaithful mate. But how many dollars would it take to mitigate the heartbreak and emotional trauma caused? That's a multimillion-dollar loss in one person's life, precipitated by one small deception that grew.

At what point does spending time socially with another woman become infidelity? It starts somewhere. Again this is why our Lord says: "There is no difference." The little white lie deception that leads to infidelity is a contributory factor. Which one of the seemingly innocuous social occasions spent with another woman was the most culpable? Hopefully we see the point. Gigantic unethical actions usually are the culmination of a collection of small, and by themselves minor, offenses against another. Many small insignificant peccadilloes snowball into horrendous affronts against fellow humans.

Our friend with the cheating college-graduate spouse might be able to rectify part of the injustice to her through a court of law, but human courts can only repay lost monetary injustice and money doesn't begin to equate to four to six years of a life lost. And can money ever dissolve the emotional pain or anguish that will be carried as excess baggage for many years to come? Again I ask, which of the long string of minor deceptions was the straw that broke the camel's back leading to an irreconcilable divorce?

That's horrible, but here's another true story. Exact same situation but this time the man and woman are not married. He professes his undying affection for her. Once he gets his degree he'll provide for her. In the meantime they have a child, a little boy. No problem, he'll continue going to school, she'll keep her full-time job and her mother (his future mother-in-law) will watch the child during the day - still no problem. As soon as he graduates and gets a great job she won't need to work.

Now why didn't they get married before? Let's just say he was a good salesman. It appears the deception started a little sooner here. Of course you and I could have predicted what would happen. Anyone could - well, anyone but Cindy, the mother. In this case he left two weeks before his graduation date. The difference here is that the courts could adjudicate a modicum of justice by increasing child support. It wasn't much since he didn't have that high- paying job yet. That came two months after the settlement. But what about the four years lost? What about the fact that a young woman with a child in tow has fewer options then a single woman never married? Where's the guy that's going to be the new father for the baby?

Human courts are incapable of sorting out this mess. But that's why I'm a Christian, that's why Paul became an apostle and that's why Habakkuk continued to be a faithful prophet. Human courts, human regents, may attempt to decree justice. Only the Lord is so capable. He will see to it that justice is done for Cindy. Rather than appeal to human courts, if she merely appeals to the highest court, the highest Judge, He will bring justice.

Her present life can still be satisfying emotionally and monetarily, if she appeals to Him during her lifetime. If not, during the life to come she has hope of receiving her recompense. For now her son can have a father, albeit a Heavenly Father, at least. Presently and in the age to come many other benefactors may be put in their paths, if the son or the mother so prays. Again, in the age to come, full resolution will be realized by mother and son. An eternity is plenty of time to work out the rectifying of what 70 to 80 years of human living has made into a mess. Never again will they ask why did God allow evil.

So once more let's follow Paul's reasoning. We've all sinned in great numbers and gravity or in lesser numbers and gravity, but we've all hurt others. If the Lord is to demand justice from your adversary when you are broken, He will just as readily demand justice from you due to your own unthinking or premeditated sins against others. Justice requires that. How could you respect a judge who demands of one repayment while not demanding the same from another, even if it was his friend? Do you see the point here? You may be working to be a friend of God but does being His friend absolve you of your sins in itself? Think about it, does God play favorites? Scripture makes it clear that God does not. Everyone has the same reward and everyone has the same opportunity. As scripture says ***"He causes his sun to rise on the evil and the good."*** (Matt. 5:45). So whether you're attempting to be God's friend (righteous) or have nothing to do with God (wicked), either out of intent or because you haven't yet been led to Him, either way you must be considered unjust. By the same token you can't expect absolution of sins just because you know the Judge, at least not when the Judge is unbiased and just.

ENOUGH OF THE NEGATIVE

Paul now clarifies the Lord's idea for all to share in His benevolence. Romans 3:24-25 tells us the Lord's side of the story. (All) *are justified freely by his grace through the redemption that came from Christ Jesus. God presented him as a sacrifice of atonement, through faith in his blood. He did this to demonstrate his justice, because in his forbearance he had left the sins committed beforehand unpunished.*

God's solution to the perpetual quandary of sin, death, suffering and pain was this. "God presented him (His Son, Jesus Christ) as a sacrifice of atonement." Do you see how this works? Paul brought us to the point of recognizing our shortcomings and in the preceding pages we've dwelled enough on the negative. The positive side of the story is this: Christ came and voluntarily gave His life as a sacrifice for anyone who wishes to claim that His suffering be considered in exchange for his or her own penalty of sin. We've all heard the story of Jesus' passion. His inhumane treatment, torture and final death were endured as a sacrifice for any who claim their value for their own personal acts of injustice.

Before I go on to demonstrate how you can use Christ's sacrifice every day, let me point out three words in this two verse passage that have similar meanings and connotations. The three are necessary for you to understand if you are to get the full import of what Jesus did for you. They are "justified," "redemption" and "atonement." All three have to do with fairness and justice and give the flavor of what Paul was attempting to convey to us.

I especially like Paul's choice of the word "redemption." That word gives the connation of being released from bondage. Living in a society where slavery was part of the fabric of the culture, that word "redemption" immediately came into Paul's mind. In his day and for thousands of years previous, people were pressed into bondage or sold into slavery with only a very slight chance of emerging with their freedom. For someone to be redeemed meant that the slave or another benefactor paid the price for release.

So the redemption that came by Christ means that Jesus paid the price, giving His life in exchange for the punishment that most of us feel we deserve. His life releases us by paying the debt of any former sins we have committed and also releases us from punishment for errors we know we will yet commit in the future. Redemption means freedom from a slave mentality. We no longer need to think of ourselves as individuals with a long chain of mistakes and errors holding us down. Just accepting and acknowledging what Jesus has done releases us from feeling like slaves to our imperfect nature. Redemption also means a clear conscience.

Freedom from pangs of inadequacy and freedom from nagging regrets of the past are all packaged into "redemption." For you personally, these are probably the most marvelous benefits from Jesus' release of you. He's unlocked the prison cell that enslaved you, but it's up to you to walk out with the courage and confidence to start anew. Many of those Paul called out for redemption had totally been enslaved physically, under the oppression of wealthy, insensitive masters, all their lives. Here the apostle was heralding a new perception. Even if they were physically still enslaved, they could live in freedom mentally with the assurance that physical redemption would come in time, in their temporal lifetime or if not, then in God's lifetime. For those who could have faith in the reality of present redemption, what a life-transforming immediate difference they sensed. No longer were they limited by their legal enslavement. At least their minds and hearts could soar. They were freed immediately to use their God-given capability to hope, to love, to persevere. What a difference - perception is everything.

Unfortunately remnants of legal slavery were present in the United States some 150 years ago and in the United Kingdom some 175 years ago. When the decree of redemption or emancipation was proclaimed in both of these countries, many of those redeemed still felt in bondage. Perception is everything when it comes to a person's actions. And unfortunately some in our time and in our country (the USA) still live in the world of 150 years ago. Their mentality is still one of enslavement, living as if to say, "I can't be free till someone like the government forces the bigoted to denounce their bigotry." Or, "I can't be free till the government gives me some monetary or other special compensation before I can get on with my life."

Fortunately millions of blacks (not just African-Americans) and Hispanics have broken the mentality of enslavement. It was no coincidence that one of the galvanizing personalities reminding the disenfranchised that they were indeed free was a Christian. Dr. Martin Luther King employed the concept of redemption for all humankind, blacks and whites alike, as the premise of his argument for equality and freedom. His followers were, of course, legally free but many did not feel mentally and emotionally free. Dr. King employed the conviction of his faith in Jesus' sacrifice to conclude he was indeed free. His Christian faith was the source of power that gave him the conviction to endure till he began to see the realization of freedom in the lives of others, first in their mental and than in their physical environment.

A legal end to slavery had been decreed over 100 years before, but many did not begin to live as free till they were touched by the perception of true freedom. Only when an individual chooses to live in freedom is he or she truly free. In our lifetime many of us have seen first hand the result of a perception of freedom. Those that accepted Dr. King's examples of living in freedom and mentally accepted the reality of freedom saw their lives transformed before their eyes.

This is a wonderful example of redemption and it illustrates what is incumbent on each of us, to realize the true freedom offered us. Christ gave His life to shake us emotionally and mentally, to perceive there are no excuses why we should be in bondage any longer. Again perception is everything. The basis of redemption occurred 2000 years ago. Have you allowed the effect of that event to register on your conscious perception? Will you live as a free person? That takes faith. We come back to what God's prophet Habakkuk said 2600 years ago. It's no different today. "The righteous will live by faith." Don't let the perception of freedom escape your consciousness. Only when people like Dr. King and millions of his followers perceived and accepted that they were indeed free and that freedom did not depend on anyone else, did things begin to happen. Likewise in your life, what Jesus did 2000 years ago is meaningless unless you first accept His sacrifice and personally claim it for yourself. Then you need to accept the challenge to live as free. I'm so thankful Paul used the word "redemption" when he spoke of Jesus' sacrifice.

Paul also used the word "atonement". That's a word not very often heard in our day. It's a remnant of a past culture and way of life. It's worth dusting it off and remembering why "atonement" was an ever-present term in Paul's world. For thousands of years before Paul's time, civilizations sought a means to "atone for" or receive forgiveness for their errors and sins. Even in Paul's day the "enlightened" Roman civilization still sacrificed animals on an altar to their own deities to request a smile of beneficence on their lives. They lived in mortal fear that in some way they might have inadvertently offended their deities. An atoning sacrifice of livestock was presented to appease the deities. Even the Jewish people, of whose progeny our prophet Habakkuk was, were instructed to make animal sacrifices to atone for their sins.

Not that these sacrifices had a major influence on the true Lord, but the tradition reminded the Jews of their predicament. Like the saying goes, "damned if I do and damned if I don't," a Jew could only indicate with his sacrifice that he was sorry for past mistakes. However if the mistake was serious like injuring another physically and irreparably, eventually he had to admit his animal sacrifice was inadequate. For example, if he had wrecked his own marriage or someone else's marriage due to his uncontrollable lust, could he ever atone for that? If the other parties could not be swayed to forgive him when he came to his senses, what could he do? An animal sacrifice was just a puny attempt to declare justice. He knew from a justice standpoint that God couldn't just wink at his indiscretion. In fact, what Paul tells us proves the point, ***because in his forbearance he*** (God) ***left the sins committed beforehand unpunished—he did it to demonstrate his justice at the present time...*** (Paul's day, shortly after Jesus' death) (Ro. 3:25-26).

Every one of us, being constructed in God's image as scripture says, has a sense of justice built within us. That's why every civilization, every culture, every isolated inhabited island has its own set of justice rules. They may vary in minor details but in most all cases the prohibition of murder and theft and regulation of marital fidelity are remarkably similar. It's this sense of justice that urged societies in the past to seek forgiveness, to atone for their sins. One of the ways they did that was by giving up something, (like an animal) which was their food and a possession of monetary value. However, as they recognized, those sacrifices could not atone for major shortcomings. For example, how many animals would you have to sacrifice or sell to the temple to absolve you from an unintentional act of manslaughter? There's no amount of money that could ever allow you to feel you had atoned for such a sin.

God knew this; after all He put that sense of justice in each human heart. And as Paul reminds us in that verse in Romans 3:25, "Because in his forbearance he (God) left the sins committed beforehand unpunished." He did this for several reasons. First He had already foreordained the solution. Second, for some horrendous acts, like manslaughter, there could be no way that such an act could be punished commensurate to the act's gravity short of executing the perpetrator. Justice would require an atonement or act of redemption but the punishment would be too steep for any one man to bear. That's why Jesus volunteered to make that sacrifice or act of atonement for each of us. He, in place of us, gave His guileless (perfect) life, so that the scale of justice might be balanced.

We've covered a lot of ground in a few simple verses (20-26 of Romans, Chapter 3). Here Paul reasoned step by step why you need a personal savior, someone to stand up for you personally, someone to look you in the eye figuratively and say, "Are you ready to start over, do you want the negative chapters of your past to just fade away? Would you like some help on the next chapter of your life? You did it on your own last time but you seem to admit your life didn't work out as well as you'd have liked. Are you really willing to admit that and ask for some help?"

Everyone is forced to make this decision sooner or later. Remember, not making a decision is a decision! I think you have enough knowledge to make an informed decision now, if you haven't yet. And if you aren't quite ready, don't delay too long. Let's review the decision we each have to make and to do that I'll quote Romans 3:25 in the paraphrased "The Word" Bible (we have used the NIV till now): ***"God sacrificed Jesus on the altar of the World to clear the world of sin. Having faith in him sets us in the clear."*** It's up to you now. You will sooner or later answer two questions; it's that simple. To be what the scriptures call "saved" you need to answer affirmatively these two questions: Do you recognize yourself as a sinner falling short of God's standard? Have you accepted Jesus' sacrifice as a full repayment to God of your past and future sins? Read them aloud verbally and in your mind word for word. Can you answer, "Yes" to both questions? If you can, and you really mean what you say, get ready for some momentous changes to happen in your life.

If you've answered "Yes" before but haven't requested Jesus to make decisions for you and open the way for you, that's no matter. Resolve now to let Him guide you and help you solve your problems. If you've already answered affirmatively and you've already experienced what a wonderment has happened in your life, I ask only that you remember today to tell the story to someone else. Can you do that? Let's all, new Christians, newly affirmed Christians and committed Christians, share the story of our blessings with others!

Let me clarify one more point. Jesus' sacrifice doesn't just work one time for us. It's not like if I believe in Jesus' death my past sins are forgiven. Though that's true, it works every time after that as well! God knows you'll continue to make mistakes (sins) but every time you realize and confess, "I erred, I'm sorry, please let Jesus' blood apply for this mistake too," - every time, every time, because we're imperfect, Jesus' sacrifice continues to be applied for us. We need only to be constantly grateful and remind ourselves of our wondrous gift. I know it's hard to believe, but it's true.

MESSAGES I HOPE YOU NOTED:

- God Will Restore All We've Ever Lost, I Believe.

- God Patiently Endures Evil By Focusing On The Good That Will Result.

- Many In Our Own Country Still Live In A World Of Unreality. They Mentally Are Enslaved Even When God Says They're Free

- Remember, Not Making Or Avoiding A Decision About God Is In Itself Making A Decision.

Paul Serwinek

Chapter Ten

GOD USES LITTLE PEOPLE IN BIG WAYS

Before we leave Paul's sermons on Jesus' sacrifice for us, I want to highlight several verses in Romans, Chapter 3. This gets us back to the principle Habakkuk emulates so well during his lifetime. As we've concluded, God uses little people in big ways. Throughout history we can observe that more often than not it is just the ordinary, average citizen that rises up to help in a time of need. I'm not talking now just about sacred and spiritual needs. That goes without saying. The Old Testament is replete with examples of ordinary men performing extraordinary deeds of courage and valor. Almost all the prophets that God energized and inspired to warn and counsel the Israelites about impending disaster facing them were just small village residents called to center stage in front of the whole nation. Rarely, if ever, did the Lord inspire the High Priest, the most powerful person next to the king, to do the Lord's bidding. No, usually an insignificant small-town character emboldened with God's Spirit had all the power necessary to do the Lord's bidding.

Many of those prophets were at first reticent to be used for a holy mission. They felt they were too insignificant. Jeremiah and Isaiah, two of God's greatest spokesmen, felt inadequate for the work assigned them. Gideon, the courageous judge of the Israelites, continued to argue with the Lord, in effect saying, "I'm a nobody, how do you expect me to perform such gigantic tasks?" God used them nonetheless. Their stories are there for all to read. When you read their stories in books such as Judges and Jeremiah, dwell on the humble beginnings as much as on the fantastic finales of God-ordained missions.

And doesn't it seem that it's not just a coincidence that our God, in our time, picks the small-town preachers and not the well-known presidents of some prestigious seminaries to lead a revival of His people back to a close relationship with Him? You might even say it's an exception when God chooses the exceptional to do the extraordinary. He prefers to use the ordinary to do the exceptional. There are reasons for this phenomenon, as we'll soon learn.

We see this phenomenon in our modern world in areas other than those of sacred, spiritual trust. Our world is driven by services more than at any time in history. We are all dependent on one another for basic services. We all serve others as productive members of society. Some of us ordinary workers have been able to help transform society in extraordinary ways, far beyond our initial vision. Henry Ford was not a university-educated engineer. He just began tinkering with his revision of the new invention from Europe, the horseless carriage. An ordinary man had an extraordinary idea of using mass production of his version of another hand-me-down invention to create the modern automotive industry. As a result, countless millions have experienced their standards of living transformed from the lower classes of society to the more comfortable middle class.

How many other small-town inventors working in their garages and homes have helped transform our society to a higher standard of living with more opportunities for education, proper health care and charitable giving? It wasn't the presidents or prime ministers who transformed modern society so much as the little-guy inventor or activist. So this is not just a spiritual phenomenon, it's a social one as well. The premise I'm building on is that each of us can potentially be galvanized for service and goodwill to our own world. We'll be talking a great deal more about how we in our own small ways can contribute to a great explosion of good deeds benefiting our neighbors and manifesting God's glory.

We may not feel adequate at times for the tasks set before us, but the apostle's words in Romans 3:27-28 might give us the impetus to persevere. Remember Paul is making these comments before and after he quotes from our friend Habakkuk. Also keep in mind, before we read the next verse, he stresses in Romans 3:22 that "there is no difference..." All of us, the little guy and the big guy, are the same before God. "There is no difference!" We all need His help equally. Now in verses 27-28 Paul says, *Where, then, is boasting? It is excluded. On what principle? On that of observing the law? No, but on that of faith. For we maintain that a man is justified by faith apart from observing the law.* Once and for all it's so clear. "Where then is boasting?" Paul asks. We're all the same. None of us can complete the "single" task of living right all the time. Maybe we can do it for a minute or maybe for 30 seconds, but not much longer. It reminds me of the anonymous prayer, "Help me, Lord! I'm about to get out of bed."

Did you get the point? We're no different; we're all the same, in the same quandary. It's just that some don't know it. And sometimes it's the ostentatious, glib and self-confident "big guy" who doesn't know. He may never have thought about it. But the sooner we learn the lesson, the better. "Where, then, is boasting?" Who can boast? Our abilities were given to us at birth. They were honed while we were thrown into a pool of experiences when we were young: at home, at school, in social settings. We were just there reacting to the stimuli of the environment around us. We were too young to know what was going on. Maybe, if we were lucky, at about age 18 we began to think and plan and strategize a little. By then we were already formed, our abilities, our personalities all handed to us on a silver platter, so to speak. So then we ask in unison with the apostle, "Where, then, is boasting?' Since we had it all given to us, we're no better than anyone else.

As I suggested, the sooner we learn the lesson, the better. And guess what? It might be a blessing in disguise that we were born a little guy or gal, from a working class or poverty level home. We learned the lesson early; it came naturally to us. We already know the answer to "Where, then, is boasting?" By the time we were age 8 or 10, even back then when looking around, we realized we may not have had as much as others in the way of resources or opportunities. But already we had gotten the concept, hadn't we? It's as the Master observed, ***"So the last will be first, and the first will be last."*** (Matt. 20:16). Those born amidst plush surroundings and granted an Ivy League education based on family names may have a little harder time learning the lesson. And this lesson of humility is one of the most profound lessons one could ever learn. We'll explain why in just a moment. Don't you feel better already just reading the four-word question of Paul and his three-word answer? "Where, then, is boasting? It is excluded." Do you get it yet? We're all little guys and when we realize that, God can make us big influences, as He did with Habakkuk.

HERE'S SOMETHING TO BOAST ABOUT

As the lesson sinks in, let's meditate on the rest of the wisdom in Romans 3:27. The apostle, after categorically stating no one can boast, divulged the other half of the boasting lesson. "On what principle?" he asked. "On that of observing the law?" Flatly he says, "No, but on that of faith." Once more I'm going to repeat the reasoning. Rest assured I'm repeating it for me as much as I am for you. We all have to have it burned into us. Paul says you can't boast because of "observing the law." You can't observe perfectly God's perfect law to man. We've discussed in another place that if we're lucky we can perfectly live the law of God to the letter for maybe 30 seconds, a minute or two at the most, but certainly not for even one day. I guess you could say, maybe while you're sleeping, depending on the dreams you have... In honesty we are not capable of living or doing anything perfectly, flawlessly at all times.

So if you ever want to boast you can only do it one way. Here's the formula: "(Boast) on that (the principle) of faith." Isn't it great to feel you now have something to boast about? All we little guys and gals can boast, "I get it, I understand the lesson, and what's more I'm just starting to get that idea of faith." That's what is going to make me "important," a "big person" in this life, because I have faith. I know that to the extent I have faith, God can use me, entrust me with important stuff.

Permit me to boast for a moment. I remember it like yesterday. I was fourteen. It was late at night and I was lying on the floor in my room thinking. And the lesson began to come through to me. I already knew the part about being inadequate. I was recounting how at fourteen I was inadequate when it came to understanding social graces, I was inadequate when it came to talking to girls, I was inadequate when it came to living on my own. I had nothing to boast about, I thought. Then it came to me; I guess the only thing I can try to do is learn the lessons for living in the Bible. Maybe God could help me grow to be mature and feel a certain amount of adequacy. That night I resolved, "I don't like feeling as I do, low self-esteem and all." I didn't know what the full meaning of the phrase "low self-esteem" was back then, but I knew the feeling and I didn't like it. I was smart enough and dumb enough to believe God's promises with no reservations. I couldn't put into words then what I can articulate now unequivocally, "I can't do it on my own." That was too complicated for me to be able to say simply, but again I knew the feeling inside and I was beginning to learn the lesson.

I trace back my modicum of life success to that night, June 30, year I'm not telling. Since then I've tried to live with that resolve to learn and build my faith. Of course I couldn't do it always (I haven't even been able to do it most of the time), but I can honestly say I have tried and am trying. I can boast that I was only fourteen when God began to teach me the lesson. At fourteen I knew what feeling depressed and low meant and I knew what the exhilaration of beginning to know about the Lord felt like. And as the poet Robert Frost said, "and that has made all the difference."

I hope you can also boast (even if not at the moment), be able to say, "I boast that I know the lesson, God has shown me the lesson. I get it!" I boast I can say with Paul, I get it, "for we (including me) maintain that any man (woman) is justified by faith apart from (trying to prove I can do it on my own by) observing the Law." Boast, "I know the secret! It's so simple, yet so complicated. I can't do it on my own, but faith in the Lord will make up the deficiency." Say it and mean it. Tomorrow when you wake up and it hits you that, "I've got a problem," just say it. "I can't do it on my own but faith in the Lord will make up for my deficiency." I guarantee you'll feel better immediately.

When you feel inadequate about bringing up your kids or inadequate keeping up on the job, just say the little prayer that makes a little guy a big guy. "Lord I can't do it on my own, but faith in you today will make up for my deficiency." That what Brother Lawrence in seventeenth century France called a "breath prayer," is all you need. If you don't believe it, just try it for one day. Then you'll begin to boast, not in your self but in knowing what it's all about. "There aren't many people who know what it's all about, but I do," you'll be able to boast. I wonder how many of you know what I mean when I say at this moment, "I'm smart enough and dumb enough?"

PRACTICAL APPLICATION

Once you've learned the lesson you'll be able to use it from now on. As I always try to stress to those with whom I share my thoughts and experiences, the wisdom from above is always practical. You can use it immediately to improve your lot and circumstances. That's one of the reasons the Bible was written, as a guide for practical living. This is so true with the lesson of "boasting" in the Lord. If you apply this one lesson you can do pretty much anything!

That's a pretty powerful statement, but I've learned from observing life events over the years, it's absolutely true. I don't flinch when I say it. I put no qualifications on this. I'm saying it is categorically true. If you have the faith Habakkuk taught us to have, anything is possible. I'd also say everything is possible. Those of you who have witnessed miracles in the lives of others and perhaps in your own lives will second my assertion. Logically if our God is all- powerful and beyond all the dimensions that humans can comprehend, then with our God all things are possible. Scripture in fact says, ***"Nothing will be impossible for you*** [with God].*"* (Matt. 16:20). If you don't believe me, look it up for yourself. Those words have been there in print for almost 2000 years. And no one has been able to refute those words' validity yet. So if all things are possible with God and we are friends of the Lord, essentially anything is possible in our lives. I know, there are things that are improbable but I've learned never to say impossible. For example, to categorically say that a seemingly permanently disabled child could never grow up to be a star professional football player is beyond the capability of any Christian to ever say with certainty. It can happen, however. It has happened.

I've seen personally and know of individuals seemingly certain to die only to make a complete recovery. I know of friends in dire financial circumstances considered impossible to rectify, in only a matter of days, see their finances transform to portions of wealth and financial wellbeing. I know of others in complete mental and emotional anguish that have experienced full recovery to a state of peace and equilibrium literally overnight - improbable yes, impossible no.

Most people of faith would tend to agree with Jesus our Lord who said, *"You may ask me for anything in my name and I will do it."* (Jo.14:14). You notice Jesus' words don't have a qualifier in fine print. It's not like the "too good to be true" ads in the newspapers, or the radio ads that make fantastic claims only to be followed by the announcer reading softly and at 100 miles an hour the disclaimer. That's the normal expectation of most people, but not of many Christians. They take Jesus' words at face value. That's the way I've tried to live my life. Who am I to limit my own personal expectations when the Lord doesn't put a qualifier other than to say, *"...Everything is possible for him who believes."* (Mark 9:23).

I do have to admit that there are very devout Christians that don't feel right about taking Jesus literally about some of His claims. I don't want to debate the issue here. Suffice it to point out that all too often scripture makes audacious and preposterous claims without back pedaling to say, "not to be taken at face value." Jesus frequently spoke with outrageous claims. See Matthew 17:20 where Jesus says, *"I tell you the truth, if you have faith as small as a mustard seed, you can say to this mountain, 'Move from here to there,' and it will move..."*

God Himself spoke with preposterous assertions often. Who are we to limit God's people, when He doesn't? In Malachi 3:10 the Lord boasts, *"...Test me in this,"* says the Lord Almighty, *"and see if I will*

not throw open the floodgates of heaven and pour out so much blessing that you will not have room enough for it." Look it up in scripture yourself. I can't find an asterisk or any fine print at the bottom of the page, can you? Of course not, that's the Lord's style; that was Jesus' style when He came to show us the way. As admen have been known to say, "Big, Hairy, Bodacious, Audacious Dreams," but those are the types of dreams our Lord can make come true.

EXPECTATIONS

So, dear friend, I beg you to be willing to go out on a limb at times. Try living in faith, the kind of faith Habakkuk demonstrated, even for one day without reservation, trusting that your Lord and Father will assist with the difficulties. But be prepared for this. The enemy will be jealous and may even try to make things difficult for you. Friends have told me when they attempted that first-day experiment they encountered a barrage of problems. However they just kept reminding themselves, "I've just committed myself to one day. I'm going to stick it out with faith." You guessed it. By day's end the problems appeared to dissipate, to be replaced by the promised peace of mind and serenity. It works. God's way, the way of faith, really does work.

This one-day experiment will give you the conviction to continue to put more trust and faith in our Heavenly Father. He desires the best for us if we patiently wait for His direction. Here's what else you can expect. You'll be able to think more clearly and incisively in your personal difficulties. This is the ***wisdom that comes from heaven*** (Ja. 3:17) promised to all people of faith. What a gift for one day of faith devoted to coming closer to God. I've already found that the comparatively little effort I muster up to draw close to God, He repays abundantly. It's never a fair exchange. He always gives much more! There's only one catch; you've got to first commit for one day.

I'm reminded of the reassurance I am granted every time I teach a class in Christian living to a group of men who had been down on their luck (that's a euphemism for living without God). One of the things they learn is you don't need luck when you have God. A person with luck comes out ahead for the moment, it's true. But you can't count on luck. You can't summon it up on demand. It's fleeting and it's fickle. All these men I talked with believed in luck, but it ran out on them! And when luck runs out, it's almost impossible to coax it back. When these men finally got to rock bottom with no money, no resources for drugs or alcohol; when they had nowhere to go, no one to turn to, they were appealed to by Grace Center of Hope in Pontiac, Michigan. First with food and shelter, and then with potential hope, they were appealed to and taken in. These men were asked to make a short-term commitment: attempting a one-year commitment to exchange trust in luck and elusive physical salvation for trust in the Lord and His spiritual bounty.

Whenever I go to share my testimony and my experiences on healthful, positive and exciting living in Christ, I invariably learn more from their collective experiences than I can ever hope to impart. But what encourages me most is when I ask them candidly. My group of students usually amounts to about 50 men (others in the program are busy working in and for the mission center). The group I teach, or more correctly, the group with whom I share, comprise individuals who have just started on the path to the Lord, maybe a few days ago maybe for a few months to almost a year.

When I ask them, "How many of you guys from your short time living in faith have found some of the 'peace of mind' God promises?" every hand is raised. When I ask, "How many of you feel better about yourself (or have higher self-esteem) than when you first walked in here?" again every hand is raised. And when I ask them, "How many of you feel God has given you more positive rewards than what you originally bargained for?" again every hand is raised. Year after year I am greeted with the same positive response.

I then ask them, "How does living with the Lord compare to living with luck?" They all say there's no comparison. From those who are infants in the Lord, getting their first glimpses of God's ways, to the veterans with almost a year of Christian living under their belts, they all exclaim in amazement, "God gives what He promises." I'm asking you to make that commitment. I know what will happen. I've seen the positive response hundreds of times! These little guys, with seemingly little to offer, become big significant men in God's eyes. Their personal experiences and examples then can help others to take that "bet" from Jesus. "Just try me!" Jesus says. These guys can tell still others, others to whom they can relate, others you or I could never reach since we may never have been part of their world of drugs and addiction. God raised up these little guys, the surrogate-like Habakkuks, to beckon others to come to Jesus. They affirm, "You won't be disappointed, I wasn't!"

HOW ABOUT YOU?

What I'm getting to here is you. Christians feel strongly that they have to make a difference. We're here on purpose and for a purpose. However, wherever it is or whenever it is that we start on the faith way of Christianity, we can never predict what we're destined to accomplish. That takes time. Often our Christian growth builds our confidence along the way. Often we learn to trust for the first time or at least expand our arena of trust, first to God and Christ and then to other trustworthy and inspiring Christians. So we pick up a measure of confidence along the way.

We have resources now, a network of friends, a congregation of like-minded confidants and most of all our own set of experiences interacting with our Father and the Holy Spirit promised and sent by Christ. Then when an assignment crosses our path disguised as an opportunity, we're willing to accept it. Our reason may be gratitude for what the Lord has done for us or it might be due to the compassion and love the Holy Spirit has built in us over the months or years. He has had the opportunity to work on us. Confidence isn't so much an issue then. Something needs to be done, some cause needs to be supported, or some special concern moves us to take a step forward.

Where that step will lead we may not know. I think you can assume, as I do, that none of the little guys and gals who have been chosen for great assignments ever imagined what they'd accomplish when first chosen. Luther was a fearful teenager wanting to know more about our Lord. Little did he realize what his earnest study of scripture would uncover. He was used to change the world. Florence Nightingale was a sickly girl driven to help others in need. Little did she realize that from a position of no training, no university credentials, she would change the structure and operation of hospitals for the whole civilized world. The modern organization of hospitals, including the profession of nursing, were essentially the effort of one woman with no political network to galvanize to action and no university research to offer as a precedent. Yet no learned doctor has ever accomplished more for hospital organizations than Florence Nightingale.

Finally, countless great preachers confess that they were first called by the Lord when they were initially confused teenagers searching and seeking to be used by God, while some had their first vision of God from a literal gutter or from circumstances that can be described as the lowest of the low. Billy Graham started his path to greatness with the Lord as that frightened teenager. Og Mandino, the writer of one of the most influential books ever written for business professionals, *The Greatest Salesman in the World*, a treatise on the life of the apostle Paul and his lessons on salesmanship, averred he remembered clearly the exact day when he made the decision to turn his life around after he had been devastated by business setbacks and divorce.

None of these "great" people considered themselves "great." None of them, when initially summoned by the Lord, ever saw a glimmer of greatness in their futures. They blindly, tentatively took their first steps trusting in a power beyond themselves. The Lord assisted them the rest of the way and they made a monumental difference. Jesus promises us we will make a difference, a great difference. In fact Jesus while on earth confidently expressed, *"…anyone who has faith in me…will do even greater things than these."* (Jo. 14:12). He was prophesying that collectively Christians, including you, if you take up the challenge of Christianity, would accomplish more than He did as the Son of God on earth. Wow, we are ordained to do great things or at least to be a part of something great.

I can't tell you what great things you are specifically destined for, but I can say you are destined to make a difference. I hope you can believe that making a lasting positive difference in someone else's life is a wonderful accomplishment, a great thing. As Jesus Himself said, ***"Whatever you did for one of the least of these brothers of mine, you do for me."*** (Matt. 25:40). When you help another fellow traveler in this life, you are doing something to God and for God. That is a great thing! The possibilities are limitless. There is enough poverty in America itself, let alone the world, to keep us busy for years. Continue to remember that giving one person your help is doing something for our Lord. That is a great thing!

If your circumstances allow you to befriend an orphan or a fatherless boy, and there are at least millions of them in the US and many millions worldwide, you are doing a great thing. You may not think so, but imagine how you'd feel, and God's sentiment surely mimics yours. Imagine years later a minority fatherless boy from an inner city environment were to graduate from college and thank you personally for the chance your camaraderie or monetary contribution gave him, as he vows to help still others by, in some way, using his education and skills. If this experience happened to you even one time in your lifetime, wouldn't you feel your life was worth living? This experience can be multiplied many times over in one lifetime. Every time you share the message of hope to one in despair and assist her in a small way to be positively oriented, you do what our Lord calls a "great deed." Every time you act to lessen the ongoing suffering of another you do a "great deed." Our world is filled with social problems that offer us endless opportunities to do what God considers "great deeds."

An interesting note here might be that we all have come into this world with a set of abilities and propensities that uniquely qualify us to serve and fulfill the needs of others. For example, I'm not a mechanic. I freely admit I'm not mechanically inclined. Every time I call a plumber, auto mechanic, heating specialist, or computer repairman, I'm using the talents of another. Those talents make my life easier and those talents of others allow me the time to do what I do best. I'm a better person, a happier person, a more contented person, which I know my

God desires for me, and it's partly due to the shared abilities of others. What is so interesting, too, is that these laborers in the service industry that I have come to count on are doing what they enjoy doing because they are using their own unique gifts and talents. Each one helps hundreds of others each year to have a more secure, less frustrating life due to their reliable talents. God tells them if they do that work of helping others (and get paid for helping others) and dedicate their service to God (the service they have done for you and me) God considers that a great thing too!

Each of us has talents and abilities, but those gifts are meaningless and useless unless they are exercised for the benefit of those around us. When we do use our gifts we simultaneously make a difference in the lives of others. Those integrative and cooperative skills can accomplish unbelievable results. Initially we have the satisfaction of being part of something greater than ourselves. We feel the joy of making a meaningful contribution to the welfare of others. Scripture makes it quite clear when it says, ***Whatever you do, work at it with all your heart as working for the Lord...*** (Co. 3:23). Again, I know some feel you can't take scripture for what it says, but I assert I can't read into this verse something that is not there. The writer, the apostle Paul, seems quite adamant here when he says, "Whatever you do." He is speaking of unlimited possibilities without putting limitations on them.

"Whatever you do," whether those tasks are what some might consider of a religious nature or of a secular nature, is not the issue here. Whatever you do can make a difference to humanity. Collectively we can accomplish great things. The possibilities for making a difference are boundless since the problems and predicaments of humankind are endless. Starvation, poverty, crime, diseases like AIDS - all provide opportunities for us to mitigate suffering. The very problems God has seen fit to allow to run their courses provide fertile fields for our work. And what greater privilege is there than to befriend an orphan or share the exciting message of salvation to someone hearing it for the very first time. These are all examples of working whole-souled, whole-heartedly to and for the Lord, a great feat indeed.

Again notice what Paul states qualifies as working for the Lord. It's not the kind of work you do that matters. He says, "<u>Whatever</u> you do," not "only certain tasks count." What he does say as a promise is simply this, "Work at it with all your heart as working for the Lord." That's what counts, doing our work as if to God and in the manner that is befitting of labor being donated to the Lord. Taking this verse at face value, we conclude that if we do a task, any task, that benefits another in any of a myriad of ways, that's being done as if to God and done to the best of our ability, we are doing something noteworthy and meaningful. From the ranks of what might be considered "nobodies" we miraculously become a "somebody." We are valuable, for our work has value. The Lord is calling us to make a difference, be a difference. Ask Him what that difference might be.

MESSAGES I HOPE YOU NOTED:

- **You Don't Need Luck If You Have God!**

- **You Are Here To Make A Difference**

- **God Doesn't Need To Use The Exceptional To Do The Exceptional**

Chapter Eleven

NO LIMIT FAITH!

I hope you've begun to see that faith is a way of life. Faith helps you through the ups and downs of life. Most of us don't have difficulties anywhere near the level Habakkuk had to endure. After his pep talk from The Almighty it was as if he had taken a deep breath and moved on. I've often thought it was probably fortunate that he did not know how long he would be required to live in faith, enduring the injustices of his world. As it was, in his lifetime he was never able to see the resolution of injustice coming full circle. After all, the full story took at least eighty years to tell. By that time he was probably long forgotten, even by his descendants. However, his song was still playing, "The righteous will live by faith." He wrote the song; he sang the song; he lived the song.

We don't know how long he lived. History tells us absolutely nothing about him. If it weren't for scripture as a personal chronicle of his own encounter with The Almighty, he would have been lost in time. Providentially for us, he wasn't. His is an enduring record of faith. As they say, he walked the walk or maybe I should say he "strutted the song." He demonstrated what it means to live by faith, enduring by faith. He felt secure and at peace in the midst of injustice. The point is clear; he kept his mind on the end result – complete justice, not just temporal justice appearing for a brief moment. I know he'd be the first to admit it's not easy, living in faith when circumstances around you are not conducive to encouragement. It's necessary then to focus on the worthwhile end rather than the pressure-filled present. That's the way the family of faithful have always lived.

In fact, to remind myself of the means employed by some famous faithful, those of Bible fame, I defer to the faith chapter in scripture. You know the one, Hebrews, Chapter 11 in the New Testament. As I was turning there I couldn't help but think it would have been fitting for Habakkuk to be mentioned by name in the "great cloud of witnesses," but I got the surprise of my life when I opened up the Bible and happened to glance at a verse just preceding Hebrews 11. You'll never guess what I found, or I guess I should say you know exactly what I found! That's right, Habakkuk's imprint right there, once again. Hebrews 10:38 says, *"But my righteous one will live by faith…"* How often I've read this section of scripture but never realized what was there. Habakkuk isn't mentioned by name there but his lyrics are! Maybe he never performed spectacular "headline" deeds to make him famous but his thoughts and ideas are fittingly recounted alongside the deeds of the famous faithful.

While that's only fitting, I can't help but think of the object lesson here. Habakkuk is my hero precisely because he was so ordinary. I can relate to him. I can't relate to Moses, Abraham or other giants of faith mentioned in Hebrews 11, but I can to Habakkuk. To think there's a place, a special place, in the preface to the march of the faithful found in Hebrews 11 for a tribute to the ordinary guy, the un-named prophet, has to be encouraging to us.

As we mused before, Habakkuk is the champion of the little guy and gal. The guy and gal who never actually get, in their lifetime, the prizes of which they might be dreaming, are those of whom I speak. But they keep going, plodding along in faith and with faith. They, like Habakkuk, never are extolled by news releases, never have a book written about them, never a chapter in a book, never even a paragraph in a book, but they are special. Their thoughts, their sentiments are the same as Habakkuk's. "Living by faith," is their song also. And as Habakkuk is part of that "great cloud of witnesses " in spirit by his words prefacing the chapter, so are the little guys and gals throughout history that get their inspiration to live from the phrase "The righteous will live by faith." They too made that list though not mentioned by name. Take my word for it, the older you get the less making a name for yourself matters, and the more the feeling of peace of mind that accompanies faith matters.

Now with that introduction, let's read some of the inspiration found in Hebrews since it continues the thread of thought put into words by Habakkuk. I'm going to start at Hebrews 10:35. Here the Bible writer, who is traditionally believed to be the apostle Paul, though he's not identified by name, is attempting to encourage the faithful to persevere in their faith. He says in Hebrews 10:35-36, *So do not throw away your confidence: it will be richly rewarded. You need to persevere...* This, in a nutshell, is what the writer is advocating. This is exactly what Habakkuk's story is advocating. Be confident with faith; persevere with faith. They aren't saying it's easy. I know and you know it's not easy, but if we are ever going to get to where we want to be, we must take one step after another confidently and continuously, stepping with perseverance.

Hebrews 10:36 continues, *You need to persevere so that when you have done the will of God, you will receive what he has promised.* Here we are introduced to one of the secrets to enduring faith. We'll speak much more of this when we look at Hebrews 11, but stop right now and repeat what is said here. "You will receive what he has promised." That's the secret; keep the reward ahead of you. "What he has promised" is not just the reward of heaven, though. As you read Hebrews 11 the writer calls attention to the fact that many of the legendary faithful actually did get the reward they sought while still physically here on earth. That's important to note. Habakkuk too dreamt of a world on earth, not in heaven, where justice prevailed. Unfortunately he didn't see it in his lifetime, though his dream did come to fulfillment and many of the generations succeeding him lived to see it. But that dream kept him going. He had faith his dream would come true. Yes, he'd see that dream come true in all its ramifications in heaven, of course, but it was enough for him to see it in his mind's eye with full confidence that an earthy reality was also possible.

I hope this thought resonates with you as it does with me. Have you ever noticed that the time of anticipation can be enjoyed just as much as the actual reward? Stop and think of something special you wanted and worked for. I can think of so many things in my life. I couldn't wait to get married to the woman of my dreams. I couldn't wait till I scaled the possible academic degrees to finally get a terminal college degree relatively few acquire. I couldn't wait to build a business that gave my family and all those associated with the enterprise a measure of security. In each case, once I attained the goal a rush of satisfaction would come. The end was worth the work and the wait, but in every case the thing I noted is the anticipation, the effort, was as much a reward as the reward itself. Do you know what I mean? The hard work, the effort, the inconvenience was part of the full package. The reward wouldn't mean quite the same without the hardship. And in every case looking back, I had to admit I remembered the anticipatory time with a great fondness. Anticipation was a special time, a time to be relished. I'd never want to give up that sometimes calm and sometimes arduous, period of waiting. It was part and parcel of the reward.

So do you comprehend the point I'm making? When we live in faith, we just know the end of that faith will be realized. If we learn to live in faith, the waiting experience, working experience can be a time of excitement, exhilaration and joy because the certainty (that comes with faith) guarantees a reality. It kind of reminds me of the Christmas gift already wrapped under the tree days before Christmas. You may know what the gift is, it's what you've been waiting for, and you know it's here even now. It's just not the time to open it yet. That's what faith is like. Remember how the Bible writer described it? *"Now faith is being sure of what we hope for and certain of what we do not see."* (He. 11:1). Habakkuk learned to live that way. The writer of Hebrews gives us the secret Habakkuk discovered.

THE SECRET

First, before divulging the secret, the Hebrews writer gives credit for the basis of his dissertation on faith. He quotes among others our friend Habakkuk. Hebrews 10:37-38 prefaces what is about to be said about faith by quoting, *For in just a very little while, he who's coming will come and will not delay. But my righteous ones will live by faith. And if he shrinks back, I will not be pleased with him.* And there it is again. The writer, no doubt the apostle Paul, is not willing to proceed on a faith discourse without first quoting our man Habakkuk. He contrasts Habakkuk's "My righteous one will live by faith," with the negative prospect of shrinking back. Faith takes courage and lack of faith constitutes an act of cowardice. Faith is forging on, not shrinking back in fear. When a person of faith feels the symptoms of cowardice coming on, he or she need only pray for God's Spirit and the attendant courage. So one more time the words of Habakkuk live on to inspire the early Christians and to inspire us to press on. No, faith isn't always easy. We can't do it on our own. Faith takes focus. But the more the Spirit from God that brings faith flows into us, the more fervently we desire to be with our Heavenly Father. Do we really want Him in our lives? If so, the Spirit that brings faith begins to flow. We feel stronger, we feel bolstered.

SECRET OF FAITH

Here's the part of building faith I want to underline. There is a formula that can be used to bolster faith. The writer of Hebrews stresses it over and over, and it's the same method Habakkuk employed to keep his faith strong. The very definition of faith in Hebrews 11:1 emphasizes the ingredients, "Now faith is being sure of what we hope for..." That's it, the clarity of something worth hoping for. It's difficult to endure without a sustaining hope or reward. What men and women of faith have always done is hope for something greater or finer in connection to the Lord. Note the description of Abraham. He is heralded as a prime example of faith throughout scripture. Hebrews 11:8 assures us, *By faith Abraham, when called to go to a place he would later receive as his inheritance, obeyed and went...* He was able to endure trials through faith in that inheritance promised by God. This is the secret you want to take with you. To sustain faith there must always be a light at the end of the tunnel, there must be a reward worthy of endurance through difficulty. To the extent that reward is clear, faith is easier to maintain.

Note how Hebrews 11:10 described Abraham's incentive, *For he was looking forward to the city with foundations, whose architect and builder is God.* What I want you to note is, "he was looking forward." That's the secret, "looking forward to." There must be something to look forward to. Scripture speaks of that ultimate reward as heaven. But in Abraham's case he had an additional incentive to keep him going, an inheritance. That inheritance was a "promised land" bequeathed to his descendants. He was privileged to see that land and his descendants actually took possession of it. They did indeed receive a physical reward for their faith and endurance, but the ultimate reward would be yet to come. So faith requires a worthy goal and a valuable reward to be sustained.

Now this secret of faith can easily be applied to any worthy goal. In fact, throughout history men and women wanting fabulous wealth or fame have applied the secret, but the problem with physical rewards once attained, is that they cannot satisfy or sustain us for long. Once a physical goal is fulfilled, if an immediate new goal is not substituted, the power of faith evaporates. An ultimate goal beyond the physical is the only kind that can sustain one for a lifetime.

Let me illustrate it this way. As I write this I have had a serious heart problem that required open-heart surgery. What keeps me going without complaint is that I have faith God can help heal, or as Romans 8:11 says, *give life to* my mortal body. Faith keeps me going through exercise; dietary changes, fighting stress, etc. I know God will see to it that the best will happen. However, once I attain that physical reward I need to find a new worthy goal for my faith to continue growing.

Hebrews 11:16 says of the faith giants, *they were longing for a better country — a heavenly one...* And the point is made. *All these people were still living by faith when they died. They did not receive the things promised; they only saw them and welcomed them from a distance.* (He. 11:13). This verse conveys so much. First the reason they, the men and women of faith, were specifically mentioned in the Hebrews Faith Hall of Fame is that they never stopped living with faith; they "were still living by faith when they died." They endured, they were successful, but only some finished what they had started. What an accomplishment - they made it to their end. That's what can put us in the midst of this select group of believers – living by faith till we die. That accomplishment insures the ultimate prize.

Further, this verse stresses that most of the people of faith fame "did not receive the things promised." They kept going without the ultimate reward granted. What an accomplishment that was, too. How could they do that? How can we do that? The next sentence illuminates clearly, "they only saw them and welcomed them from a distance." The reward was so real and so clear they could almost see and touch in reality what was promised them. They kept God's promises before them as if they could see them from a distance. This emphasizes what each of us needs to work on. You must be certain God has a promise for you. By reading scripture you see it clearly. It's got to happen; it's impossible to fail. Remind yourself of the aspects of the promise that especially appeal and apply to you. Imagine being there to see the ultimate fulfillment of all history. Imagine a reunion with friends and family. Imagine exploring the mystery and beauty of nature from a different vantage point. Bible authors freely shared what parts of the promise they especially valued. Be specific about what personally excites you relating to God's ultimate promise for all mankind.

Some of the faithful had endured *"...so that they might gain a better resurrection."* (He. 11:35). Scripture doesn't elucidate, but you can be sure these faithful were certain what a "better resurrection" meant for them. I can share that one of the prospects that keeps me going is to stand before my exemplar Christ and hear Him commend me personally, *"Well done, good and faithful servant"..."Come and share your master's happiness!"* (Matt. 25:21). Meditate and dream of what God's promise means to you. The more detailed it is in your mind's eye, the more natural faith becomes.

Paul Serwinek

DON'T LIMIT OUR LORD

To be sure, our life's work is to remain faithful in our actions and resolve for what has "been promised." However, the elements of faithful living can be employed to enhance our lives now. Scripture avers (Hebrews 11:33) and leaves no doubt that many faithful including David, Gideon, Barak, Samson ***...gained what was promised.*** Not talking of the ultimate reward here, we're informed that God granted them individually fulfillment of dreams along the way, dreams that did come true in their lifetimes. Just as Abraham was granted his desire to walk and reside in his "promised land," the Lord is open to grant us promises along the way. In fact, much of scripture recounts how, on many occasions and scores of times the Lord aided the righteous faithful to attain what was so dear to them, whether the reward sought was to be blessed with a child, to have health restored or to be granted material blessings. Scripture specifically says they "gained what was promised."

I firmly believe God doesn't say that to tease you or to discourage you, as if to say, "Some of these faithful 'gained what was promised' but that's just them, they were special, I don't mean that for everyone." What kind of God is He anyway? I know some Christians don't feel it's proper to presume that God will ever assist us with our comparatively mundane desires. But why would scripture relate the countless stories of those prospering with God's power? I, along with many faithful Christians, can testify to countless instances when we have felt special, unusual power and ability to accomplish any type of meaningful goals. We have "gained what was promised," in our own lifetimes, though not as yet having attained the ultimate promise.

I've made a big issue of this several times in this volume because I personally am certain that some Christians sell our Father short by discouraging other Christians from "gaining what was promised" now. I know every time our Father grants me a promise it gives me another opportunity to testify to His love and kindness. I consider it a necessity to glorify the power from above for every promise as it comes true. No one can take those joys away from me. They serve as further proof to me of God's love and they bolster my faith in God and in the future. The operation of the "faithfulness secret" in our lives today can only draw us closer to God.

Many seekers of truth over the years have stumbled upon and discovered the "faith secret" and used it to manifest dreams. I consider these cases examples of how our Creator set up the universe so that anyone armed with faith can experience dreams coming true. The wonderful thing about being a believer is we can ask for the help of Someone all-powerful and yet benevolent and kind.

So as the book of Hebrews shows, for any promise to be granted, the recipient must first act in faith, must be absolutely certain that he or she deserves the goal. Christians are absolutely certain they have a loving Father who cares for them. That gives them absolute certainty. They know they deserve their goals since they have no desire to hurt others but only to help them. They know they are trying, not just praying, but also acting in accordance with their prayer requests. They know their Father wants them to be happy. So when they pray for the fulfillment of a promise, they act in faith and follow the faith secret. They also let their Father know, "I ask for this only if it glorifies You. I promise to give credit to You for the goal fulfilled and I will share the bounty with others by either material sharing or by sharing the encouragement that comes from hearing and seeing a dream come true."

A Christian then acts in faith. She is "sure of what [she] hopes for" and "certain of what [she] does not yet see." Also she is clear in mind and emotion as to what reward is desired. She sees "from a distance" the end result in all its glorious detail. Then she acts confidently knowing that the goal is certain to come true as long as others are not inadvertently hurt by the fulfilled request. And every time the faith principle works in her present life, she is that much more certain it will work on a grander scale in her future beyond the here and now!

CAN YOU ACCEPT A REWARD?

I firmly believe from my experiences with our Father that he wants the best for us. He desires happiness for us. When He senses your excitement about a project or undertaking that means a great deal to you, He wants that for you. Here is something else you probably don't realize; when something we fervently desire comes to fruition, not only do we benefit but others around us benefit! That's the way our Father envisioned the universe. Good begets good. Satisfaction begets satisfaction. Love begets love. This works even in the most mundane of situations. For example, in business when an entrepreneur is excited to market a new product, that product has a great chance of succeeding if the product fulfills the unrealized needs of others. This rule works for Christians and non-Christians, for those seeking the Lord and for those unconcerned about spirituality. But it especially flourishes when a business owner consciously applies this Law of the Universe. Stop to realize in your own life experiences, isn't it true that whenever you have done something that brings great satisfaction it will invariably either help, be of benefit or bring satisfaction to others? This works with personal relationships, business transactions, all aspects of life. If this is true, and it is, don't you think your Father wants that for you? He knows any good flowing to you will automatically flow to others. So don't be so hesitant to live in faith, wishing the best, expecting the best. That's what our Father wants, too.

I firmly also believe our world was constructed to run on this principle. As long as a desire will benefit others and will not be harmful to others, our God blesses those efforts. As long as a Christian or seeker of the Lord desires something that will not be hurtful to others and take away from others, our God blesses those prayers of faith. He sees to it that the forces and circumstances around the faithful ones will work in harmony with the actions of the person of faith. You supply the ingredients in your power; God takes care of the rest. You supply the fervent desire, you be certain to the best of your understanding others will not be hurt as you supply the actions in harmony with your prayers of faith, then God will do the rest. Any analysis of every Bible story of faith and every history of faithful experiences will highlight those same steps: fervent desire, the presumption of good (not hurt) to others, harmonious and steady action in conjunction with those prayers and God supplying the rest.

LIVING FAITH

I can't do any better than repeat the words of the writer of Hebrews here. After quoting Habakkuk on faith, he summed it up this way: *And without faith it is impossible to please God, because anyone who comes to him must believe that he exists and that he rewards those who earnestly seek him.* (He. 11:6). Could that be any clearer? Without faith we are nothing. Without dreams of something beneficial, there is no life. Without certainty that something good is on the way, there is no joy. And without hope there is no will to go on.

Life with abundant happiness is impossible without faith. I hope I'm making this clear. Christians talk about faith this and faith that. Those are words. Do you know what you're saying? Faith is a bubbling, overflowing hope. Faith is the certainty something good is on the way. Faith is the excitement that I just can't wait; it's going to be great! Is that what you mean by faith? That's what the Bible says. Those are not my words "anyone who comes to him must believe that he exists and that he REWARDS those who earnestly seek him." (He. 11:6). Faith is inextricably linked to rewards.

Based on what scripture preaches I wonder how many of us have more than a modicum of faith. What rewards are we looking forward to? What joyful project that you know will help others and benefit you are you excited about? What prospect do you have that you just can't wait to tell others about? What meaningful task do you wake up exclaiming, "I just can't wait to get started on this."? Someone with perfect vitality and perfect faith would be a "ball of energy" with such faith. Unfortunately I know only one person who ever walked the earth like that, but His example (Christ) is enough for all to strive for. Healing people, helping people, talking about God's good things filled His days and nights. That's what faith does. Faith says, "I'm having problems but I just know things are going to get better." Faith says, "I may not be doing anything exciting but I know my just being here is going to be a blessing to someone else." Faith says, "I know God has a plan for me." Faith says, "I can't wait to find out some of the good that God is using my life for." Faith says, "When my time comes, I can't wait to hear the Lord say to me, "Well done, good and faithful servant.""

So what projects are you involved in that energize you to excitement? What talents given to you would you like to use to benefit you, others and, of course, God's purpose? If you are between such projects at the moment, pray in faith that your Father directs you to see what projects will interest you. Maybe you are required to work to provide for yourself and family and can't do all you'd like. But God can give you the insight to make your job meaningful or show you at least one hobby you enjoy that brings good. Remember Habakkuk now. He had to work physically in the maintenance of the Jewish temple no doubt, but if he did nothing more than be a good friend to others, be a contributing family member and write down his story to encourage us, he made a fantastic contribution to the annals of faith. Don't worry about what contributions you'll make, just be assured (that's faith again) that your life will prove to have meaning. Pray now for insight from God on how your life has already brought meaning and help to others, because it has and it will. That's faith.

Don't shortchange yourself. I didn't say it, God did. **You *must believe that God exists and that he rewards those who earnestly seek him.*** (He. 11:6) Those rewards are not just limited to the afterlife. What we read in Hebrews 11:32-35 leaves no doubt. Scripture makes it a point to highlight that the faithful witnesses chronicled here in Hebrews, ***administered justice,...gained what was promised,...and received back their dead.*** Their desires, big and small, did come true. The writer adds this exciting prospect in Hebrews 11:39-40, ***(yet none of them received what had been promised. God had planned something better...)*** Wow, all those rewards in their earthly lives, but still the writer says, "none of them received what had been promised." As if to say, they couldn't even fathom all the rewards yet to be showered on the faithful. Rewards now but "You ain't seen nothin' yet." Something even better is still coming.

So please don't be so lacking in understanding to think that desire for rewards from God is selfish. That's what God wants for you. Don't let anyone ever ask you to tear out Hebrews 11:6 from your Bible. You MUST BELIEVE He REWARDS those who earnestly seek Him. God constructed us to want good things. What would you think of someone who was given a gift, but would ungratefully disdain accepting it or not at least acknowledge the thoughtfulness of the giver? How ungrateful; that's just common manners to say, "Thank you," you'll agree. Yet some would have you say, when a benevolent desire of prayer comes true, "It was just a coincidence, it had nothing to do with God, He doesn't care about me." No, He does care. He does reward. He is doing it every day, all the time. Can't you see it? You must believe He rewards you. Notice too the tense of the inspired Bible writer's remark. "You must believe…He rewards (not will reward or will reward in the future). HE REWARDS," that's present tense. He rewards those who earnestly seek him. That's faith!

Don't those words just make you feel good? Don't you feel special that Someone cares so much about you? He wants to reward you. Don't reject those rewards, those so-called "coincidences" that seem to happen. It's not selfishness to accept what God has given to you and say, "Thank you." That's just common gratitude. Pray that your faith will expand when you have the insights demonstrating that your Father is (present tense) rewarding you now, with much more in store.

So you say you have faith. God says it's impossible to have faith without that fervent appreciation of God's rewards. What human father doesn't like to surprise his kids by granting their wishes and even doing something unexpectedly special? What normal child wouldn't be so appreciative and say, "Thank you"? The child would not be expected to say, "I can't accept that, I don't deserve that. " You'd say, "What's wrong with you, boy, don't you see your father loves you?" That's absurd!

I say this only to shake you. I believe some of you are unnatural to deny that your loving, kind, benevolent Father rewards (present tense) those who seek Him. I want you to have living faith, vibrant faith, extraordinary faith but it's going to be "impossible" (God's word, not mine) unless you highlight the rewards of God, rewards now and in the future. Now, with your faith, tell someone what excites you. What do you want others to say about you and your vibrant faith when you're gone? What unbelievable things coming into your life would you want to boast to others that God did for you? "This is what my Father did for me, I know I don't deserve it but that's just the kind of God and Father He is." I wish you'd consider letting Him adopt you into His spiritual family as a "son (or daughter) of God."

Let me leave you with a couple verses from the Message Bible, a translation that takes liberties with word usage but is faithful to the meaning. I'll quote Hebrews 11:1, 11:6, 11:33, and 11:39-40: *The fundamental fact of existence is that this trust in God, this faith, is the firm foundation under everything that makes life worth living...It's impossible to please God apart from faith. And Why? Because anyone who wants to approach God must believe both that he exists and that he cares enough to respond to those who seek him...Through acts of faith, they toppled kingdoms, made justice work, took promises for themselves. They were protected from lions, fires, and sword thrusts, turned disadvantage to advantage...Not one of these people, even though their lives of faith were exemplary, got their hands on what was promised. God had a better plan for us; that their faith and our faith would come together to make one completed whole.*

I'll just add a few words to this. The translator, Eugene Peterson, called "trust in God" the equivalent to the term faith and who is there who knows God that will deny that His faith is the foundation for all else, that life can't be worth living without faith. Faith has its essence in the belief that "He cares." God deigns to think enough of us to respond to our cries and petitions. This translation also indicates the members of the family of faith were bold enough that they "took the promise for themselves." They weren't presumptuous, just so trusting as to accept God at His word. And God responded, they were protected, and given the insight and ability that "turned disadvantage to advantage." Finally, though these faithful may not have "got their hands on what was promised, God had a better plan for us (that's all of us)." This is to say, God's conception of His promises is far better than what any human can imagine that those promises of God would consist of. I can only implore you, when hit head-on by your next problem or roadblock, ask for and look for how God can turn your "disadvantage into advantage."

CONCLUSION

So Habakkuk is inextricably linked with the topic of faith in scripture. The very passages Christians consult to find the definitive answers to faith questions in Hebrews Chapter 11 are prefaced in Hebrews 10:35 by Habakkuk's contribution to faith. Habakkuk's life example is one of confidence that is bolstered by faith. He kept the reward before him and though he didn't actually see his reward in his earthly life, he continued living in faith, confident the reward would be realized. He demonstrated the secret of vibrant faith is centering on the reward ahead. No amount of adversity derails a divine reward when it's in our souls. The clearer, the brighter the reward ahead, the more vibrant is our faith. Keep remembering, keep reminding yourself of the reward. Remember why you are willing to endure. Only if you truly believe the reward is worth the effort will you persevere in faith. So I ask you again, "Why do you claim to have faith? Do you have real faith? Is it connected with a reward? Can you state what the reward is? Is it a transcending faith? Can you see others benefiting from those rewards? Does your faith have a value component (like God's glory, your pure satisfaction) along with a 'thing' component (heaven, or present earthbound reward)? Finally, do you believe God "rewards" those who earnestly seek Him?"

MESSAGES I HOPE YOU NOTED:

- **Faith Turns Disadvantages Into Advantages**

- **Rewards From Your Lord Give You The Opportunity To Testify To Others About His Love**

Paul Serwinek

Chapter Twelve

TURNING DISADVANTAGE TO ADVANTAGE

In most cases we'll probably agree that our best teachers are those to whom we relate. As was mentioned previously, that's what makes the Bible such a source of wisdom and inspiration. Most all of the writers were ordinary guys with an average education eking out a living no different than their peers. Remember all Jesus' apostles were just average Joes - tradesmen, fishermen, farmers, with only Matthew, the tax collector, having significant wealth. King David and Solomon were the other writers with wealth. However, David didn't start out in a royal family and he never forgot his roots or humble beginnings. That's why his prayers and songs are so timeless. Such a man is our confident Habakkuk, just an average guy with no pretensions or presumptions. So when I suggest the book of Habakkuk as a primer on prayer, you'll find you can readily relate to these prayers. As we've seen, much of Habakkuk is a series of prayers, interspersed with replies from God.

You'll find his prayers will teach us how to pray if we've not been properly taught, or help us to enunciate more effective prayers if we are veterans of supplication. Let's first note that Habakkuk does not pray in a "preachy" style. What we hear is what we get. He bares his soul and speaks from his heart. What he feels, he speaks. What bothers him is clearly what he announces in the form of complaints to God. He speaks his mind to the Lord. Rather than search for tentative, "proper" terms when addressing his Heavenly Father, he talks the way we'd expect a son or daughter to talk to a human father with whom he or she feels comfortable. Habakkuk holds back nothing. Can you imagine talking to God like this? "How long must I call for help but you do not listen?" (Ha. 1:2) and "Why do you tolerate wrong?" (Ha, 1:3) he asks. Then again in Chapter 1, verse 13, Habakkuk in effect says, "I thought you were pure and holy, so why do you tolerate the treacherous?" One of the things I've taken note of and applied in my prayers is Habakkuk's bold style. Rather then couch my thoughts to God in cowardly or detached, non-emotional phrases, I've been encouraged to discuss, complain, importune my Heavenly Father as I did my human father when he was still here for me.

Remember, if we think it, we're speaking it anyway, since our Lord can "hear" what we think. Nothing is concealed from Him, so why not speak to Him that way, as if you believe He's listening. What I've found is that when we bring our inner thoughts to conscious language and terms, we are immediately helping ourselves. Baring one's soul is therapeutic in itself. Immediately by putting thoughts into words or just letting those words come out unedited and to conscious recognition, we release pent-up negative emotions. We free ourselves of the debilitating negative energy churning in our beings. Putting those emotions into words, acknowledging them to self and to God, releases the bondage they have over us. Have you ever cried and screamed and finally blurted out loud to yourself or others a pent-up source of suffering, something you should have done long before but were afraid to? What a release of negativity is felt! What a sense of catharsis is experienced. That's exactly what Habakkuk is teaching us in his prayers. What you hear is what you get, no sugarcoating, or hidden agenda. For between God and us it's impossible to have hidden agendas.

One of the salient truths I've learned in my studies of social psychology is that you can't trick yourself and you can't trick God. You can trick friends, associates and antagonists, but God and self, never. If you keep suppressing your valid feelings you hurt only yourself, since deep within the self, the soul knows the truth no less than God, Who is all-knowing. The healthiest practice for mental hygiene is to tell yourself the truth. This is where prayer comes in.

Prayer is an avenue of communication: a vehicle to get what's deep inside out into the open between you and God. Nobody else needs to hear. You need only say it in silence without an audible sound. No one else need ever know unless you ever feel comfortable enough to confess it to a mentor or friend. There is no other mechanism ever invented that serves the same purpose or works as efficiently. Unfortunately the closest thing many have to this divine therapy is psychotherapy using the aid of, in many words, a paid alter ego. Unfortunately again, such a mechanism still doesn't allow you to be truly honest since you feel the practitioner may be judging you secretly as he or she listens. NOT to say psychotherapy is to be avoided. It very often is absolutely necessary. Bouncing off feelings and ideas and hearing feedback is very beneficial.

Human psychotherapy without soul therapy is incomplete as far as our spiritual self is concerned. To be able to, at a moment's notice, make an appointment with, have an audience with the wisest Being in the universe is unbelievable. When I write these words, I admit, I can hardly believe it either, but I keep reassuring myself; based on past experience it's really true! God listens, He cares, just give Him a chance. That's what Habakkuk did.

Habakkuk modeled something else that is part of prayer, in fact, an integral part of prayer. Prayer is not just talking; it's listening. Notice how Habakkuk teaches this from his example in a series of conversations with God. First Habakkuk complains but then he waits for a response. He complains again but then he waits for a second response. Finally Habakkuk replies again, this time to say, "I get it. It makes sense to me now. Thanks for being patient with me. I admit I'm a little slow at this, but thanks again for waiting till Your thoughts finally got through this dense skull!"

Yes, thanks be to our Lord for putting up with us, being patient till we get it. It does take some of us longer than others. There are times we just aren't ready to accept the truths of life. For example, I've found with some of my younger friends it's only when they suffer a loss, a friend or parent dying, that they begin to understand that the spiritual part of their lives is missing. Not infrequently have I gone to a funeral home to hear a sorrow-filled lament. "This is really hard on me, I was close to my mother. I've got to get back to church again, maybe that will make this a little easier for me." I always leave them with the encouragement that it's not too late.

Dwelling on spiritual things isn't usually confronted with reluctance when one is forced to admit he doesn't have the answers concerning the cycle of life and death. But that's what it takes for some to begin walking on the path to spirituality. The Lord sees to it that the ability to sort out those issues that inevitably arise with the death of one of the family is available. I remember the wife of a friend of mine being overjoyed and confiding that her husband really did start coming to church with her regularly not long after the funeral. Bill is now one of the most valuable volunteers at his church. When I see him now on occasion, I can't help but note the striking contrast. It wasn't so long ago at the funeral he was desolate and despondent, but now I see before me a new life brimming with confidence and being positive, upbeat and clear about his and his mother's future.

And what we've related here is no different from what Habakkuk's confession demonstrates. Habakkuk, however, knew God but he wasn't, as he admits, looking at his society and its predicament from God's viewpoint. Once he did, the fog began to clear for him. So thanks be to Our Lord and thanks be to Habakkuk for willingly giving us our simple scriptural example of the commendable and the not so commendable.

Remember, here is a blessed Bible writer and character showing by example, "I'm no different than you." I get it wrong sometimes, that's when I look at things through human eyes, but when I stop and meditate and be quiet, I begin to be receptive to God's thoughts. Now it begins making sense." This is really encouraging to me. I can relate to Habakkuk; he's not so different. His experience is a message to me. Now, do you get the message? Here's a guy who was close to God, blessed to write a portion of the Bible, but he admits he was very off base at times. He didn't have all the answers. But when he got so confused and so upset with his world and took the time to pray and listen to his inner thoughts, that's when answers started coming. Hey,

I've been there, too. I can admit, because Habakkuk showed me it's OK to admit, I don't have all the answers, I didn't get it right every time, my life isn't always running perfectly. But I've learned to do what Habakkuk teaches. When we're done cussing and fussing, start "fessing up" to our oversights. Start reconnecting with our Father in prayer.

Habakkuk says, in effect, "I cussed and fussed and got angry with God, I'll admit, but God's the kind of friend that takes up a friendship where it left off." I'm sure you have friends like that. Haven't you met a friend you hadn't seen for years and you just seem to take up where you left off? No one complains, "Why haven't you kept in contact with me, all this time lost?" No, you just start getting caught up on what's happened and then start reminiscing and the friendship bond continues growing. That's the way it is with our friendship with God. When we're ready to come back to work on restoring our friendship, whether it be a day, a month, a year or even years, He doesn't scold or complain. He doesn't say, "So, now that you need Me you're finally coming back. Where were you when you thought things were going so well for you?" That's not God's way. Nowhere in Habakkuk's conversations does he ever mention God acting as if He was being used. God's above all that. He just wants us back. He just wants to do for us what He did for Habakkuk, to encourage and bolster him.

Spend a little time with our Father in prayer or reading His biblical words. You'll be encouraged as Habakkuk was. A little time with God and Habakkuk could swing from the depths of depression to the heights of ecstasy proclaiming, *...I will be joyful in God my savior.* (Ha. 3:18). By God letting Habakkuk's writing be preserved all these thousands of years, He's saying in effect, "Habakkuk was a good man in spite of the fact he didn't always look at life from My perspective, but that's okay, he's only human. I'll treat you no differently than I treated Habakkuk. Come back when you're ready and I can get you back to a life of joy and peace in no time."

Habakkuk testified he went from "Oh woe is me" to *...I will rejoice in the Lord.* (Ha. 3:18). This transformation took place only after Habakkuk started praying. And this works for all of us. Just start praying. When Habakkuk started praying he didn't have the answers.

The second time he prayed he began to get some clear insight. So don't expect the heavens to open to you immediately as if the world revolves around you. You know it doesn't, so don't expect it. But do expect answers will start coming when you persist in praying.

MIRACLES EXPOSED

Now let's examine how Habakkuk prayed. You'll be surprised again; he put into words what you and I would like to say to God but are afraid to say! No doubt it was because Habakkuk knew his God well enough that he could importune as he did. I know if you're a thinking person you've asked the very same question, but probably never to God. Habakkuk's question might appear too presumptuous. Thank you, again, Habakkuk, for asking what I've questioned but was afraid I'd be putting God on the spot. Thanks, Habakkuk. I've wondered this myself but thought it too presumptuous to ask God directly.

Ready? This is his question and request at the same time. Ha. 3:2 records Habakkuk's bombshell of a request. First he introduces his thoughts to the Lord and then it comes out, ***Lord, I have heard of your fame; I stand in awe of your deeds; O Lord.*** And then what you and I would like to say, ***Renew them in our day, in our time make them known...*** In reading Habakkuk you could have easily glossed over this. But what Habakkuk was saying is, "I know you've done miracles in the past but what about now, what about our time? Will you do more miracles? Am I going to see how miracles can affect my life, in my time?"

Habakkuk elaborates and says in effect, "I know about the miracles like the plagues of Egypt that set the Israelites free." (Ha. 3:5). "I know about your dividing the Nile River so the Israelites could pass through and how you churned the water to deluge the Egyptian armies." (Ha. 3:15). "I also know about how you made the sun and moon to stand still so Joshua could fulfill your purpose." (Ha. 3:11). Those were all miracles I admit, confesses Habakkuk. But what about now? Will there ever be miracles again? Will I be able to see them? We'll all stand in unison with Habakkuk now asking, "Will I ever be able to see these miracles? I know I'd believe if I could just see some miracles. I'd know I was on the right track. It would be so much easier for me, just show me some signs, do something!"

Now get ready for God's answer. This is the other bombshell from Habakkuk. The whole book of Habakkuk screams back the answer to him, to us. YES, yes, yes, there are miracles today! This is what God was saying to Habakkuk, our surrogate spokesman, and to us by extension. God knew we'd all want to know the answer to the miracle question, so He allowed Habakkuk's writing to come down to us after more than two thousand years. Habakkuk heard God saying, in effect, "there are miracles all the time but you just don't notice them. Look at things from My perspective and you'll recognize that miracles are happening all around you, all the time."

From my own perspective I believe I've let some learned Bible scholars confuse me into misunderstanding what a miracle is. I've heard many scholars interpret "MIRACLE" in the Bible to mean, "an act by God than cannot be explained by the laws of nature or that circumvents the laws of nature." However, search as I have through scripture, I can find no verse that substantiates that definition. Not that the laws of nature haven't been revoked by God at times. Joshua's experience of seeing the sun and moon stand still would certainly be an example of that type of miracle. But those are not the only types of miracles of which the Bible speaks.

God, speaking through Habakkuk, tells us of other miracles, miracles Habakkuk wasn't recognizing because he was just looking for some glitzy, dazzling, daring act by God that evidently meant miracles to him, too. However, as Habakkuk shows, when God maneuvers events to let nature take its course, that's a miracle too. God told Habakkuk, "What appears to you as a coincidence, is actually Me working behind the scenes. That's a miracle and you don't even see it." Habakkuk's eyes were opened and frankly my eyes have been opened like never before, due to God's revelation to Habakkuk. I'm just beginning to see all the miracles I didn't recognize before and I can't wait to see more!

Let's let God explain to you what He did for Habakkuk's sake. You remember Habakkuk had been praying for justice. The men in power had prevented justice. The average dweller around Jerusalem could not compete with the tribes of the wealthy. Legal cases were decided based on wealth rather than what was fair and just. Habakkuk begged for God to do something. That's when God let him in on the secret. The secret was this: World events were at that very moment occurring that would eventually lead to the toppling of the unjust Jewish system of justice and the installation of a fair system in the future. All this would occur at the Lord's behest; His will would be done. In this case He would use the Babylonians, a bloodthirsty nation in the Middle East who were intent on achieving regional hegemony. This is how God announced His plans to Habakkuk in Ha. 1:6, *"I am raising up the Babylonians, that ruthless and impetuous people, who sweep across the whole earth to seize dwelling places not their own."*

I think it's critical that Christians understand how God sometimes works. This Bible passage is one of the few in all scripture that lets us be privy to God's mind. And this is His point. In many cases, in most cases, God need not directly intervene in human affairs. He simply uses the forces of nature and the natural inclination of humans to do His bidding. God explains it that way to Habakkuk. The Babylonians are by their very culture a ruthless people. Their intention is to become a world empire, "to sweep across the whole earth," as He puts it. And this is the critical point you must understand. God says, "I am raising up the Babylonians." Do you get it? God didn't groom the Babylonians to become ruthless, power hungry just to punish the wayward Jews, did He? No, yet He says, "I'm raising them up."

Can you see what He means? Of course, He is merely saying I'm going to "allow" them to do what they'll naturally, predictably do anyway. I am doing it in the sense that I will not prevent them from following their natural inclinations. I'm not making this up. God says this in scripture. He in effect says to us, "I'm letting you in on how I act. I don't need to personally visit each and every situation where My presence is needed and personally manipulate the details. I may want the natural course of events to unfold for My will to be done. I can, if I wish, intervene. I can, if I wish, prevent a natural outcome. I can speed it up or delay it. The fact that I predict it years in advance, something no human can do, is proving this is divine will."

Personally I glean from this personal explanation from God a world of possibilities. I would never have understood this facet of God's control were it not for Habakkuk's encounter with The Almighty. To me the Babylonians coming to destroy a nation and then for the Babylonians to be overthrown, allowing the Jews to rebuild their cities was a miracle. But you say, "God didn't have to circumvent natural events. This can't be a miracle. I think of miracles as when a laser light comes from the sky to zap someone or when you turn water to wine before my very eyes - that's a miracle." God says to Habakkuk in effect, "Give Me more credit than that. There are a lot more miracles going on around you; you just can't see what's happening behind the scenes. Scripture is showing that the fact I, God, predict it in advance is proof My endorsement is on the event. If necessary, take the prediction or prophecy that comes true as proof it's a miracle, even if I didn't have to lift a finger." Someone might counter, "This Babylonian affair was just a coincidence. That wasn't necessarily proof of God's divine will. No way is it a miracle." However, to predict or prophesy it in advance is indicative of God's decreeing the event. He need not circumvent physical nature or human actions to call it a miracle.

HOW IT ALL WORKED OUT

Now, let me tell the rest of the story that first began during Habakkuk's lifetime but was played out after his death. Then you'll realize it was all part of a gigantic miracle, though on the surface, it was deemed just coincidence. As prophesied by some of God's holy men, Habakkuk included, Babylon did indeed invade and ransack Judah. Jerusalem, the holy city, with its temple was razed. The wealthy families, who compounded their wealth by unjust means couldn't use their wealth to buy freedom. They were slaughtered or taken captive as slaves to Babylon. The land of the Jews lay desolate some seventy years. Justice triumphed and the Lord's will prevailed.

This wasn't the end of the story, though. When God writes a story it always has a happy ending. This was just a chapter in the saga of those who were truly God's people. God wants happy endings for all His children. That's why those close to God, like Habakkuk, are always optimistic. They don't find it difficult to believe, as Habakkuk admonishes us, that "The righteous will live by faith." When one gets Habakkuk-style faith and believes that righteousness always wins out in the end, he or she can endure even a lifetime of trials. If you can believe that God wants a happy ending for you, too, you'll work with Him while always looking for His guidance and for little coincidences that indicate divine providence coming your way.

Some would say it was just a coincidence that Daniel, a young Jewish captive in Babylon, was recognized by the Babylonians to have extraordinary wisdom and mental abilities. Of course, it was just a coincidence that he and his three Jewish friends were enrolled in the king's "fast track" educational program. Then coincidence again, only Daniel of all the king's wise men could reveal and unravel a terrifying dream that King Nebuchadnezzar had. (See the book of Daniel in the Bible for details).

Finally there was an "actual miracle," the kind traditionalists classify as a real miracle. Daniel, Chapter 5 tells about the terrifying events during a party of the successor Babylonian king. A mysterious hand began writing on the wall of the banquet hall. Then, when none of the king's seers could decipher the writing, Daniel was summoned to read and interpret. The message from God announced the end of the Babylonian Empire and the ascent of the Medes and Persians to power. Of course, it was just a coincidence again that that very night while the guards around the city were drunk from participating in the Babylonian festivities, that the Medes and Persians diverted the river running through the city and were able to charge into the city, capturing it without a fight.

Later when the Persians learned a Jew predicted the imminent rise of the Persians as the new world superpower, they were only too happy to decree the freedom of the Jews to return to their homeland, a land desolate for some 70 years. Of course, that decree wasn't a miracle since naturally the Persians would be obliged to the Jews for their prediction foretelling Persian prominence. Those returning were dedicated people of faith who vowed to restore a government based on justice for all inhabitants of Judah.

That's the happy ending we were waiting for. Some would say it took a lot of coincidences for that to happen. Others would say, of course, that it was God's doing but He didn't need to use any overt miracles to accomplish His will. Then there are others like me that call it all one big miracle. God didn't have to go outside the laws of nature to arrange events. Just an adjustment here and a slight intervention there was all that was needed. Justice was restored to Judah with a fresh start for a new generation of Jews vowing to live by God's laws of fairness. I call any event where God's hand is evident a miracle. It's up to you to decide. The reason I make such a big thing of this is that unless we realize the workings of "coincidences," I call them "miracles," we'll miss the hundreds of potential interventions of God in our lives today. I personally consider it an affront to God to claim, as many traditionalists do, that God's allowing events to naturally unfold where He doesn't have to directly intervene but allows the laws of the universe to control - those can't be miracles. Who says? Not God. Miracles are occurring all the time, only to the untrained eye they don't look like miracles.

Let me give the synopsis of one more Bible book before I apply this to you personally. This is the Bible book of Esther. This book recounts another miraculous deliverance of the Jews. Since the whole story is a series of coincidences some Christians might not see God's hand in the events. Not one miracle. Some have questioned this book as a valid Bible book since there are no seeming miracles to be found. The book of Esther never even mentions God! I'd say, and many other Christians with me, those aren't just coincidences recounted, that's God working. Remember Habakkuk even asked God (Ha. 3:2) why He wasn't doing those spectacular glitzy miracles He used to do. All the while God was telling Habakkuk, "What you see occurring, these are miracles, too." Especially since the advent of Christ, God now deals more often with individuals and not just nations like the Jews. The little every day miracles now are much more effective. To herald the coming of the Messiah and the validation of His reinterpretation of the Old Jewish Covenant were the spectacular, highly visible and publicized miracles essential for a time. The Lord has not seen fit to employ the spectacular miracles that can be caught on TV as yet, but rest assured miracles from God are occurring daily in staggering numbers.

Now to Esther's story. You can read the whole true story in one short sitting on your own. Just look up the book of Esther in the Bible, remembering when you read it, God is nowhere mentioned as an active participant in the drama and never is the word "miracle" used to describe any event. Tell me what you think...

Esther's story actually played almost 100 years after Habakkuk's story. Habakkuk's happy ending, the restoration of justice in Jerusalem, had already occurred. But life is not static; hence a new drama confronted God's people, the Jews. Fortunately this story was resolved in short order, unlike Habakkuk's resolution of justice that took generations to come to fruition. Esther and Mordecai, her uncle, lived during the reign of the Persians over all the Middle East and adjacent civilizations.

The true story goes like this. You might say Esther was in a beauty pageant with the top prize being crowned as queen to the newly divorced Persian King. For some reason (coincidence one) the official over the beauty pageant took a special liking to Esther, the Jewish girl, and became her mentor. Under his tutelage, she, of all contestants, was chosen queen (another coincidence maybe). Shortly after, Esther's uncle Mordecai uncovered a plot to assassinate the king, when he just happened to be in the right place at the right time (coincidence?) The plot was foiled and Mordecai's loyalty to the king was duly noted in the royal records.

In the meantime a powerful Persian prince, Haman, hatched a plot to exterminate the Jews from the Persian Empire, not knowing Esther, the queen, was herself a Jew. Shortly before this date set for the Jewish genocide, the king "just happened" to remember he hadn't ever rewarded Mordecai, the Jew, for his loyalty. Thereafter Esther gained a special emergency audience with the king that was completely against all official protocol (coincidence, right?) In the nick of time Esther revealed the plot of Haman and begged for the king's protection. Having become so enamored with Esther, the king certainly acquiesced and the villain, Haman, himself was executed. Once again a major plot to destroy God's chosen people, the Jews, was foiled.

Now tell me, do you think these seeming coincidences were nothing more than chance occurrences? You might be able to explain away one or two but not so many at such critical moments. God's will was being accomplished behind the scenes. However, only those with discernment as to how God works are privy to the true workings of God upon all the players in the drama. A dazzling spectacle did not constitute a miracle here; little interventions did the trick.

I'd call this drama of deliverance a miracle, wouldn't you? The Lord didn't have to do anything unusual, just a little adjustment here and a slight intervention there. It was that simple. Yes, the Jews were God's special people and you'd expect such consideration from a Father to His adopted children. But now remember the current reality introduced by Jesus and amplified by the apostle Paul (with the help of Habakkuk's insight). We are all, who live by faith in Christ, considered God's special children. We as individuals and as a group are no less special than the Jewish nation, specially chosen by God.

The coincidences experienced by Habakkuk, Esther, Mordecai, and every Bible writer can be expected by you. Just take a moment right now and think about all those beneficial coincidences that just happened to bring you to God, how you just happened to find a true set of Christian friends, how God protected you through sickness, accident or negative events. Habakkuk's story, Esther's story implore you to treat them as more than just coincidences but more like little (actual big) miracles with you as the beneficiary!

Permit me to relate to you several of my coincidences (for those of you still on the borderline and unsure of what to make of them) or as I would prefer to look at them, encounters with something beyond myself and divine. I remember so clearly a time I was in a quandary not knowing whether to move to a different area of our state, Michigan. My wife and I realized the decision we were to finalize would have long-term ramifications on ourselves, our children and their education. What were we to do? We explored several possibilities but still couldn't decide what was best. In a moment of frustration, but really wanting divine guidance, I got down on my hands and knees and prayed. "What's best for my family?" I begged. No sooner had I said my "Amen" than the phone rang. On the other end was the landlord of a rental house saying he decided to let us rent his home for a fee we could afford, which was well below his original price. My wife and I could feel divine presence and guidance than. Just a little thing you say, yes, but there have been quite a few times when I've felt so especially cared for.

Let me tell you one more little occurrence. I remember not too many years ago having finished a major self-imposed assignment and wondering where I should be turning my focus next. There are always projects to keep me busy. But I was beginning to feel I needed to make more of a difference (more on this topic in the next chapter). I prayed and looked for options. I prayed for several months with no indication of direction. I have to admit I was getting discouraged, but having learned that faith means optimism, I kept expecting some kind of answer. In the last chapter we examined how faith requires expecting a reward for our efforts. I believed it then and I believe it all the more now. Regardless, after several bouts with discouragement I happened to attend a banquet sponsored by one of my business partners. We took our assigned seating and during the course of the evening I talked extensively with a gentleman directly across the table from me. How we got to talking about my predicament I can't recall, but he excitedly told me about a book he had recently read that gave him what he needed when confronted with indecision similar to mine. He even promised he'd send a copy of the book to me. His animated story of his past year with purpose, and his unselfish desire to help, proved to me I was in the right place at the right time. No, not just a coincidence; I know I was in the place I was supposed to be at the time appointed! By the way the book he sent me was *Half Time* by Bob Buford, perfect for anyone halfway through his or her lifetime and in search of a game plan for the last half.

Enough about me; how about you? Do you want more of those appointments with coincidence, more invisible interventions? Wouldn't it be nice for your friends to think you're crazy, but you have proof in your own life that somehow, some way, Someone seems to be looking out for you? I can give you the formula; it's so easy. Rather, not I, but Habakkuk gives you the simple two-step formula. Do these two things and watch for the miracles. And don't argue with anyone. If they prefer to call them coincidences, let them. You and I and anyone that has put himself or herself on the path of spirituality knows the truth.

A PRAYER HABIT

Just follow Habakkuk's example. NUMBER ONE, pray as Habakkuk did. In fact, if you're not sure what to say, use his exact words. "Renew your deeds in our day." It's that simple; that's what he said. "God, I know there were miracles in the past, I have heard of them. I'm just one person but I'd like a couple miracles just to assure me You're there. Please renew Your miracles (acts) in my day, in my life, as You did in the past. All I need are a couple tiny little miracles in the form of coincidences or whatever pleases You. Father, I know there once was a simple man named Habakkuk, he put it so simply to You. I'm doing the same. Renew Your acts in my day, in my life." Doing that for the first time may make you feel nervous and a little out of your comfort zone. Don't worry, those words were written by an ordinary man that found his much-needed answers and desired to pass on the results of his encounter with God to you.

Do this every day, then follow Habakkuk's NUMBER TWO step. Remember what Habakkuk said about faith. "The righteous will live by faith." Taking this literally it simply means living each day with faith and optimism, looking for that divine encounter, knowing it's going to happen. As Paul the apostle said shortly after uttering Habakkuk's words about faith, he embellished on Habakkuk by saying, "You've got to believe that God is and He'll reward you." Well he really said it this way, *"...anyone who comes to him must believe that he exists and that he rewards those who earnestly seek him."* (He. 11:6) If you pray for help, you must start looking for that help. Faith means knowing it's going to come. When and how or through whom you don't know, but it will come.

Those are the one-two steps to divine intervention in life. I don't want to appear trite. This is profound and beyond any human imagination. I feel like pinching myself every time I write or speak this advice. I don't ever want to treat this profound formula with less than the value and reverence due. Having said that, just remember "alms and anticipation." Endlessly say your alms of praise to the Divine and daily live with a sense of anticipation; something good is going to happen, I just know it. One without the other won't do it.

Saying your alms (prayers) in endless repetition is not enough. Just anticipating something good from someone won't do it either. But alms of praise and acknowledging the divine Source of miracles in the universe, God, and excitedly anticipating something good, a reward, is the two-step process. And, by the way, if you really believe it's going to happen you should start acting in accordance with your requests immediately. Start taking the next actions as if the miracle, the intervention, has already occurred. Simple ideas (or at least simply understood ideas such as always anticipating the best) from simple writers (Habakkuk and Paul) in a simply written book (the Bible) are really the most profound ideas by profound thinkers written in a profound and timely masterpiece of guidance. Prayers are powerful and can lead to powerful, life-transforming, life-shattering events in your time, your life.

MESSAGES I HOPE YOU NOTED:

- **Remember: Alms And Anticipation**
- **Those Coincidences Are More Than Just Coincidences**
- **When God Writes A Story It Always Has A Happy Ending For The Faithful**

Chapter Thirteen

WHAT A DIFFERENCE IT MAKES TO MAKE A DIFFERENCE

I like to keep repeating to myself this simple phrase, "What a difference it makes to make a difference." It's simple but it reminds me of something that is all-important. I'm reminding myself what a difference it makes in my life when I live knowing I'm making a difference. Stop and think about that for a moment. There is much more there than you might think at first impression. I'd have to say it's taken me years to be able to communicate so simply and succinctly what I knew, yet didn't know. This is one of those statements that packs a lifetime of searching into it. "What a difference it makes to make a difference."

Let me explain why this is so valuable to me. You see I've always been a thinker. This, like any other character trait can be a blessing or a curse. I have always found myself asking, "Why?" This is especially a curse when I find myself analyzing motives too critically and the reasons why others act as they do. I'd stop and ponder at times, "Why don't I just stop thinking and enjoy the ride, so to speak." Some of my friends seemed to go from one moment to the next enjoying themselves, seemingly oblivious to what happens behind the scenes. When I was young I wished I could be like that. Later I realized my analytical nature could be a blessing.

Fortunately, one thing I promised myself when I was a teenager was I'd always search for truth. I probably only realized it then because I was so young and hadn't had the time, the years needed, to perfect suppressing my actual feelings. What I admitted (when I promised myself that I would always seek truth) was that I felt fear. Every time this resolve to seek truth came to mind, I felt a little twinge in my stomach. Since I hadn't learned how to suppress thoughts yet (and that's a blessing I've come to realize is a blessing in itself), I admitted, "I'm afraid, but why?"

A little bit of analysis engaged in, as I admitted a practice I gravitated toward, enlightened me as to why. Of course, you already know why I was afraid and why you may have had similar feelings of fear well up when you've lived through major change. I was afraid seeking truth might force me to change my life, maybe to admit I was wrong, maybe to admit I didn't have the answers and what's more scary yet, to come to find in the end there were no answers. That's scary. To come to a dead end, driving down the back dusty roads of life, after dark, where there are no streetlights and then you hit a dead end. What do you do then? I admitted my fear of that happening. I had to either decide to never go on those back roads after dark and have a hard time living with myself, or plunge ahead. Again, I say thank You, God! I was young, naïve and hadn't learned how to play psychological games with myself yet.

There was one thing, though, that helped me through my plights, my fear. Every time I'd start feeling nervous about what I'd find I could remind myself about all the wonders in life around me. I was still young and the new ideas, exciting stories, astounding beauty everywhere pinched me to admit, "There must be something behind this all." There's got to be a Mastermind in the universe and with all the beauty and good in amidst the suffering pain, this Mastermind wouldn't, just couldn't, play tricks on us (me)." So armed with two ideas I believed self-evident, at least to me, I muddled on, somewhat tentatively, still nervous, still lacking in confidence, a typical teenager. The two "self evident" Ideas being – there is such a thing as truth and there is a benevolent higher Power.

FORTUNATELY for me, again as I look back, I initiated this quest while still a teen. If I had waited till college to start my search my two self-evident ideas would have been blown up in my face. College philosophy proved to me beyond any doubt nothing can be proved true with 100% surety. Being a seeker of truth I had to admit that unsettling discovery. However, I did have to take exception to the next statement coming from the college textbook. If you can't prove anything with 100% accuracy, therefore there can be no truth. But that's simply not true. This is where reason allowed me to draw the line. Yes, I can't prove certain tenets true beyond any doubt but that doesn't negate truth. At that moment, for the first time, I understood why the Bible made such a big thing out of faith. Yes, I can't prove it, I have to take it on faith but that doesn't deny or negate the idea of truth's existence. I was able to move on with my search, my two self-evident truths still intact.

However, while wandering in the "no faith" college environment I was introduced to other thinkers who were willing to take the suggestion of a nineteenth century Swedish philosopher, Soren Kierkegaard, who himself grew up in a world of doubt. Where he yearned for certainty, the only solution was the necessity of taking what he called "a leap of faith." In essence he was saying, "I can't prove it but I can't live in a world with no certainty, no answers. Here's a source, the Bible, which claims to offer certainty. But the catch is, you have to take a chance." He said, in effect, "I'm willing to take a chance even though it's like jumping off a precipitous cliff hoping that you'll be saved somehow, some way during your free fall." I've met people who admitted they suffered through such an experience, free falling. That's scary. I thought I was scared when I started out testing truth in the world around me, but what they had to do, that's really SCARY. But they survived. They took the jump and started living their lives as if there was a God. Though they couldn't prove it, somehow, some way they all survived to testify, "I've proved it to myself. The risk was worth it."

I've continued searching, continued seeking. Living as a Christian all these years, having taken a less scary leap of faith since I was taught the Christian philosophy when I was young, I've researched all the evidence in my field of study - sociology and social psychology. I can truthfully report with a deep sense of confidence, never has the Bible's guide for living ever been debunked when all evidence is considered. I am ever amazed because in my field most of my peers are atheists or agnostics. They keep spouting theories about how antiquated scriptural ideas are. However, every time they put their replacement guidelines to the test of rigorous scientific research, they invariably admit they haven't found better guidelines for living than the Bible. In fact, with all the talk in psychology in the 70's and 80's about the primacy of love in life and then in the 90's about the healing power of forgiveness, my peers talked as if they had made momentous discoveries, without admitting they unwittingly were just verifying the ancient wisdom of scripture.

Now getting back to my problem, my penchant for analysis, my attempt has always been to put my beliefs in simple, practical terms I understand myself and then am able pass on to others in easy-to-digest bits and pieces. I admit to a methodical search for purpose in life. I desired above all else clarity in this one life area. My study of scripture made it abundantly clear that the biblical perspective is the conclusion of Solomon, purported to be the wisest philosopher in history. Solomon so succinctly stated in Ecclesiastes 12:13, *Now all has been heard; here's the conclusion of the matter: Fear God and keep his commandments; for this is the whole duty of man.* I have always cherished that simplicity, but as any reader of scripture soon finds, simplicity is very often deeper than deep. When I've gone to implement that in my life I have questions. I've come to find that "fear of God" is something you learn to understand more fully. For example, when Jesus came He taught us to interchangeably substitute the word "Father" for "God" in prayer, a whole new dimension in inclusiveness. As a social psychologist I really have appreciated His clarity. Now when I hear from Solomon with Jesus' help, "Fear God, your caring loving father" I get a much more assuring directive.

Then with Jesus' own observation, and suggestions on living crystallized by His life example, I have broader insights into what is expected of me. For example, while scripture for thousands of years hailed the necessity of forgiveness, only with Jesus' advent do we have a complete picture of what is expected. Recall how Jesus' disciples questioned Him on how often to forgive. Seven times, Peter suggested, but by Jesus imploring "forgive seven times 70," He highlighted the sublime nature of God's forgiveness.

Still I admit I'm continuously perfecting myself in what I should be doing and to what I should attain. I freely admit I'm not a Mother Teresa. I can't evince the joy she could just by heralding the urgency of helping the needy. I freely admit when I heard Christian missionaries from civil war-torn Africa relating their excitement for befriending, teaching and truly rescuing starving, terrified children, I've often shaken my head saying, "I'll never make it, I'll never be able to serve God, I don't think I have that kind of zeal in me. What's more, I can't even get excited about doing that kind of work. What's wrong with me? I must be defective as a caring human."

Fortunately, when going through that bout with self-examination I still had faith, and faith means optimism as we've learned from studying Habakkuk. I kept saying somehow God will change me. Maybe I can't be a Mother Teresa, after all I still think of her as a saint, but maybe God will make a light bulb go on in my head and I'll have this burning desire to sell everything, move to India and walk barefoot through the streets of suffering and squalor to spark some joy. I had been waiting for decades for this transformation, but it never happened. So here I was plodding away, reasonably happy with life, still excited about possibilities but not being able to put into simple terms, "My purpose in life is… and I'm doing it right now this way…"

The closest I got to enunciating my thoughts was to say "I just want to feel 'settled', that's all, feel settled and calm about who I am and the direction I'm taking." Over time little insights would be offered to me almost like someone inviting me over for a truly scrumptious homemade dessert that you couldn't believe could taste so good (I've had some of those and those are my number three reason why I believe in God). I remember reading one psychologist writing from his experiences in private practice making an observation, again so simply and so succinctly, just as I've found all truths of living to be so packaged, neatly, simply wrapped in a pretty, unpretentious colored bow. His conclusion was, based on his lifetime of work, what every one wants is simply to get to the place in their lives where they have "peace of mind." That rings true for me. I had to admit he put it so clearly. I've analyzed that, researched it, interviewed others randomly. I'd have to say that everyone - when you keep asking, keep peeling off each layer of the onion so to speak - what we all seem to desire is that simple destiny. All said and done, I want to calmly sit back, take a deep breath and say deep down inside, "All things considered, I feel good about myself, I feel peace of mind."

I'm not going to dwell on that now; that's a study in itself. I only ask you to accept it as one idea worthy of future reflection. I know this may not sit well with some literal, traditional thinkers, but please don't make an issue of it. Accept it as a piece in the puzzle of life I discovered in my journey to search for purpose. At least now I could put into words and prayers what I was looking for. "Lord, I want that, peace of mind." I suddenly knew what Paul had been describing, *the peace of God, which transcends all understanding*. (Ph. 4:7). That's what I want, that something I could never explain completely. It's beyond all words, beyond all thought, but one little particle of it is that feeling of sitting back, sighing and saying, "I feel good about myself, I tried, I feel peace of mind." I finally knew for what to pray. I also knew guidance would soon be forthcoming to know what my Lord wanted me to do.

GETTING THERE

Still, what course will lead us to that hallowed ground of such an open, unthreatening relationship with God, our Father? Habakkuk's own experience points us in the right direction. Remember how Habakkuk started out his meditation? "How long, O Lord, must I call for help?" "Why do you make ME look at injustice?" "Destruction and violence are before ME." Do you get the picture? Do I have to say more? Those I's and Me's are interspersed in his complaints. "Woe is me, why me, when will something be done to help me?"

Contrast that to how Habakkuk ended his proclamation. Ha. 3:17-18 summarizes what he learned. Note the difference, ***Though the fig tree does not bud, and there are no grapes on the vines... and no cattle in the stalls, yet I will rejoice in the Lord, I will be joyful in God my Savior.*** Clear, isn't it? When we read Habakkuk's first words, and compare them to his last, a salient contrast emerges. At first Habakkuk dwelled on his predicament, his pain, his problems, how hopeless he was. After listening to God's inspiration, the center of attention had shifted. Here he spelled out what he had learned. Can we take this away as a principle of living?

MY POSITION ON PERCEPTION

Habakkuk confessed he has learned, "No matter how bad things appear for me - no food, no property, no prospects - I'll center my attention on my work. I'll be joyful knowing He can transform the situation. I'll rejoice in the Lord, knowing He can help me extricate myself from the quicksand I find myself in or at least He'll help me to float on the quicksand. Just trust in Him, for my position or my perception will be transformed. Either way I can claim victory through my God, for either my position, my situation, will miraculously seem to improve or my way of looking at the mess will miraculously take on a new, positive perspective. Either way the sun is on the horizon." Don't doubt the possibilities in your life. You need this for yourself. In three short chapters you read how Habakkuk was transformed from a complainer to a confidant with the Lord. During the course of his writing his contribution to scripture, his circumstances were no different, but his viewpoint had shifted. Rather than looking down at his pitiful state, he was convinced to look up to God's realm. From clouds and rain to sunshine in the blink of an eye!

I'm certain, if you don't see the sunshine yet, you will, if you just do this. Reread Habakkuk, Chapters 1-3. When you consciously relate to Habakkuk, his qualms and his quandary, and say, "That's how I feel most of the time. I've dwelt on myself, my suffering, but I'm going to let God talk to me in these very words He spoke to Habakkuk." When you come to the end of Chapter three, pay particular attention to Habakkuk's very last words. "The sovereign Lord is my strength", and then his final refrain we might paraphrase in this manner, "with God's strength, I feel I could do anything, confront anything." You know, someone else declared almost those exact same words. It was Paul who concluded, *I can do everything through him who gives me strength.* (Ph. 4:13)

So one of the first steps to that prize of "the peace of God, which transcends all understanding" is steering in the right direction. Don't stare down at self but up toward God. Look at it this way, how far could you get on a walk anywhere, to a garden, to a park, if you attempted to walk looking at your feet or your hands only? How often would you find yourself stumbling or veering off track? It's so much easier walking with eyes affixed on the destination ahead, the garden, the park. The same principle is true with living life. Pay attention to where you're going, not who's going. Be more conscious of the journey, more so than the act of walking. The paradox of Christianity taught by our Lord Jesus is more attention to self yields less benefit to self (less happiness, less self peace), but more attention to others' welfare brings a greater abundance to self-welfare. Every Bible writer, including Habakkuk, learned the same lesson, "less is more." Live it and pass it on.

THE GIANT STEP

So much for our perception, now the other side of the coin, which is purpose. You and I need both, proper perception and powerful purpose. Each feeds on the other. Concentrating on the two allows God's Spirit to energize us in multiple ways. Can you see that it's difficult to keep our thoughts centered away from self and on God's welfare without keeping busy? But busy doing what? Here's where purpose comes in. What does God want us to do? And before you blurt out as you may have been taught, "Praise God" or "Glorify God", or "Worship God," think of this. The end result will always be those ends. Unfortunately to many Christians those phrases have become pleasant platitudes. They are ends but I asked, what does God want us to do? There's a difference. The neophytes, the new believers will ask what does this mean, glorify God, how do I do that? Unfortunately I've seen too many believers left in that state. Scripture says, "Praise God." But what do you mean by that? The response you'll get from many is, "You know, just glorify God." But how do you do that?

I submit that these goals are the means, not the ends. God will be praised by you, God will be glorified by you, and you will be worshipping God if you do something. Again I ask, what is that something? What should you and I be doing? In deference to other scholars and with fear of stepping on someone else's viewpoint, please let me submit this thought. Scripture tells us God will be praised and glorified by us, His workers. In spite of our differences, differences in abilities and differences in circumstances, we'll come up with a million ways, each adding our own spin to the directive, with the end result being the praise of God. How will we personally do it? Very simply, we'll each find our own way to "make a difference." That's not my idea; it's found in scripture. Habakkuk made a difference to his fellow citizens and to future generations. He used his talents, his circumstances and he acted and spoke humbly but convincingly of what he learned from God, about God. He made a difference by helping us see how we can make a difference and then seemed to say, "This is my contribution, so for now pass it on."

Our Master, Jesus, put the facts this way in John 15:16-17. *"You did not choose me, but I chose you and appointed you to go and bear fruit—fruit that will last. Then the Father will give you whatever you ask in my name. This is my command: Love each other."* Jesus had a knack for explaining a complex idea simply and understandably. God chose you, God expects you to "bear fruit." Do something with your life. Know that your life is meaningful, lived with a purpose.

He explained the paradox of Christianity a little differently here. Jesus was famous for talking in parables, what some listeners thought were riddles. For example, He said, "...many who are first will be last, and the last first." (Mark 10:31). And, "... whoever loses his life for my sake will find it." (Matt. 10:39). But in John 15:16 He explained what

He meant. He assures us our Father (He taught us to call God that) wishes to see us happy. He wants good things for us and will even "give you whatever you ask" (those are Jesus' words not mine). Yes you can have whatever you need to find fulfillment, but you must understand and live by this paradox of Christianity. Jesus stressed here the "me" part comes second; the "them" part comes first. You are destined to make a difference, as Jesus asserts, "I chose you" and "I appointed you." Then the task..."go and bear fruit – fruit that will last."

It's first things first. You take your mind off yourself and do what you're appointed to do and rest assured then you can have whatever you require for happiness and fulfillment. Our project per our Lord is to "bear fruit." Insist that the result of Christian living will pop up everywhere your life touches. How do we do that? Jesus' answer, simple and succinct as usual is, "This is my command: Love each other." There you have Jesus' recipe for success. Make a difference in the people and the world around you and do it by sharing the kind of unselfish concern (love) Jesus demonstrated while here. Then the other things (everything) you may need to sustain your individual happiness will automatically follow, once you ask your Father.

Isn't that so clearly, so simply put? You were chosen, you were appointed to bear fruit with your life. You can only do that by turning your mind off self and displaying a true concern for the welfare of others, making a difference in their lives. You must continue doing this for as long as it takes to get "me first" out of your thoughts. Then and only then can you turn with full assurance asking your Father for what you think you need. I like to remind myself, "I make a difference by helping others make a difference in their lives." I can "bear fruit" or make a difference by assisting others to make a difference in their lives. Care for others to the extent the fruits of love spring up all around you, then step back and ask yourself, "How do I feel now?"

I equate making a difference in other lives to bearing fruit. The way one makes a difference is by showing care. That act of love bears fruit as the seed of love cultivated in others in turn is passed on bearing more fruit. The recipients of our love begin to make a difference in the lives of those close to them. The fruit continues to multiply. Put still another way, we transform our lives by helping others transform their lives. The motivation is love, simply caring and demonstrating real concern. That ingredient can't be faked. You notice Jesus qualified his direction to "bear fruit" by adding, "fruit that will last." Here He reminds us that only really caring will result in "fruit that will last." Saying "I care" or doing something kind for a stranger is a start, but bearing fruit that lasts, or really touching others meaningfully takes effort and perseverance. For our caring to last we must last (persevere) in our caring and concern.

I've attempted to put what I've learned in a number of different ways. Let's reflect and meditate on the stages. First Jesus said, "bear fruit.... then the Father will give you whatever you ask." How do we bear fruit? Jesus said, "This is my command: Love each other." I believe our whole mission and purpose is now before our eyes. Any questions? What will produce happiness in my life? Bear fruit. How do I do that? Show love. What does love mean? Read Jesus' life story for examples of how love is displayed to others. Any more questions? We can see our life's purpose is simply and clearly identified for us. We need only be cognizant when circumstances put someone to care for in front of us. The end result is praise to God, glory and honor to God. We can't "do" glory and honor. The "do" is to bear fruit and demonstrate love. That makes a difference. That's our purpose.

What you truly want is that God will be praised and thanked profusely by all those whom our lives touch. When you show compassion to your neighbor, Donna, when she is suffering, Donna will pray, "Thank you, God, praise you God, for bringing Linda into my life. When I really needed the encouragement, you sent her." That's the end, praise to the Lord. That's your part, to "bear fruit." The second ancillary benefit is that our Father promises you whatever you ask for. But let me give you a little hint here. A strange thing happens on "the yellow brick road to happiness." What you decide to ask for is transformed. You may start out asking for material things, but in time you'll find yourself asking for more spiritual gifts, compassion, the peace of God, joy. You'll begin to ask for what you really need for personal fulfillment, not what you may think you need now. But this adventure, on the yellow brick road, is yours to experience and enjoy. I'll be happy to compare notes with you on that once you've started on the path by making the commitment to follow it wherever it leads. All you need to do is resolve to bear fruit.

Hoping I don't confuse you, let me mention a few ideas that helped me. But one more time, Jesus' formula for getting what you really want (and know it or not, what you really want is to make a difference, to be one of the ***fellow workers in Christ Jesus*** Paul mentions in Romans 16:3), is this. Bear fruit by showing love to others; then afterwards ask for yourself, too. Give of yourself to others, then ask to be replenished and you'll get more in return than you could ever imagine.

SIGNIFICANCE

I try to remind myself of the simple formula each day by repeating, "Help me make a difference by helping someone else make a difference". I continue to center on "making a difference." I believe the reason is that my work with others has taught me that all of us are insecure. Let's face it - the most powerful person in the world today is probably the President of the USA. Can you think of anyone more insecure than he? He is at the mercy of his constituents. His future in the history of this world will depend on whether future generations appreciate what he did and what he stood for. That's the epitome of insecurity. But we are all insecure. We all worry about how we are judged by others. We desperately seek to be noticed, to be appreciated. I've learned you feel appreciated once you sense you have some significance. You're more than an insignificant grain of sand in your backyard. I've learned we become significant if, and only if, we feel we've made a difference, any difference.

Permit me to go through the psychological underpinning for you. I believe that most of us sense at some primal level that life is not just a chance occurrence. There is an abundance of beauty and creativity in nature and that beauty and creativity is mimicked by humankind. All of us yearn to be a part of the incredible vibrancy of life and nature surrounding us. We yearn to be a part of something greater than we are.

This is only natural. From the time that we first recognize we are individuals, as children, we sense our obvious inferiority in status and ability. Then we're socialized by family, school and peers, which often highlights our weaknesses and inferiorities. Hardly a day goes by that we aren't reminded there is always someone who can do whatever we do better than we can.

Yet all the while something within us yearns to be accepted as being a someone, someone special. We seek to fit in with friends and peers, first in school and then at work. Yet there is always someone, due to his or her own insecurity, who insists we really don't belong. For many of us, it becomes a never-ending battle.

From as far back as we can recall, we have this desire to be included, but there are always circumstances that force us to question our appropriateness in our world. Do we belong? There's always some reason to feel we don't quite measure up. Even the most accomplished of us has his or her moments of insecurity. Given these all too common experiences, is it any wonder that most of us long for belonging, being a part of something but especially a part of something much greater than ourselves (there's that insecurity again). Coupled with this is the desire to have our lives matter, to have value.

What is important here is the desire to not only feel I belong, but that I have a place. I'm part of something and I'm an integral part. I've contributed. I've done my part. I'm therefore significant. I'm not lost in the crowd and, by the way, there is a big difference between being part of a crowd and being part of a special group. This is what most of us want, to be part, a meaningful part, of a select association. We can say we feel the security of being a part but we want to contribute, to matter, to do our part. This is significance – I belong and I'm contributing. Having this provides me with meaning, a purpose, a direction, a sense of value. "I am a valuable person after all." We long to enunciate, not necessarily to shout it for all to hear but to announce it quietly within ourselves. "When I'm gone, I'm going to be missed, missed by someone, at least." Tell me that you haven't thought these thoughts. Maybe because it's too difficult or painful to meditate consciously on your place in the scheme of things you've avoided the topic. But now don't you at least feel that desire resonating within your being?

Once again, just a few verses before those we quoted in John chapter 15, Jesus put it again so simply and elegantly in John 15:5, *"I am the vine; you are the branches. If a man* [woman] *remains in me and I in him* [see the idea of belonging here!], *he will bear much fruit;* [do his part, have purpose, meaning and feel he or she has made a significant contribution to the cause]." And as He concluded previously, we are bearing fruit by following Jesus' model of unselfish caring for others, loving those with whom we're put in contact.

So if you are prepared to follow the path that you are ordained and psychologically equipped for (to belong and to contribute) you need only fill your life with opportunities to help others as Jesus did. And don't worry about how many there are or how much time is required. Just start small and see to what extent the habit grows. Jesus and God don't put any quotas here, in fact, Jesus said, *"For my yoke* [for you to carry] *is easy and my burden is light."* (Matt. 11:30). Just start looking for the opportunities put before you weekly. Comfort someone who is hurting; say something positive and encouraging to a friend. Heal someone suffering depression, if only for a moment, by pointing out something positive about his or her circumstances. Take a few minutes, after taking a deep breath, to relax yourself in preparation to bring calm to another's life. Go out of your way to open a door. Just smile and make eye contact when you walk by. This may be the hardest thing to do given your own level of insecurity, but you might make just smiling as someone walks by your first goal. Once you become stronger, and with God's Spirit, you'll feel empowered to do more. After all, God is more than happy to watch you take one simple step at a time.

From there, you can progress to other projects. These may infringe on personal time, but every minute given is worth the vitality you'll feel in return throughout your being. Here are some of the ideas my friends and acquaintances have given me on how I might be more significant. Bill volunteers his time to help coach the middle school football team, even though his own children are grown and on their own. Mary takes her little girl with her down the street to keep an elderly neighbor company while Mary spends a couple hours cleaning for her neighbor. Ken is his church's unofficial handyman. He can be found Saturday mornings making repairs or improvements. Terry volunteers his time at the local YMCA to organize activities for young boys, though he doesn't have children of his own as yet. Joan spends Wednesday early evenings at the town soup kitchen preparing and serving meals. A married couple, Frank and Linda, volunteer their time weekly to help teach immigrants how to speak English. And then there's Ray who makes his weekly rounds at one of the local hospitals, going from bed to bed cheering and commiserating with those in the cancer ward.

I'm sure you could add to this list many times over with examples of friends you know who have learned to nurture the nascent desire to show we care, a desire found in each of us. You'll most certainly find an activity that you enjoy and that fulfills your need to share of self, once you admit it's important to you. It's also a contribution to opening another dimension in your own life. Expanding beyond self is a prospect for every Christian as he or she grows in a relationship with the Father. Each simple act of making a difference in the lives of others irrevocably makes a difference in us. We begin to realize that these simple acts of kindness accumulate. Each small particle is an infinite world of possibility that contributes to our Lord's praise and helps to accomplish His will. Suddenly we realize we are "fellow workers" with God as scripture encourages us to be. Each little difference contributes to the mountains and mountains of benevolence our Lord has inspired in the world. "I took a part, a very small part, but I did do something to further the cause of God's love in our world. I contributed something," we can all hope to say.

I have the inclination to believe, though I don't have the statistics to prove it, that some of those acts of kindness we've committed, some of those little seeds of caring that we spread, have made a huge difference in the lives of others. Remember Habakkuk never dreamed he would ever have had the impact on the world that he had. His few pages of written commentary compared to the billions and billions of pages and volumes written since are seemingly insignificant but as we've seen, they are invaluable pieces in the puzzle of coming to know the "unknowable" God. His seemingly insignificant thoughts have inspired millions of people since. That's significance. I don't know about you, but I'd be happy to think my life could help, could inspire even one other person to better know and mimic the love of our Father. I have faith that it will.

How do I know? Well, I remember a teacher. I just happened to be in her class when I was nine years old. I can't remember her long Polish name but I can still see her rather rotund personage before me today. She told me I was special (I'm sure now that she said the same thing to her other students, too) but I was young enough to believe what she said. I took that little treasure with me unconsciously for many, many years. I know it made a huge difference in my future. I attempted projects beyond what I consciously thought I was capable of because subconsciously I knew I was special - at least that's what my teacher said and after all, she was older and wiser and she must be right! My teacher, I'm sure, never dreamed that her words would have such a profound impact on even one life, but they did. To me, that one continued act of kindness on her part (I had her as a teacher for only six months) more than justified her existence in this world.

I wonder how many other seeds of kindness sown by her have taken root in the lives of others. I'm a better person because she crossed my path. Her example assured me that each one of us, though we may not make a difference in hundreds of lives as she did, can influence at least a few lives for the better due to our considerate contact. I firmly believe some of those contacts we experience, either by intention or by sheer chance, will bear the kind of fruit Jesus spoke of. Though we act because we truly are interested in others, we, at the same time, are insuring our own significance. We have a purpose; we matter because we make a difference.

MESSSAGES I HOPE YOU NOTED:

- IT'S NOT LOOKING DOWN AT SELF BUT GAZING UP TOWARD GOD, THERE IS WHERE THE POWER EMINATES.

- WHAT A DIFFERENCE IT MAKES TO MAKE A DIFFERENCE

- DON'T EVER BE AFRAID OF TRUTH

- WE NEED BOTH PROPER PERCEPTION AND POWERFUL PURPOSE

Chapter Fourteen

HABAKKUK'S INDISPENSIBLE PLACE IN CHRISTIAN THOUGHT

What I want to do now is review some of the spectacular insights Habakkuk has given us for building a familial bond with our Father and Lord. Then I'll offer a few parting thoughts on a productive habit, courtesy of our friend, Habakkuk.

I hope I've painted a realistic picture of our hero, Habakkuk. I can call him a hero in the strictest Christian framework. He was a hero, an exemplary historical figure in both his strong suits and his shortcomings. We've learned from both. True to the tone of every Bible writer, and I mean every Bible author, Habakkuk has portrayed both actions of which he could be rightly proud and actions for which he should be rightly embarrassed. We see his strengths and his peccadilloes, his fine points and his rough edges. The wonderful truth is we learn from both. Our study of the book of Habakkuk has highlighted one man. As is true of the personal history of any Bible personality, a balanced, not a surreal picture emerges. His was an obscure place on stage and in the limelight for but a relatively brief moment of time. Though he lived some 2600 years ago, nevertheless he made a contribution to humankind that directly affects each of us who reads these words.

One of the ideas I'm certain the Guiding Hand of the Bible wanted us to learn from his story is this: Habakkuk's writing is preserved as if to say, "Look what we can learn from one man's life, an obscure man at that." Yet if he, in almost complete obscurity, has affected millions upon millions of lives, how many lives can you, yes you, an obscure individual Bible reader affect? Maybe not millions upon millions, but is it an exaggeration to expect 10, 20, 100 or a thousand? That's realistic. For example, I mentioned my fourth grade teacher with the long Polish name. I'm sure her school kids, their children and perhaps their grandchildren, were affected by her positive compliments to students in class. I'm certain now she is aware of the fantastic work she did, though she may never have been singled out as "teacher of the year." I can't even remember her name. But a name, like Habakkuk's, doesn't matter; it's the work, the affect, and the positive influence that counts. As I've suggested previously, this is what each of us wants, just to know that we made a difference, our life counted for something!

BIG THINGS ARE ACCOMPLISHED BY LITTLE PEOPLE

This is what's so fantastic about Habakkuk's chronicle. He was a person similar to you and me. To our knowledge he was not an intellectual, not physically striking, not a powerful leader and not an especially prolific writer. The extent of his writing coming down to us is a mere of three or four pages in the Bible. As I said, I'm certain one of the reasons God saw to it that his story would be preserved is as an object lesson for us. In calling attention to Habakkuk, God is saying, "Look what you can do!" Though other Bible characters might have been especially courageous, prodigiously wise or had legendary faith, our servant leader Habakkuk was not singled out as one with those special talents or attributes. Just being himself he accomplished so much. You can do the same. You can make a difference; you will make a difference! There is no telling what you might accomplish. I'm certain you'll surprise yourself just as Habakkuk surprised himself looking back over the centuries to assess what his work has wrought.

To me this lesson of Habakkuk is most profound for proving a seemingly insignificant person can accomplish great things with the Spirit of the Lord. Little people can make a big difference. Interestingly this maxim was never specifically stated in Habakkuk's writings. You can understand why, though. As an average person in the community, Habakkuk never called attention to himself. Just from his writing style you get the impression he was rather unassuming and low key. No doubt he was thrilled to have one of his compositions chosen as a temple song for worship. He doesn't even specifically reveal that fact about himself. We only are aware of this from the song instructions edited at the end of his prose writing. That small accomplishment was no doubt considered by Habakkuk to be a highlight of his life.

Habakkuk would have had to live over 600 years longer to ever imagine that his lyrics would be translated into Greek and other languages during the time of the apostles. It was still another 1500 years further in time before his lyrics were popularized and translated into German by Martin Luther and shortly thereafter into English. These lyrics, "The righteous will live by faith," were the rallying cry of the Protestant Reformation and Wesleyan Evangelism.

As has been noted, it has taken countless years to see the full blossoming and exposition of his insight. The full ramifications of Habakkuk's work could never have been imagined when first penned. It has taken these 2600 years to fully manifest the magnitude of Habakkuk's contribution to Jesus and Christianity. Not a word or inkling of speculation about the historical impact of Habakkuk from Habakkuk himself.

OUR GOOD IS NEVER GONE ONCE WE'RE GONE

Though Habakkuk never mentioned it and though scripture doesn't single out his effort, unfolding history has underscored another lesson, an object lesson for all to behold. As we learn from Habakkuk's example, we personally may never know during our lifetime what good has been accomplished through us. Your children may live on long after you. Their full story, with all their good deeds, will not be tallied, in most cases, till long after you are gone. The full effect of your nurturing and caring will not be revealed either. What about the friends, the co-workers and other acquaintances that you touched during your brief journey through this life? You'll never fully know during your lifetime the effect you had on others. I like to think that the average person with even a modicum of caring capacity and even a minimal amount of compassion has passed on more good than sorrow.

Little did I ever dream that the weekly visit I made with my wife and children to my parents (my children's grandparents) would have such a profound affect on my children's lives. Long after my parents' passing, their memory and effect has not passed. My children, all grown and on their own, still speak fondly and affectionately of the pleasant times shared. I would never have guessed the good I was accomplishing by taking them to their grandparents to baby-sit once a week so my wife and I could be together alone for a few hours. The security and connection my parents contributed to my children's growth is only now being understood. The affection, love and sense of belonging they exhibited to my children only served to accentuate the love and security my wife and I were attempting to pass on to our kids. Before each of my parents left this world I was fortunate enough to tell them I loved them and how thankful I was that they were such caring parents to me. What I feel sorry for now is that I never thanked them for being such good grandparents. I didn't realize it at the time. I don't think they realized at the time what good they had passed on. Only now may truth be told. The legacy my parents passed on was tremendous. I wish I could have shared with them what I know now. When you're gone the good you circulate is never gone.

FROM THE DEPTHS TO TOP OF THE WORLD

Let me review another major lesson learned from the adventures of Habakkuk. In this chapter I have been recounting some of the major insights Habakkuk presents to us. These are all major and profound pearls of wisdom, not counting the scores more of corollary insights branching from the major arguments. Here again is one of these major insights that only a humble "nobody" could make so clear. Habakkuk teaches how to go from the depths of despair to being literally on top of the world in one easy lesson. Remember, when we commenced our study of Habakkuk we were introduced to a rather negative, complaining and dejected individual. When we closed the book on Habakkuk's commentary we left him literally on top of the world. Exhilarated and excited by what he was reminded his God could do, he confessed he felt like a mountain deer on top of a spiraling peak surveying the landscape below. Far from the reach of anyone who could harm him and close to his God who would protect him, he was at peace and in power. How did he get that way? Very simply, he stopped worrying about himself and started contemplating God's awesome goals and purposes.

It can't be that simple, you say. But it is. Habakkuk proves it. When a person, with God's help, stops dwelling on how miserable he is or could be (that was Habakkuk, depressed but slipping into deeper depression as he conjured up images of how much more horrible the future appeared) the appearances might be transformed. Suddenly during his meditations he was slapped with the idea that wallowing in his miseries is counter-productive, like crying that he had fallen into a mud puddle rather than getting out of it. Dwelling on how bad things are only perpetuates the misery. Habakkuk demonstrated you can (and you need to) get out of the pit and into the sky. Dwell not on our majesty but contemplate HIS MAJESTY. I know it's simple to articulate and more difficult to master, but whenever you consciously realize you are dwelling on self, make the conscious decision to exclaim, "I'm going to take the focus off me and my past and start thinking about my future with God's help from now on." Recall Habakkuk's transformation in the third chapter of his book. He implies, "If I can do it, you can too!"

THY WILL DOESN'T MEAN MY WILL

Habakkuk next Introduced us to one of the "catch 22" situations that comprises life, the "damned if you do, damned if you don't" variety. Habakkuk taught by example how to pray and the attitude necessary to commence effective prayer. Now, whether Habakkuk understood the ramifications of proper prayer and meditation attitude before he encountered the Lord in these sets of prayers and meditations, we don't know. But from his response to God's answers it appears he learned a lesson from his personal God encounter. Remember the situation? Habakkuk prayed about the injustice and outright criminal activity of the powerful community leaders. God's response was not to worry, in short time the Babylonians would come and lay siege to the whole region, the Judean political leaders would be eliminated. Though the Babylonian themselves may not be more merciful in the short run, in the long term change for the better would arrive. Habakkuk complained, you'll recall, that this solution wasn't his preference and in fact, he became quite indignant with the Lord before he fully understood how God works.

Now the lesson Habakkuk learned, the one I hope we can all learn, is the attitude required to embark on in prayer. This is the one Jesus taught prolifically in His ministry, ***"...not as I will, but as you will."*** (Matt. 26:39). Even the Lord 's Prayer with ***"...your will be done,"*** (Matt. 6:10) that we're all familiar with, stresses the point. What Jesus is saying, and what Habakkuk learned, is that when we pray we must be prepared for answers that may not at first be palatable to us - not what we had in mind. However, when we pray for something and then add the phrase, "thy will be done" or "your will be done, not mine" we are going in with the resolve that we'll accept God's answer whatever it is. In other words, "thy will be done" is not always going to be "my will be done."

God in His wisdom, may have something else in mind than the "my will" you or I may be praying for. I remember, and again I can confess now, that when I was younger I prayed at times asking for the Lord's guidance but deep inside knowing that some of the possible answers God could give, I wasn't prepared to accept. Needless to say, I didn't get any answers. I wasn't praying, "Thy will be done," I was wishing, "My will be done." Only after years of prayer in one instance did I finally receive an answer, but I first had to admit to self and God, "I'm now prepared to accept any answer, not just the one I choose in advance." If I had understood Habakkuk's message fully back then, I could have saved years of unfruitful prayer in one particular area of my life.

I've learned, as Habakkuk did, that unless I begin a new chapter of prayer in my life, feeling with all my being that I really am prepared to accept whatever answer is best, without reservation, even if it doesn't first appear to be in my personal best interest, the prayers have little possibility of success. Thanks again to Habakkuk for reminding us of this requisite of prayer. Few Bible writers make the issue as clear as Habakkuk does with his personal example. A prayer answer, even if it's a disappointing answer, is still an answer. Better to be thankful that My Father deigned to give an answer, any answer, to me personally, one of His billions of earthly subjects, than to insist either consciously or subconsciously on an answer only if it meets first with my approval. I've been forced to admit, as Habakkuk was, that prayer is far more powerful when I pray, "Thy will be done," and "God, I really mean it with every ounce of my being."

FAITH ALWAYS OVERCOMES FATE

The hallmark of Habakkuk's message is his example of faith. His example is especially meaningful to us since most of us can relate to it so easily. We can say, "He reminds me of how I feel at times." Most of us will probably never be asked to do something we consider spectacular with our faith. We won't be asked to gather an army of 300 to fight a national army of many, many thousands as Gideon was ordered to do. We'll never be required to display the faith necessary to raise someone from the dead, or to walk on water for that matter. Faith to most of us means having the faith to live our lives daily through difficulties or perhaps suffering. Economically we may be hurting; the pain of physical illness may be getting the better of us. Faith means endurance and optimism in the face of adversity. Now that's the kind of faith Habakkuk modeled. We say, "I know how you felt, Habakkuk, I feel that way now." But he says, by his testimony, "I endured it and you can too."

Habakkuk's short phrase, the one he framed from his meditations with God gave him the impetus to endure. "The righteous will live by faith," has been the rallying cry of people of faith for several thousand years now. Habakkuk proved to us that that phrase can help us through any imaginable difficulty, despair or dysfunction. Habakkuk was called upon to endure an age of violence, injustice and inhumane treatment. Only with faith could he be assured there was an end in sight. You see, without the faith, the assurance that there is an end in sight, it would be nearly impossible to endure endless suffering. Faith gives the assurance that even against all odds and as unlikely as it might appear, better days are ahead. Habakkuk demonstrated that faith is a daily affair. Daily obstacles and difficulties arise. Daily we are required to fight back against disappointments and perhaps disapproval focused on us. Habakkuk's encouragement is especially meaningful to us under these circumstances.

You see, Habakkuk initially understood the treasured phrase on faith to be taken literally. In other words, just to live or function adequately the righteous person must have faith. Just to get through the day and keep your sanity, the righteous person must muster up faith. Faith is a way of life. Habakkuk was saying faith gets us through the day. God's people, Christians, are probably more sensitive to injustice, suffering and mistreatment than others. Very often Christians are discriminated against or objects of jealousy by unbelievers. Those added impediments make living at times more difficult for spiritual believers. Habakkuk's encouragement is that faith that something better is coming will help you through. How else or what other explanation is there for why Christians in suffering can possibly be so optimistic and actually happy? It's their faith.

Faith is a daily way of life. Just as readily as it can be said a human lives by food and nutrients, so it can be said Christians live by faith. Faith is the secret (secret in the sense of not being understood by the majority) ingredient that causes Christians to be happy and excited regardless of external circumstances. Before you have your bowl of cereal in the morning, why not give yourself a dose of faith by repeating as Habakkuk did, "The righteous will live by faith." "Today I will live by faith. With God's help this day I believe my relationship with My Father will grow."

FAITH AND FORGIVNESS GO HAND IN HAND

Remember too in our previous studies the apostle Paul asserts something Habakkuk might be surprised to learn; that his original treasured phrase of faith has an extended meaning that he (Habakkuk) would never have dreamed of. Paul asserts that not only is faith needed to live now and each day, but faith is what is needed to secure our future. Not just our present life but also any hope of a future life depends on faith. When Habakkuk wrote, "The righteous will live by faith," he didn't know when the Messiah would come or Who He would be or what He'd make available. Habakkuk had faith that a Messiah, an anointed, special messenger of God, would be coming but that event was not yet for some 600 years. Habakkuk didn't realize his faith directive for living would take on a fuller dimension. Then Paul, having the advantage of living during the exact time of the Messiah's appearance, was able to discern faith's added dimension.

Paul, too, had the experience of living first outside of a relationship with his Lord and then through special consideration was invited and instructed into a fulfilling and close friendship with his God. Living at times on both sides of the fence, so to speak, he could appreciate there being no comparison between living with God and living against God. That relationship became the most valuable treasure Paul had ever discovered. What's more, that marvelous relationship was to endure endlessly to a level without bounds. Scripture is replete with the promise of endless, eternal life for those who want an unending association with the Master of the Universe. Such a prospect is beyond the dream and invention of any human. To even imagine being a close friend of the most powerful, yet most compassionate, Personage in the universe is beyond imagination. Yet this majestic Personage conceived and then took steps to share His treasures with all who desire them. Habakkuk believed this too, but couldn't imagine how the plan would all unfold.

First, Habakkuk recognized his utter inferiority when comparing himself to God. If we, each of us, realistically assess our situation compared to God's, we must admit our inferiority, our abject poverty,

Paul Serwinek

as every prophet of God has confessed. Humans don't deserve to be ranked in the same class as God. Our mistakes, our sins, our imperfections set us far outside the realm of true godly creatures. How could we ever be forgiven for our past and future inevitable breaches of God's perfect standards? Here God Himself conceived a method, a means to free us from our imperfections and help us feel somewhat worthy to be spoken of in the same breath as we speak of God. We all know God's answer was the coming of Jesus, the Son of God, to redeem the world. In one great act of forgiveness Jesus sacrificed His life for our sins and shortcomings. The life of one guileless, perfect human was given in exchange for all who would beg to apply that sacrifice to obtain their forgiveness of all sin. Being forgiven for all past and future transgression gives us the opportunity to feel, at least in a small degree, worthy to approach God.

And what do we need to do to avail ourselves of this privilege for forgiveness and this invitation to approach God? The answer Paul found was hinted in the words of Habakkuk. "By faith the righteous will live." In other words, forgiveness, friendship with God, special communion with our Savior is a free gift. You need only acknowledge it and accept it. That is what faith allows. Faith has this other dimension. If we truly believe that this impossible is possible, that the impossible breach between God and man can be connected, forgiveness and peace of mind instantly come to us. So when Paul now takes up Habakkuk's herald call, "The righteous will live by faith," he is adding that the righteous one who lives by faith in Jesus and God's plan of redemption will experience a new life, what Jesus called *"...life and have it to the full."* (Jo. 10:10). Living with forgiveness, living with intimate friendship with God, living with an endless life of adventure and privilege in view is a whole new dimension. In other words, the righteous will be living the kind of life, eternal and meaningful life that not just anyone can have. That's real living. And how do you attain that? Faith, that's all, faith, faith in God's promise, faith in Jesus' sacrifice. It's totally free, but faith that leaps to believe in the unbelievable is all that's needed. Take the leap and prove for yourself that a sense of forgiveness goes hand-in-hand with faith.

214

SIGNIFICANCE FOR THE INSIGNIFICANT

Probably the most inspirational aspect of reading the book of Habakkuk to me is the idea that each of us is significant. Each of us has value to God. Each of us has ahead of us opportunities to be used by our Father. Each of us can make a difference. Habakkuk's life proves that. Here was a guy, ordinary by any standards. So ordinary that the Bible doesn't tell us exactly what his occupation was. So ordinary that an impressive biography was not provided in the book of Habakkuk itself or anywhere else in scripture. But to be chosen to be the one to pen the immortal words of faith that have inspired millions is indeed a great honor and a great privilege. Habakkuk became a "somebody" by his association with the Lord. The same is true of each of us. On our own we may feel like a "nobody" at times. But with God we are powerful; we can do great things. We can make a difference. In fact to someone we may make the greatest difference.

I always marvel at the many sports heroes who volunteer that the most influential person in their lives was their mom or dad. They speak in such glowing and affectionate terms of that one mentor. "My mom kept encouraging me" or "My dad kept telling me I'd be somebody someday." I just know these heroes would not be where they are today without that one influential person in their lives. I often ask who is the real hero in each of these instances. Certainly a case can be made that the mentor, the mom, the dad, is in a sense a real hero. Their tireless encouragement made a difference, in fact, made all the difference in one person's life. We have opportunities to make a difference. And Habakkuk's story gives us the incentive by proving it's really possible to be raised up, designated by God to make a big difference.

A HAPPY END

We can close our examination of Habakkuk's book by reviewing a few verses from Habakkuk's third and final chapter. As most all of God's prophets were required to do, incumbent on Habakkuk was the task to warn those with whom he was in contact of God's coming judgment on those living diametrically opposed to God's way.

Judgment will come. As surely as the Lord promised judgment and recompense on the Jews, Habakkuk's people, and just as surely on the Babylonians (Habakkuk's enemies), a judgment is in store for each of us. Now what that judgment will entail is a matter of speculation but that there is a judgment is certain. We can only hope that judgment will go well for us. Habakkuk put it so beautifully and succinctly when he prayed for himself (but actually for all of us) when he prayed, …[Lord,] *in wrath, remember mercy.* (Ha. 3:2). In your justified anger with us, give us the benefit of the doubt. Following Habakkuk's example, this is something each of us needs to pray. Ask for forgiveness; ask for mercy. But as you ask have no doubt that as long as you are attempting to follow His path, the Father will most certainly deal mercifully with you. Jesus himself assured us of this.

There will be a happy ending. This is what Habakkuk is so certain of. Though when Habakkuk began his writings he wasn't so certain, over time we witnessed his transformation. Such a process of transformation has occurred millions of times and even from time to time needs to be replicated in the same individual. Being human, being a work in progress, we need to be reminded of the path we chose. That was true of Habakkuk and it's true for each of us. Habakkuk began his writing as a dirge; he moaned and complained. However, along the way he was transformed. We can only explain this as a consequence of coming under the influence of God's Spirit and power. Willingly opening up our being, welcoming God's presence, brings with it this transformation. How else can we explain such a stark contrast? Witness first his questioning and complaining to God, "Why are you silent while the wicked swallow up the righteous?" Then note his contagious optimism at the end, "Though the fig tree does not bud and there are no grapes on the vines… I will rejoice in the Lord, I will be joyful in God my Savior." As we've noted before, optimism is a trademark of God's Spirit. When one is looking at things from the vantage of the Highest Power, a happy ending is certain!

PARTING THOUGHTS

This is what I've learned over the years and Habakkuk confirms it. Whenever I'm not optimistic and hopeful and excited about the end result (the rest of the story), I'm outside of the spirit of the Spirit at that moment. I need to pray there and then for the wisdom of the Spirit. I beg to be helped to look at circumstances from the Spirit's vantage point. I might tell myself, "I'm tired at the moment, and I'll feel better in the morning." Or I might say, "I'm upset now, I need to calm down!" When I'm not hindering the flow of the Spirit, optimism and positive expectancy returns.

I mention this as a suggestion; use your disposition as a gauge to the flow of the Spirit in your life. If you can't mimic the positive expectancy of Habakkuk when he says in effect, "I might be down and out now but I can still rejoice, I know something good is coming," then you know for some reason there is a hindrance to the Spirit flowing into your life. Could it be stress? Could it be that your body (the temple of the Spirit according to 1 Corinthians 3:16-18) is not functioning at its optimal level? Could it be your subconscious needs to confess something to your conscious mind first and then perhaps confess it aloud? Any number of issues can be the root of the problem. This is where you ask for wisdom if the answer is not apparent. Pray in earnest with an honest sentiment and the problem will be clarified. The Lord cares and will reveal the impediment. He wants the best for you and He'll help find a solution.

Such a metamorphosis is exactly what Habakkuk underwent, from negativity to optimism. With God's Spirit freely flowing in his being he could exclaim with confidence, "The Sovereign Lord is my strength." I wish the same for you. As an added incentive, remember the words of the writer of Hebrews (traditionally the apostle Paul) in Hebrews 11. After starting out his dissertation of faith by quoting Habakkuk, he recounts the men and women of faith from scripture. He then observed that each of these faith-seekers found God, and here I quote the Message translation of Hebrews 11:33, and ***turned disadvantage to advantage.*** That's just the kind of God we have. This is just another one of those paradoxes of life – always, if you stick it out, an advantage (a positive) is created by a disadvantage (a negative). I can testify, knowing this has helped me stay the course with optimism. I just repeat to myself, "God turned disadvantage to advantage." Every problem encountered is just that, a disadvantage, and that's the way it should be categorized in our minds. A problem is never a dead end; it's just a detour and while taking the detour you're sure to find an unexpected positive advantage along the way that more than makes up for the inconvenience of the disadvantage. Then you can aver with Habakkuk, "The Sovereign Lord is my strength."

I really feel privileged to have taken you on this journey through Habakkuk's experiences and mind. I feel we were helped to understand the spiritual mind of our Lord in a deeper way. His experience was unique among all Bible writers, just as your life experience is unique in all the world. As such, Habakkuk's suggestions give a different view, an added dimension, to our understanding of spiritual matters. We concede Habakkuk was a remarkable person, though in his own estimation he was just an ordinary person. But as he proved once again, the ordinary combined with God's strength equals extraordinary.

By any assessment Habakkuk had an extraordinary life. Following the principles highlighted in his life course and his writings can do the same for each of us. Let God's Spirit do the same for you. Let the Spirit transform your ordinary life to one that can be called extraordinary. You still have doubts? We all do at times. Living a life of faith is a work in progress, we don't always have it right but as a Christian you find you'll have more up days, optimistic days than down days. And for those down days… I don't want to be trite here, but I remember what the doctor says, "Take two aspirin and call me in the morning." For a spiritual malady the advice can be similar. All I can say is take a deep breath, repeat Habakkuk's refrain, "The righteous will live by faith," (faith meaning the ability to believe the unbelievable) have a good night's sleep, and call on God again in the morning.

MESSAGES I HOPE YOU NOTED:

- **God Turns Disadvantage To Advantage**

- **Significance Comes From The Insignificant With Our God**

- **Our Good Will Never Passes Away, Though We May For A Time Pass Away**

- **Thy Will Be Done Is Not The Same As My Will Be Done**

Paul Serwinek

APPENDIX

THE PLAYER WE MISSED
(Research By Jason Mach)

From time to time it is necessary to reflect on and examine one's life. There is another figure in history inextricably linked to the quest for righteousness and the solution of faith. You've heard of him - Martin Luther. I thought it would be fitting to chronicle his search for a true relationship with our Lord. After all, he unraveled and then published his discoveries about Habakkuk, St Paul and faith. Our story begins with Luther's resolve to maintain a course of personal righteousness, hoping to win God's approval. Since long before Luther's time and continuing into today's society, God's subjects have always sought a pristine, clear, righteous standing before the Lord. Luther was no different. He even resolved to make the performance of good works a central theme in life in order to maintain that righteousness. To a human way of thinking, this would be an excellent and honorable course of action. However, when examined biblically, no such thinking could be farther from the truth. It is through no course of human action that one can become righteous. This is the great discovery that changed Martin Luther's life, and which then changed the life of the Church in the West forever.

Martin Luther, one of the prominent Reformation theologians, was born in Eiselben, Germany in 1483. The course of Luther's life was greatly affected by his family life, in particular his relationship with his father. Luther's father was quite strict, often punishing Luther with severe physical beatings. Even his schoolteachers would discipline him harshly. Not surprisingly, Luther's life took on an austere tone and was characterized by depression and anxiety. (Gonzalez, 15).

The course of Luther's life was shaped by his father; not only in terms of physical discipline, but also in terms of vocation. Luther's father was a peasant who worked as a miner and throughout the course of his career came into ownership of several foundries. It makes sense, then, that he desired for his son Martin to enter the professional world as well, though as a lawyer, not a miner. Luther had no intentions of making a career in law and instead followed the leading of his faith. In 1505 he joined the Augustinian monastery in Erfurt, Germany (Gonzalez, 15-16), and later continued on to earn a Doctor of Theology in 1512. (Hastings, 243).

Historical Framework

To grasp the full impact of Luther's discovery, it is necessary to begin with a look at the historical, religious framework in which he existed. Luther wrote in his *Large Catechism* that in the Church, under the Papacy's control, "faith was wholly done away with and no one recognized Christ as Lord" (Luther 1935, 122). What conditions or events prompted him to make such a bold statement? The answer lies in examining the religious culture and practices of the Western Church, and by considering how the state of the Church affected and shaped Luther himself.

A study of the religious culture and practices of the Western Church can be traced way back to the thoughts and theology of second and third century Christian writers like Tertullian and Jerome. These early Church writers maintained that the correct attitude of the Church was necessarily one of legalism and moralism. Concepts such as sin, repentance, forgiveness, grace and salvation were all seen through the filter of legalistic thinking. One historian writes that this attitude "led to a higher emphasis being placed on the judicial metaphors of the Bible than on the more appropriate personal ones in [the] understanding of the way of salvation" (Yule 1985, 5). The "justice of God" was thought of as the "demand of God the judge" (12). Sin, in this legalistic atmosphere, became a "list of particular transgressions of the law of God" when it had formerly been thought of as an "attitude of hostility to the love of God" (Yule 1985, 5). Sin went from a singular condition of the human soul to a plural list of legal wrongs for which penance must be done.

With this view of sin in mind, repentance was then defined as similar to "a duty required of the guilty party in the Roman law courts" (Yule 1985, 5). Thus a process of repentance was developed in the Church: all sins must be confessed by the sinner in a state of contrition, followed by the performance of a "satisfaction." Only after completion of this process could forgiveness be granted to the sinner. The terrible flaw in this process is that "God's forgiveness...was thought to be conditional" upon the efforts of the sinner. Even a person only casually acquainted with the Reformation Era of the Western Church can see what drove Luther to protest.

In a broader context, grace and salvation also became contingent upon the Church's legalistic process. Grace was "given through the sacraments," which then allowed a person to perform "works that were worthy of salvation" (Yule, 6-7). In this process the grace of God was still an essential component in a sinner's salvation. However, it was a component in a "non-personal religious" sense rather than as the free gift of God, given to humanity through His Son Jesus Christ. Finally, an idea still prevalent in the human mind of this twenty-first century is the Church assertion that "an initial act of love on man's part, (that is doing the best one can on the basis of natural ability), was rewarded by God with an infusion of grace."

Thus it can be seen that the theology of the Western Church was centered on human works and legalistic thinking. Christians required the grace of the sacraments to enable them to do good works, which only then would lead to their salvation. They were required to arduously confess all of their sins with an adequate sense of contrition in their hearts in order to be forgiven and maintain their righteous status before God. They had to do the best they could with the abilities they had been given in life in order to win and keep God's favor. For a person who doubted his or her own success at fulfilling the requirements of any part of this legalistic process, life could become quite miserable and hopeless.

Luther was one such person who found himself in this predicament. Initially, he bought into the Church's penitential system and tried his utmost to receive God's grace and forgiveness (H.G. Ganss). He labored intensely to confess all of his sins. He rigorously maintained the ascetic lifestyle of the Augustinian monastic order of which he was a part. He even sought out the power of holy relics to assist him in escaping from the prison of his sin. To his despair, however, all of these efforts were of no avail. He still found himself buried under the immense weight of his sin and saw no means of escape anywhere at his disposal.

Steeped in the Western Church's mindset of confession with a heart of contrition, Luther placed the blame for his continued entrapment in sin solely on himself. By his thinking, he must not have been doing enough to warrant the complete forgiveness he was so desperately seeking. Through his own strength he had proven himself entirely unable to earn forgiveness from God, and therefore felt himself unworthy of it. Whatever means of forgiveness and salvation there were to relieve him of the burden and guilt of his sin and free him from the despair in which he was living had to be sought elsewhere.

Justification By Faith Alone

As Luther studied the Bible, particularly the Psalms, he began to see the love and righteousness of God in a different way. He began to see Jesus Christ in them. For example, in Psalm 85:11, which reads, *Faithfulness springs forth from the earth, and righteousness looks down from heaven,* Luther saw Jesus Christ as the faithfulness that springs forth as the fulfillment of God's promises from of old (Luther 1961b, 75). This new point of view on the Psalms served as the preparation for what was soon to come, the unexpected discovery that would change his life, and that of the entire Western Church, forever.

It was in his studies of the apostle Paul's epistle to the Romans that Luther came to the realization that the forgiveness he was so earnestly seeking *had already been given to him*. He was indeed right in previously believing that he was both unworthy and incapable of performing enough works and exerting enough effort to earn God's forgiveness for his sin. In fact, as it turned out, he did not need to.

Romans 1:17

Luther encountered in the first chapter of Paul's letter to the Romans the verse that changed his thinking and attitude about forgiveness, righteousness and faith. Paul writes: ***For in the gospel the righteousness of God is revealed, a righteousness that is by faith from first to last, just as it is written: "The righteous will live by faith."*** (Ro. 1:17). This is the song of Habbakuk, as you recall. Here in this verse Luther found the solution to his despair. It was the righteousness *of God* that would forgive him, not the righteousness of humanity.

The Western Church had disembodied the grace of God in its process of justification. Grace was a means to the end of attaining salvation through good works. But here in Romans 1:17, Luther came face to face with the grace of God as it was meant to be experienced – through the person of Jesus Christ. As Luther writes in his *Lectures on Romans*, "'The gospel' is not only what Matthew, Mark, Luke, and John have written...[it] is the word of the Son of God, who became flesh, suffered, and was glorified" (Luther 1961b, 15). The apostle Paul was thus essentially stating in Romans 1:17 that the righteousness of God is revealed *in Jesus Christ*, the living Gospel.

Luther now saw a distinction between the righteousness taught in the Bible and the righteousness taught in the Church through its system of penance. On the one hand, the righteousness of humanity teaches how a person becomes righteous in the sight of oneself and others, and that (in the view of philosophers such as Aristotle) righteousness is produced through good works and actions (Luther 1961b, 17-18). This established the foundation for the legalistic mindset in the Western Church. On the other hand, the righteousness of God, which in Romans 1:17 is not to be understood as a character quality of God, but rather as that power from God "by which we become worthy of His great salvation, or through which alone we are (accounted) righteous before

Him" (Luther 1954, 24-25). In other words, the righteousness of God is Jesus Christ. Therefore God is no longer the angry judge who requires His people to fulfill the legal process of confession, contrition and satisfaction in order to be forgiven and declared justified before God. He is instead the God who lovingly bestows righteousness on His people through Jesus Christ His Son.

Luther realized that the righteousness of God was not the product of good works. On the contrary, it was the *predecessor* and *enabler* of good works, and the very cause of salvation itself (Luther 1954, 25). Moreover, righteousness and salvation were granted by God to the sinner through the sinner's faith in the Gospel, in Jesus Christ (Luther 1961b, 18). Faith *alone* was necessary to be justified before the Lord; thus Paul writes, "The righteous will live by faith." And lest anyone think that this newfound justification by faith is based on a human decision, Luther writes that, "faith…is something done to us rather than by us…for it changes our hearts and minds" (Yule 1985, 15).

Righteousness Further Defined

The distinction between the righteousness of God and the righteousness of humanity was a major breakthrough for Luther. It went against the mainstream thinking of the Church and held major implications for Luther's life and relationship to God.

Luther notes in the preface of his commentary on Paul's letter to the Galatians that several kinds of righteousness exist. He names four types of righteousness: political/civil, ceremonial, the righteousness of the Law, and Christian righteousness (Luther 1998, xvii). Of these four types, only one – Christian righteousness, the righteousness of faith – is of any consequence in a sinner's salvation and forgiveness from sin. The others, Luther says, "are quite contrary to this righteousness… because they consist in our works" (xvii).

Political / civil righteousness is the righteousness of politics and society's laws. This is the righteousness which "emperors, princes of the world, philosophers, and lawyers deal with" (Luther 1998, xvii). Ceremonial righteousness is that of human tradition and pertains to "the correction of manners and certain observations concerning this life" (xvii). The righteousness of the Law is the Ten Commandments in the Old Testament. Though Christian doctrine also teaches these Commandments, it does so in the context of faith, not merely of satisfying legal commands (xvii).

Set against these three types of righteousness, which focus on human strength, effort and works, is the Christian righteousness. This righteousness, as noted above, is not dependent on human works, but comes from God and is bestowed upon sinners through their faith in Him. In his *Two Kinds of Righteousness*, Luther calls it "alien righteousness" (Luther 1961c, 86) because it comes from outside of humanity. He provides an example of its external origin by referring to Paul's words in 1 Co. 1:30: *It is because of him* [God] *that you are in Christ Jesus, who has become for us...our righteousness, holiness and redemption.* As this righteousness from God is not one generated or initiated by humanity, but rather is received from God, Luther also deems it "passive righteousness" (Luther 1998, xvii).

Luther speaks quite boldly about the glaring flaw in the Church's reliance on human works to produce righteousness. In his *Large Catechism* he says, "all who...try to merit it through their own works, have separated and excommunicated themselves from this Christian Church" (Luther 1935, 124). In *Lectures on Romans* he says that those who rely on works are merely "simulators and hypocrites" of the Christian faith (Luther 1961b, 123). Clearly, Luther's discovery of justification by faith alone soured his attitude regarding the Western Church's mainstream doctrine of penance and its theological implications.

Sadly, however glaring the flaw in the Western Church may have been, it was not done away with through Luther's discovery. The problem is the flesh. In Luther's theology, the flesh is the part of the human that encompasses the physical body, the immaterial soul and the capacities of reason and will (Yule 1985, 9). The flesh seeks after its own desires and concerns, often at the expense of others, and it tries to attain everything for itself through its own abilities. Taking this into account, one can see the reason for the repeated human tendency of reliance on works for salvation. It is ingrained in the very fiber of human nature.

As deeply ingrained as physicality is in human nature, it must still be overcome in order for a person to stand justified before God. Speaking of the importance of the work of the righteousness of God in a sinner's life, Luther says in his *Commentary on the Epistle to the Romans*, "Everything turns about the point that our righteousness and wisdom must be destroyed and rooted out of our hearts and our self-complacent minds" (Luther 1954, 12). This cannot be done by human strength, however. It is solely the work of faith, and is of the utmost necessity, for "God does not require a magnitude of works but the mortification of the old man" (Luther 1961b, 290) that comes only from justification by faith.

The reason that all of Luther's labors in his earlier monastic days could not relieve the guilt and anguish he felt over his sins is now revealed. He was striving against a part of himself that he could never overcome, no matter how hard he tried or what methods he employed. The more he tried to overcome his sin with his own strength, the more disturbed by it he became. This is because, in his own words, the works of human righteousness do not allow the soul to "look up to see the passive or Christian righteousness but [rely] altogether on [human] righteousness – so deeply is this evil rooted in us" (Luther 1998, xviii). And this is why the righteousness of God, accepted through faith in Jesus Christ, is so valuable. Only He, by His death and resurrection, can overcome the evil condition of sin that so strongly infects humanity.

Galatians 3:11

The phrase "The righteous will live by faith" is not isolated to the letter to the Romans. It occurs again in another Pauline letter, the epistle to the Galatians. Luther drew upon this epistle in his theology for much the same reason as he used Romans. The phrase occurs in Galatians 3:11, which reads, *Clearly no one is justified before God by the law, because "the righteous will live by faith."* We can't help but notice how Habakkuk's words radically changed the thinking of one man and the movement toward faith was inspired.

At the beginning of Galatians, Chapter 3, Paul is reprimanding the Galatians for abandoning their reliance on faith in Jesus Christ to make them justified before God. Instead, they were choosing to seek justification through human efforts to observe the Law (Ga. 3:1-5). As Luther states, with a hint of "Kierkegaard-ian" humor, this endeavor of justification through human effort is akin to a monkey trying to become human by imitating human actions (Luther 1961b, 101). Try though it might, the monkey will never become human by simply imitating a human. It can only be human and "perform human actions in the right way" if it is *made* human, and this transformation can only take place by the action of God (101). So it is with humans and their justification before God. It is only through the act of God in bestowing righteousness upon a sinner that the sinner can be justified; he or she must be *made* righteous.

So Paul reminds the Galatians that their efforts are futile. "Clearly no one is justified before God by the law." This is because "the law is not based on faith or anything belonging to faith; nor are the works of the law faith or based on faith" (Luther 1998, 149). Real faith, writes Luther, is "a true and certain faith that does not doubt God or his promises, nor the forgiveness of sins through Christ" (148). Justification comes only through faith, a faith that believes God apart from all works, for truly "The righteous will live by faith."

Habakkuk 2:4

In two separate references within his theology, Luther has pointed out that the righteous, those justified by God, will live by their faith. Romans 1:17 and Galatians 3:11 both contain this key phrase. But there is more to the issue of justification and faith than what is contained in the writings of the apostle Paul. The phrase "the righteous will live by faith" originates not in the New Testament writings of Paul but in the Old Testament prophecies of a man named Habakkuk, as we've learned. As Luther writes, "It is Habakkuk's desire or aim…to keep the people in faith, to strengthen them with much consolation…so that the people in affliction might not doubt" (Luther 1974, 119). This was comfort in the face of destruction .

Habakkuk's exhortation to live by faith and thereby be counted as righteous is used by Paul in both Romans 1:17 and Galatians 3:11. In the story of Habakkuk, the exhortation to faith was directed at the promise of the coming Messiah and the people's deliverance from their current danger, which was political/physical in nature. In Paul's letters, the exhortation to live by faith is also directed at the promise of deliverance, though not in the same sense as that of Habakkuk. The promise in Paul's letters pertains to deliverance of a spiritual kind, the ultimate deliverance from sin. In both cases, though, God declares His people righteous and delivers them by their faith in His promise. And in both cases, it is faith specifically in the Messiah, the Christ, which delivers and justifies them.

Luther's life reveals the struggle over the choice between the righteousness of God and that of humanity. His quest to attain forgiveness for his sins and justification before God began with his choice for the ways of human righteousness. These proved fruitless, and he was soon immersed in seeking forgiveness and justification in a different way, one that changed his life: the way of the righteousness of God by faith alone. He no longer saw the need for, or effectiveness of, the Church's penitential system or its sale of indulgences, which were purported to save a sinner's soul from its sins. As he writes in thesis #37 of *The Ninety-Five Theses*: "Any true Christian…participates in all the benefits of Christ and the Church; and this participation is granted to him by God without letters of indulgence" (Luther 1961a, 494). Additionally, Luther writes of the life and death nature of the doctrine of justification by faith alone. In the preface to his commentary on Galatians, he makes the following claim: "Once we lose our belief in justification, all true Christian doctrine is lost. There is no middle ground between the righteousness of the law and Christian righteousness" (Luther 1998, xxi).

Luther's personal struggle for exoneration of sin and his tireless searching of scripture moves us to appreciate the wonderful plan of our

Lord. We've seen how the prophets, starting with Habakkuk, culminating in Jesus, illuminated by St Paul and resurrected by Luther, have developed this major doctrine of faith. We can never take for granted the righteousness that comes from God and the awesome power of faith.

Paul Serwinek

BIBLIOGRAPHY

Ganss, H.G. "Martin Luther." The Catholic Encyclopedia, Vol. 10 Online Edition, K. Knight, 2003.

Gonzalez, Justo, Story of Christianity, Vol.2. New York: Harper Collins Publisher, 1985.

Hastings, Adrian, editor, A World History of Christianity. Grand Rapids, MI: William B. Eerdmans Publishing Company, 1999.

Luther, Martin. *The Ninety-Five Theses.* John Dillenberger, editor, Garden City: AnchorBooks,1961.

Luther, Martin. Com*mentary on the Epistle to the Romans.* Translated by J. Theodore Mueller. Grand Rapids: Zondervan Publishing House, 1954.

Luther, Martin, *Galatians.* Edited by Alister McGrath and J.I. Packer. Wheaton:Crossway Books, 1998.

Luther, Martin, *Large Catechism.* Translated by Dr. Lenker. Minneapolis: Augsburg Publishing House, 1935.

Luther, Martin, *Lectures on Habakkuk.* Edited by Hilton C. Oswald. St. Louis: Concordia Publishing House, 1974.

Luther, Martin, *Lectures on Romans.* Translated by Wilhelm Pauck. Philadelphia: The Anchor Books, 1961.

Luther, Martin, Commentary on the Epistle to the Romans. Translated by J.Gonzalez, Justo, *Story of Christianity, Vol.2.* New York: HarperCollins Pub.1985.

Paul Serwinek is available for interviews and/or author appearances. For more information, contact Leila at:

Paul Serwinek
C/O Advantage Books
P.O. Box 160847
Altamonte Springs, FL 32716
info@advbooks.com

To purchase additional copies of this book or other books published by Advantage Books call our toll free order number at:

1-888-383-3110 (Book Orders Only)

or visit our bookstore website at:
www.advbookstore.com

*A*dvantage
BOOKS

Longwood, Florida, USA
"we bring dreams to life"™
www.advbooks.com

Printed in the United States
136467LV00003B/1/P

9 781597 551885